# Germans Divided

GERMAN STUDIES SERIES
General Editor: Eva Kolinsky

ISSN: 1354-3571

**Previously published titles in the Series:**

Volker R. Berghahn and Detlev Karsten, *Industrial Relations in West Germany* (cloth and paper editions available)
Eva Kolinsky (ed.), *The Greens in West Germany: Organisation and Policy Making*
Eva Kolinsky, *Women in West Germany: Life, Work and Politics*
Eckhard Jesse, *Elections: The Federal Republic of Germany in Comparison*
Richard Stoess, *Right-wing Extremism in West Germany: Its Roots, Development and Organisation*
Alan Kramer, *West German Economy, 1945–1955*
J.K.A. Thomaneck, *Workers and Trade Unions in the GDR*
Russell J. Dalton (ed.), *The New Germany Votes*

# Germans Divided

*The 1994 Bundestag Elections and the*
*Evolution of the German Party System*

*Edited by*

**Russell J. Dalton**

**BERG**
*Oxford • Washington, D.C.*

First published in 1996 by
**Berg**
Editorial offices:
150 Cowley Road, Oxford, OX4 1JJ, UK
22883 Quicksilver Drive, Dulles, VA 20166, USA

Berg is the imprint of Oxford International Publishers.

**Library of Congress Cataloging-in-Publication Data**

A catalogue record for this book is available from the Library of
Congress.

**British Library Cataloguing-in-Publication Data**

A catalogue record for this book is available from the British Library.

ISBN  1 85973 160 0 (Cloth)
1 85973 165 1 (Paper)

Typeset by JS Typesetting, Wellingborough, Northants.
Printed in the United Kingdom by WBC Book Manufacturers,
Bridgend, Mid Glamorgan.

In memory of our colleague, for all his contributions to
comparative electoral research

Rudolf Wildenmann

# Contents

*Contents*

# List of Tables

# List of Figures

# Acronyms

| | |
|---|---|
| A 90 | Alliance 90 |
| CDU | Christian Democratic Union |
| CSU | Christian Social Union |
| DVU | German People's Union |
| FDP | Free Democratic Party |
| FRG | Federal Republic of Germany |
| GDR | German Democratic Republic (East Germany) |
| NPD | National Democratic Party |
| PDS | Party of Democratic Socialism |
| REP | Republicans |
| SED | Socialist Unity Party (East German Communist party) |
| SPD | Social Democratic Party |

# Preface

Scholars of the democratization process often argue that it is the second election after a democratic transition that begins to show the enduring features of the new political order – this was the German Bundestag election of 1994.

This book has two goals. Our first objective is to provide a historical record of the Superwahljahr of 1994. During this year there were nineteen separate national or subnational elections, culminating in the Bundestag election in October. This concentration of elections was unprecedented. It created a unique electoral dynamic, as exceptional attention was focused on Germany's past politics and its future choices. This was a year of multiple and fundamental choices for the German public, even if the implications of these choices remain very mixed. The contributors to this book thus track the issue choices that faced the Federal Republic, the parties' reaction to these issues and their programs for Germany's future, and the factors which ultimately guided the public's electoral decisions in 1994. In this sense, this book contributes both to our understanding of contemporary German politics, and to the broader field of comparative electoral research.

In addition, we see this as more than a study of a single election or even a Superwahljahr. Our second major objective is to investigate the evolution of German politics since unification by using elections as a tool for study. The merger of two different societies and two different political histories has created substantial economic, social, and political challenges for the Federal Republic. The framework of partisan politics and elections provides, we feel, a valuable method to monitor the nation's success in addressing these challenges. Thus various chapters in this book discuss some of the social problems that flowed from German unification, how the political parties responded to these challenges, and how the public viewed the choices facing the nation. This larger interest also means that our time perspective begins with the first all-German election of 1990 and extends to the future of the German system after the Superwahljahr.

Elections are a measure for gauging the passage of time, for taking stock at what has transpired recently. This measure has a special meaning for many of the contributors to this book since one of our valued colleagues, Rudolf Wildenmann, passed away between the 1990 and 1994 elections. Virtually all of us owe a direct and special debt to Rudolf. He was one of the principal investigators on the path-breaking 1961 German Election Study. Starting from this beginning, he was a mentor to many of us, a source of data and critical thought, and he played an essential role in the creation of the infrastructure for empirical social research in Germany that benefits us all today. The study of German politics would not be at its present state without Wildenmann's own scholarly contributions, and his ability to nurture younger German (and American) social scientists. We think he would have found many positive features in the political developments we chronicle in this volume, but he also would have insisted we need to expand our thinking, collect more data, and ask new questions. We will miss this encouragement, and thus dedicate this book to his memory and his contributions to the study of German politics.

Finally, we want to close with a note of thanks to the many people who helped in the development of this book. This volume continues a series on the evolution of the German party system that we began with the 1990 Bundestag election (*The New Germany Votes*, 1993). Many of the contributors to this volume were participants in the earlier study, and our goal has been to provide students and scholars of Germany with a chronology of electoral politics. We also want to acknowledge Eva Kolinsky's enthusiasm for this project, and her willingness to include this book in Berg's German Studies Series. Kathryn Earle has been a very supportive editor at Berg, and Nigel Hope provided a critical eye in the preparation of this manuscript; we appreciate their assistance.

We also want to express our appreciation to the Center for German and European Studies at the University of California for their generous support for the preparation of this manuscript. The Alexander von Humboldt Stiftung and the University of California, Irvine have supported the collaborative study of the German party system by Wilhelm Bürklin and me that is presented in Chapter 9. Many of the authors draw upon the public opinion data collected by the Forschungsgruppe Wahlen in Mannheim as part of the Politbarometer series of the Second German Television network (ZDF). The Forschungsgruppe has generously shared its data with the academic community; these data are a national treasure for the Federal Republic and social scientists interested in German elections and public opinion. (These data are available from the Zentralarchiv für empirische Sozialforschung at the University of Cologne.) Several contributors also would like to thank the Federal Press Office and its director, Wolfgang Gibowski, for hosting them on a study visit of the 1994 campaign.

In the last book I noted that unification had closed a door on part of Germany's past, and opened a door to a new political future. This book continues to describe the nation's course along this new path, its successes and failures. Certainly the path has been steep at times, and the outcome of the 1994 election was not a ringing endorsement of the government's or the parties' past performance. But progress has been made, and the prospects for the future are even more promising.

Russell J. Dalton
Irvine, California

# I Introduction

# 1
# Unity and Division: The 1994 Bundestag Election

## Russell J. Dalton

The 1990 Bundestag election was a unique event: a referendum on the historic unification of Germany and the Federal Republic's newly-won status as a sovereign state. Because of the exceptional events that mark the (re)formation of a nation, it is often the second election after a democratic transition that begins to identify the true nature of partisan competition and the electorate's values. This was the Bundestagswahl of 1994.

The 16 October 1994 election to the thirteenth Bundestag of the Federal Republic of Germany (FRG) resulted in a victory for the conservative/liberal coalition of Christian Democrats (CDU/CSU) and Free Democrats (FDP). Yet, the margin of victory was razor thin. Although Helmut Kohl thwarted the surge of the opposition parties, the governing parties lost a substantial share of the vote compared to their 1990 poll. The CDU/CSU and FDP entered government with only a 10-seat majority in parliament. Kohl's won his re-election as chancellor in the Bundestag by a single vote!

This volume chronicles the events leading up to the 1994 Bundestagswahl, and the reactions of the voters and the parties to the election's outcome. We hope to continue the tradition begun in *The New Germany Votes* (Dalton, 1993), which tracks the formation and initial development of the new German party system. There are many important elements to the process of German unification. We feel that the party system is an important reference structure for judging the workings of this process. Germany is widely regarded as a "party state" (*Parteienstaat*) in which political parties are the key actors in the political process (Dalton, 1992a: ch. 9; Padgett and Burkett, 1986). On the one hand, the political parties and their leadership have been instrumental in guiding the course of German unification. On the other hand, the parties have themselves been affected by this process. The merger of East and West has added 8 million new voters to the electoral rolls, created new opportunities and challenges for the political parties, and created new policy problems for the Federal Republic.

We also feel that elections are an important method for measuring the political process of a nation. Elections provide a periodic opportunity for the nation to assess where it – and its leadership – stand in addressing its goals. Elections encourage people to discuss politics, and think about the goals and needs of the nation. Elections also force political elites and the political parties to stand on their past record, and offer a choice for the future. And, of course, elections decide who will lead the nation for the next legislative period.

Beyond the vote counts, the contributors to this volume are interested in electoral politics as a barometer of the political forces now affecting German society and politics. German unification has granted freedom and a new life to 16 million new residents from the East. But unification has also created severe economic problems for the nation, problems of cultural and political adjustment between two diverse publics, and strains on the parties and other institutions of democratic governance. Elections are a celebration of the democratic process, but they also provide a setting in which to evaluate the workings of that process.

The goal of this volume is to track the evolution of the German party system since 1990 as a measure of the progress of German democracy in dealing with the challenges of unification. In 1990 the party system and democratic politics itself was new to eastern voters. Voters in the new Länder were only superficially familiar with the FRG parties that had expanded eastward. The pattern of interest group competition and intermediation that underlies the western electoral process was still forming in the East. The 1990 election was a tentative test of what partisan politics would look like in the new Länder. What progress has been made by 1994 in integrating these new voters into the Federal Republic's party system, and how has Germany and the German party system been changed as a result of this process?

## The Long Campaign: 1990–1993

For party officials, the campaign for the next election starts as soon as the votes are counted for the last election. By this measure, the Christian Democrats and their Liberal party allies began the 1994 campaign in difficult straits. Kohl promised Easterners that no one would be worse off in the short term because of unification; he promised Westerners that this could be done at little cost through a new eastern Wirtschaftswunder. Reality was different. The inefficient and undercapitalized eastern economy made a transition to a western market economy extremely dubious. As these inefficiencies were corrected, the number of jobs in old state-owned industries decreased, and unemployment skyrocketed. The Kohl government was forced to admit that it initially overestimated the economic vitality of the East and the ability of eastern industry and manufacturing to compete in a world market.

The critical problem for the East, however, was not the loss of old jobs but the inability of the economic system to create productive new jobs in their place. A variety of factors contributed to this economic record (Sinn and Sinn, 1992). For example, the initial advantage of substantially lower labor costs in the East evaporated as eastern wages rose to reflect the cost of western-produced goods. The Kohl government tried to create new investment incentives through grants and tax benefits, but this was not sufficient. Besides cost factors, the property restitution laws and the unclear property titles on eastern land discouraged potential investors. Potential environmental liabilities also discouraged investment. The uncertain political and social situations in the East were additional disincentives to western investment.

Instead of a rapid integration of the two economies, economists extended the target date of economic parity between West and East until early in the next century. Moreover, a massive infusion of western funds was needed to sustain the eastern economy and the living standards of the population. Despite Kohl's promises that German unification would not require new taxes, the government initiated a 7.5 percent surcharge on income taxes (*Solidarbeitrag*) almost as soon as the votes were counted (January 1991). The Social Democrats (SPD) quickly labeled this as Kohl's tax lie (*Steuerlüge*), and intensified their warnings about the costs of unification.[1] Moreover, most of the initial funds going East were used for consumption rather than investment. In 1992, for instance, more than DM 200 billion in public funds were transferred from the western Länder to the East, and two-thirds of these funds went towards social services and the basic operation of state and local governments (Sinn and Sinn, 1992).

In addition to the tremendous economic costs of German unification, a series of other political and social problems arose in the wake of German union. Even before unification, the Federal Republic was receiving a growing stream of individuals seeking to settle in Germany: ethnic Germans from Eastern Europe and asylum-seekers.[2] This stream of immigrants grew because of the increasing instability in Eastern Europe and the rest of the world. The political and social tensions associated with these immigrants was a major factor behind the rise of the Republikaner party in 1989. The social and economic dislocations accompanying unification intensified tensions over immigration issues in the new (and old) Länder. Starting with sporadic attacks against foreigners by small right-wing groups and youth gangs, there was mounting opposition to foreigners in areas where they had been relocated in large numbers. Foreigners were criticized not because they were responsible for the situation in the East, but because they were vulnerable targets of attack for frustrated and worried Germans.

Unification also revived debates about the structure of the Federal Republic's welfare system. Westerners were concerned about the high costs of social benefits being provided to Easterners; Germans on both sides of the border criticized the generosity provided to asylum-seekers, who often were viewed as economic refugees rather than political refugees. Similarly, immigration into Germany and migration from eastern to western Germany created severe housing shortages and worries about a new housing crisis of the 1990s (*Wohnungsnot*). Indeed, the present financial demands on the social welfare system are far greater than during the 1970s, when debates about the crisis of the welfare system were commonplace.

As these social and political problems mounted, the CDU/ CSU and the FDP suffered losses in public support. State election results signaled the declining fortunes of the governing parties (see state results in appendix). Between January 1991 and March 1994 the CDU lost votes in Hesse, Rhineland-Palatinate,

Hamburg, Bremen, Baden-Württemberg, Schleswig-Holstein, and Lower Saxony (Dalton and Bürklin, 1993; Bürklin and Roth, 1994). Even more ominous for the FDP, the party fell under the 5 percent hurdle required to win parliamentary representation in the 1993 Hamburg and 1994 Lower Saxony state elections.[3]

These state election results weakened the Christian Democrats. By mid-1992 not a single state among the ten western Länder was headed by a CDU-led government with the SPD in opposition. These losses meant that the CDU/CSU–FDP coalition no longer controlled the Bundesrat, where SPD-led state governments held a majority. Furthermore, public opinion data from the Forschungsgruppe Wahlen and the Allensbach Institut indicated that since early 1991 the SPD held the lead over the CDU/CSU in voting preferences in the western and eastern Länder.

Helmut Kohl was fairly sanguine about these developments. He called this a period of difficult passage (*Durststrecke*) for the party, claiming that the Union's fortunes would improve with economic growth in the East; hopefully before the next election. These reassurances were unconvincing to many people, however. The CDU's commitment to free market principles helped the Federal Republic rebuild in the postwar period, but the same principles appeared ill-suited to the problems of creating a functioning capitalist economy in the East (Smyser, 1992). Beyond the economy, the CDU was ineffective is addressing the other social and political problems stemming from German union, such as anti-foreigner violence and health care reform. The government's commitment to stay the course it charted in 1990 diminished hopes that the situation would improve.

The Free Democrats shared many of the CDU/CSU's problems because they were part of the governing coalition. The party and Foreign Minister Hans Dietrich Genscher quickly took credit for the foreign policy accomplishments of German union; they were equally hesitant to address the social and economic problems flowing from unification. In addition, Genscher's resignation from the ministry in early 1992 robbed the party of its most visible and popular figure. The party struggled first with a leadership succession, and then with the new leader, Klaus Kinkel.

The SPD should have been the major beneficiary from these developments, and indeed the party's standing rose in Land elections and the public opinion polls (Dalton and Bürklin, 1993).

Björn Engholm assumed the party leadership after the 1990 election, and he was a popular and effective representative for the SPD. However, Engholm was forced from office in May 1993 by an admission of complicity in an election scandal in his home state of Schleswig-Holstein. He was replaced by Rudolf Scharping who was viewed as an effective and electorally successful politician. Public opinion surveys in late 1993 and early 1994 found that most Germans favored Scharping over Kohl as the next chancellor.[4] As the next Bundestag election approached, SPD strategists forecast the party's inevitable return to government as part of a multi-party coalition.

## The Superwahljahr: 1994

All political observers agreed that 1994 would be a decisive year for the German parties, and the nation. A total of nineteen elections were scheduled for the year: a European Parliament election, eight state elections, the October Bundestag election, and assorted local elections (the appendix to this volume presents election statistics). In addition, the Federal Convention would select a new president of the Federal Republic. This would be the *Superwahljahr* (super election year).

This series of elections was primarily important because of the number of significant political choices that would be made in 1994. In addition, the clustering of elections could affect the dynamics of the 1994 Bundestagswahl. Election analysts often considered the European Parliament and Landtag elections as indirect measures of the government's standing with the public. Success in early elections could provide a party with momentum that would carry through to the Bundestagswahl. Conversely, a party that stumbled in early elections might be harmed to an extent that it could not recover by October. Thus each election was a sign of what might lie ahead in the fall.

As late as spring 1994, most indicators pointed to a loss for the CDU/CSU in the Bundestag election. The Christian Democrats continued to trail the SPD in the polls. There had been progress in addressing the immigration issue (see Chapter 11) and in defining Germany's new international role, but many of the overshadowing problems of German union remained unresolved.[5] Even the CDU-leaning media and political analysts were pessimistic that Chancellor Helmut Kohl could (once again) snatch victory from the jaws of apparent defeat.

The Lower-Saxony elections in March seemed to confirm this prediction. With a popular state leader, Gerhard Schröder, the Social Democrats increased their share of the vote and retained the control of the state government. More ominous for the CDU-led government in Bonn, the FDP was unable to surmount the 5 percent hurdle, continuing its slide from power. This election created a euphoria within the Social Democratic camp, with expectations of assuming control of the federal government after the Bundestag election in October.

The next election was for the federal presidency in May. The president is not directly elected by the people, but is selected by a Federal Convention (*Bundesversammlung*). Nevertheless, the public and political observers closely watched the course of this election.[6] The election initially created a liability for the CDU when Kohl first nominated an eastern German, Steffen Heitmann. Heitmann's nomination was heavily criticized by Kohl's opponents, but also by members of his own party. With intemperate and impolitic comments, Heitmann appeared to diminish the significance of the Third Reich and to display feelings of political intolerance. Kohl eventually withdrew Heitmann's nomination, and substituted the name of Werner Herzog, the highly respected chief justice of the constitutional court. The Social Democrats nominated the popular Johannes Rau, and the FDP nominated Hildegard Hamm-Brücher. In the end, Herzog was victorious in the presidential election. The Social Democrats' bitter reaction to the inevitable (since it controlled only a minority of votes in the Federal Convention) tarnished the party's image. This was the SPD's first stumble in 1994.

The first national poll came with European Parliament elections in June. Normally, the opposition parties fare better in the European Parliament elections, as voters feel more freedom to express their doubts in this "second-order" election. The Social Democrats thus counted on the European elections to build their momentum for the Bundestagswahl. But it was not to be. The CDU/CSU recorded a surprisingly good showing in the elections (38.8 percent), which was 1.0 percent higher than the party's 1989 result (Table 1.1). This victory thus shifted the momentum of the Superwahljahr to the CDU, and buoyed the party's hopes for the fall.

*Introduction*

The other clear winner in the Europarliament election was the Alliance 90/Greens, the newly formed party uniting the western Greens and the eastern Alliance 90. The western Greens had failed to win Bundestag seats in 1990 because they fell below 5 percent in western Germany. Thus, the 10.1 percent vote in the European elections, and the accompanying seats in the Europarliament, signalled the party's national recovery.

**Table 1.1** European Parliament Election Results, 1989 and 1994

|  | 1989 | 1994 West | East | Total |
|---|---|---|---|---|
| Christian Democrats (CDU/CSU) | 37.8 | 40.5 | 34.2 | 38.8 |
| Free Democrats (FDP) | 7.0 | 4.2 | 3.8 | 4.1 |
| Social Democrats (SPD) | 37.3 | 34.0 | 25.4 | 32.2 |
| Alliance 90/Greens | 8.4 | 11.0 | 5.5 | 10.1 |
| Party of Democratic Socialism (PDS) | – | 0.6 | 19.2 | 4.7 |
| Republicans | 7.1 | 4.2 | 3.0 | 3.9 |
| Other parties | 3.8 | 5.5 | 9.0 | 6.2 |
| Total | 100% | 100% | 100% | 100% |
| Percent voting | 62.3 | 59.4 | 64.1 | 60.0 |

*Source: Statistiches Jahrbuch der Bundesrepublik 1994, p. 96.*

The CDU/CSU and Greens emerged from the European elections as the victors, but there were many losers. The smaller or more radical parties normally do well in the EP elections, but not in 1994. The FDP failed to reach the 5 percent barrier and thus lost its seats in the European Parliament. This result, and poor showings in public opinion polls, heightened worries about the party's ability to survive the Bundestag election. The right-wing Republikaner had garnered 7.1 percent of the vote in 1989, and seats in the European Parliament. In 1994 the party fell below the 5 percent hurdle. Similarly, the left-wing Party of Democratic Socialism (PDS), the reformed successor of the East German communist party (SED), failed to surpass the 5 percent hurdle.

The big loser in the election, however, was the Social Democrats. Instead of a trial run for their Bundestag victory, the party garnered only 32.2 percent of the vote. This was a fall of more than 5 percent since the 1989 European Parliament election. The party's showing in the West was only marginally different than in 1989, but it had lost badly in the East – and the PDS was attracting a growing share of the leftist vote among Easterners. Instead of building momentum, the Social Democrats had stumbled in this nationwide election.

Several of the chapters in this book will discuss the events leading up to the European Parliament results, but it appears that two factors were paramount in explaining the relative showings of the CDU/CSU and SPD. First, the German economy began to display clear signs of recovery in the spring of 1994. Kohl and his government loudly proclaimed that the awaited recovery had finally arrived, and the public caught their optimism. Second, the prospect of a real change in government likely raised doubts about whether the SPD opposition could provide a better future. The SPD had criticized the costs of unification, but had not presented viable alternatives. The SPD had openly struggled in deciding its position on asylum rights, redefining Germany's defense role, and other issues. Even the SPD's earlier support in the polls had to be read with a note of caution. For example, Westerners voting against the tax increases introduced by the Kohl government did not really see the SPD as the anti-tax party; voters worried about the influx of foreigners and the erosion of social order did not expect the SPD to take up these positions. Thus, the SPD's strength during the inter-election period often reflected a negative vote against the CDU, rather than a positive endorsement of a Social Democratic alternative.

The next measuring event was the Saxony-Anhalt election in late June. The Land had been governed by the CDU, but seemed ripe for an SPD gain. The Social Democrats received 34.0 percent of the vote, an 8.0 percent increase since 1991. Conversely, the CDU vote share decreased to 34.4 percent and the FDP vote fell to 3.6 percent (and the FDP dropped out of the Landtag). The CDU and FDP had collectively lost 14.5 percent since the prior Landtagswahl. The SPD and Greens held a plurality of parliamentary seats, but not a majority. The federal leadership of the SPD agreed to form an SPD–Green minority government in Saxony-Anhalt, which would signal the coming *Machtwechsel* (power change) in Bonn. However, this government depended on the latent support of the PDS. Quickly the CDU turned the SPD's victory into a liability, by painting the Social Democrats with the red brush of PDS affiliation.[7]

By late summer the CDU/CSU had consolidated its lead over

the SPD. The Christian Democrats led in voting preferences and Kohl held a clear lead over Scharping in Germans' chancellor preferences (see Chapters 8 and 10). To broaden its support, the SPD emphasized a leadership troika – Scharping, Schröder and Lafontaine – that would govern if the Social Democrats gained power. The Land elections in September yielded mixed results. The SPD gained an absolute majority in Brandenburg, but this was largely attributed to the popularity of the state party leader, Stolpe. An equally popular CDU leader in Saxony, Kurt Biedenkopf, led the Christian Democrats to a majority. The Christian Social Union also retained control of the Bavarian government in the September elections.

## The 1994 Bundestag Results

Few election experts would have correctly predicted the outcome of the 1994 Bundestagswahl twelve months, or even six months, before the election. As the date of the vote approached, there was still great uncertainty in the air. It was not clear if either the FDP or PDS would gain enough votes to enter the Bundestag, which might greatly alter the calculus of coalition building. The polls projected that the CDU would emerge as the largest party in the new parliament. But the polls could not assure the Christian Democrats that they would have sufficient votes to reform the government.

If 1994 was a referendum on the progress of German union, then the public's evaluations were decidedly mixed. Political analysts could legitimately claim that every party had gained from the election – and that every party had lost. Although the CDU/CSU vote dropped by 2.3 percent since the last Bundestagswahl, the Union parties retained control of a governing majority (Table 1.2). The victory was rewarding for Kohl, but his huge parliamentary majority had diminished to ten seats; even this majority depended on the peculiarities of German electoral law that generated twelve "overhang seats" ("Überhangmandate") for the CDU.[8] More than ever, the CDU/CSU will have to depend for its governmental power on the small(er) FDP. Moreover, there must be a bittersweet taste to the CDU's victory. After leading Germany through the tumultuous period of 1989–1990 and guiding the unified Germany toward

democracy and economic stability, Kohl was rewarded by
watching the party's vote share sink in each of the last two
Bundestag elections. The 1994 outcome represented the Union's
worst showing since 1949.

Table 1.2 Bundestag Election Results, 1990 and 1994

|  | 1990 | 1994 West | 1994 East | Total | Seats |
|---|---|---|---|---|---|
| Christian Democrats (CDU/CSU) | 43.8 | 42.2 | 38.5 | 41.5 | 294 |
| Free Democrats (FDP) | 11.0 | 7.7 | 3.5 | 6.9 | 47 |
| Social Democrats (SPD) | 33.5 | 37.6 | 31.5 | 36.4 | 252 |
| Alliance 90/Greens | 5.1 | 7.8 | 4.3 | 7.3 | 49 |
| Party of Democratic Socialism (PDS) | 2.4 | 0.9 | 19.8 | 4.4 | 30 |
| Republicaner | 2.1 | 2.0 | 1.3 | 1.9 | – |
| Other parties | 2.1 | 1.9 | 1.1 | 1.7 | |
| Total | 100% | 100% | 100% | 100% | 672 |
| Percent voting | 77.8 | 80.5 | 72.6 | 79.0 | |

Source: Statistisches Bundesamt. The CDU/CSU seats include 12 *Über-hangmandate*, and the SPD seats include 4 *Überhangmandate*.

The Social Democrats, however, were the major losers in the
Bundestagswahl. From the threshold of victory in early 1994, the
SPD agonized its way to another defeat by October. The party
received only 36.4 percent of the total vote – better than 1990, but
worst than any other election since the early 1960s. The blunders
and strategic mishaps during the campaign, as well as the
closeness of the loss, deflated the future ambitions of many Social
Democrats. In addition, the SPD's institutional – as opposed to
electoral – weakness in the East showed no sign of abating.
Among Easterners the SPD gained only 31.5 percent of the vote,
and in many districts it ran third behind the CDU and PDS.
Furthermore, public opinion polls have tracked a further erosion
in public support for the party since the election.[9] The SPD's
struggles in opposition will seemingly continue.

The 1994 Bundestagswahl results hold even more ominous
implications for the FDP. The party's very existence appears
threatened. The Liberals' early successes in the five new Länder
had largely dissipated by 1994, and the party won only 4 percent
of the eastern vote. The Liberals received only 7.8 percent of the
western vote. The FDP has all but disintegrated into a function, a

vehicle that allows the CDU/CSU to govern the country, while moderating the conservative CDU/CSU agenda. Even the role of maintaining (and moderating) the government has not protected the FDP in Land elections. Since the Bundestag election, the FDP has selected a new party leader and tried to revitalize the party organization. Nevertheless, the party is still suffering in the polls. The Liberals' existence has been threatened in the past, but never has the threat been more severe than the party's present predicament.

The Greens, in contrast, had reasons to rejoice after the ballots were counted. The Greens had come back from the grave of parliamentary death they suffered in 1990. The new Alliance 90/ Greens won 7.3 of the national vote in 1994, and 7.8 percent in the West. The only shortfall for the party was its dropoff in support within the new Länder. The Alliance 90/Greens are now the third largest party in the Bundestag, holding 49 seats. Together with the internal partisan changes described by Gene Frankland (in this volume) the Greens are transforming themselves into an important actor in the party system and the governing of Germany.

The other major victor in 1994 was the PDS. Counted out by everybody and vilified by much of the (western) German public and political establishment, the party proved these critics wrong. By winning four direct seats in East Berlin and carrying nearly 20 percent of the eastern vote, the PDS established itself as a genuine voice for eastern interests in the Bundestag. More important still, its showing confirmed the party as a legitimate representative of East German identity in the Federal Republic's public debate. At the same time, however, the PDS failed in its attempt to broaden its appeal to leftists and critics of the regime in the West; it received only 0.9 percent among western voters.

Finally, the Republikaner failed to win representation in the Bundestag. Their 1.9 percent in 1994 was even lower than the 1990 total, and below their earlier showing in the European Parliament elections. Alexandra Cole (Chapter 7) describes the internal conflicts that have burdened the party, and led to these results. The Republikaner forced the established parties to address some of their issues, albeit with policies the Republikaner did not always endorse. But having prompted this response, the party might disappear as did the NPD in the 1970s.

As this narrative makes clear, the 1994 Bundestagswahl yielded mixed results for the specific parties. Each party gained and lost to some degree. Thus rather than a defining election on the future of specific parties and the German party system, this seems like an interim step in an ongoing process of political change following German union.

## Germans Divided?

Counting votes and determining the winners of the 1994 Bundestagswahl are important. In addition, however, we are interested in studying the Superwahljahr for the lessons it provides on the development of German politics and the party system since unification.

One of the most apparent, and important, lessons involves the growing partisan division within Germany. This book adopted the provocative title, *Germans Divided*, because the pattern of partisan division that we first observed in 1990 has widened by 1994. Despite the many positive aspects of German unification, the 1994 election displays an expanding gap in the electoral behavior of Germans in the East and West, and a growing separation in partisan politics across the two regions. The partisan and electoral analyses of this book describe this division in many forms.

One clear example of this division involves the levels of partisan support in West and East. Although Germans are voting within the structure of a single party system, there are clear regional contrasts in the strength of the parties. The PDS is the most apparent example. It is a party of the East, reflecting both the ideological values of the former regime, and now also serving as a rallying point for Easterners disaffected by the course of German union. The PDS garnered almost a fifth of the eastern vote, but it gained less than 1.0 percent in the West. Similarly, the PDS has a strong organizational base in the East, giving the party a cadre of workers and a local patronage network, but its organizational presence in the West is nearly non-existent.

The eastern strength of the PDS is mirrored by the decidedly western base of other parties. The Alliance 90/Greens, for example, are developing a decidedly western base that is reflected in their vote share and membership base. Similarly, the

FDP is becoming a party rooted in the political values and political networks of the West. Moreover, these patterns strengthened in 1994. Both parties lost vote shares in the East, while maintaining a significantly stronger electoral base in the West.

When one looks beyond these quantitative measures, there are also signs of regionally based ideological or philosophical differences within each of the established parties. Representatives of the eastern CDU are more likely to favor liberal social programs that often contrast with the conservative economic values of the party's western leadership. The working class orientation of the western SPD is less developed in the East, where the party activists are drawn from the middle class. The eastern wing of Alliance 90/Greens is more moderate in its policies than its western counterparts. Many of the chapters in this volume present evidence of these growing intraparty policy tensions that follow regional lines.

These differences in party orientations and political bases are also evident in the chapters on voter behavior. The two major parties – CDU/CSU and SPD – have contrasting voter bases across regions. The western CDU is a party of the middle class and the religious; the eastern CDU receives the majority of its support from the working class and the non-religious! The SPD in the West gains most of its votes from the working class; the eastern SPD is disproportionately supported by middle class voters. Other chapters in this volume point to the different issue interests of Westerners and Easterners, or their different electoral calculus in determining their vote.

In short, the results of the 1994 election suggest that the new Germany contains two different party systems and two distinct electorates. Although the party labels may be the same throughout Germany, the parties advocate and represent different political views across the regions and attract different bases of support.

If this portrayal of two party systems and two electorates is an accurate description of contemporary German politics, then several consequences will follow. These contrasts will heighten the tensions already existing within the German party system, as voters realize the interparty and intraparty tensions produced by German unification. The electoral gap between West and East may further deepen, as parties respond to different constituencies in both regions. The major parties' rejection of the PDS that occurred in 1994, and the sympathy that this generated for the party among Easterners, are signs of this increasing divide.

Such regional differences create basic strains in the German system of party government. The intra-party tensions on issues that span the East/West divide – such as abortion, the management of Treuhand, or economic development policies for the East – have severely tested the system of party governance. If eastern deputies vote to represent their constituents, it often places them in conflict with the party leadership in the West. Such tensions become even more problematic when the government's majority in the Bundestag is so slim. Moreover, one can see that many prominent eastern party leaders, such as the minister-presidents in Saxony and Brandenburg, are developing a political base independent of the national party. It is difficult to sustain a system based on disciplined parties if such tensions exist within the electorates, party organizations, and party elites.

This pattern of regional division is also significant because it reinforces a second trend in German party politics. Over the past decade there have been increasing signs of a dealignment within the party system (Dalton, 1992b). Unification has increased the burden on the governing (and opposition) parties, and this has apparently accelerated the dealignment process.

The dealignment pattern can be seen in the public's declining involvement in electoral politics. Despite the historic event of the all-German election in 1990 or the very close contest in 1994, voting turnout is now substantially below the highwater marks of the 1970s and early 1980s. Furthermore, there has been an even more dramatic dropoff in turnout in Land elections in the 1990s. The parties' organizational base is also eroding, as party membership rolls have dropped off in both the East and West. Similarly, Helmut Norpoth and Dieter Roth (Chapter 10) describe the weakening of the electorate's psychological attachments to political parties over this decade.

These weakening party bonds went hand in hand with growing public hostility toward the parties during the 1990–1994 period. As many chapters note, the German term "Parteien-verdrossenheit" (frustration with the parties) became the political catchword for these developments (see Chapter 13). Skepticism of the parties is not a new development, but it seemed to intensify during this period. For example, in a 1990 EMNID survey barely a third of the public expressed trust in political parties; the second to the lowest rating of the dozen social institutions included in the study. After this survey, a series of party scandals and the parties' collective inability to deal with the new challenges of German unification deepened the public's doubts about the parties and the system of party government.

Several of the contributors to this book see the 1994 Bundestag election as reversing, or at least halting, this trend of partisan decline. The governing parties rebounded from their negative ratings during the inter-election period and (barely) retained control of the Bundestag. Turnout increased slightly in 1994, up 1.2 percent over 1990. The pattern of growing party fragmentation and losses for both major *Volksparteien* seems to have peaked. The election provided the opportunity to assess past progress and make choices about the future – as it should in a democracy.

There has been progress, but the evidence of democratic renewal still seems ambiguous. Turnout dropped off significantly in the Land elections of 1995, and broader signs of partisan dealignment have not reversed. Indeed, monitoring the regional polarization in the German party system and the public's support for the system of party government should be our major concerns as we track the evolution of the German party system after unification. This book provides an evaluation of past developments, and a basis for this future monitoring.

## Plan of the Book

Although we are specifically interested in the elections of the Superwahljahr of 1994, our broad interest is to track the evolution of the German party system since unification. We have approached this task from several perspectives in the chapters that follow.

The first section of this book (Chapters 2–7) consists of six chapters that analyze electoral politics in the context of specific parties: David Conradt (CDU), Gerald Braunthal (SPD), Geoffrey Roberts (FDP), Gene Frankland (Alliance 90/Greens), Henry Krisch (PDS), and Alexandra Cole (Republikaner). Each chapter considers how the political party approached the 1994 election and reacted to the events of the campaign. These chapters describe the motivations behind party actions, as well as the anticipated and unanticipated consequences of these actions. The authors also discuss how the unification process has affected the parties internally. Each chapter closes with a discussion of the future prospects for the party that looks beyond the results in October 1994.

The second set of chapters examines the election from the perspective of the voters. Hans-Dieter Klingemann and Juergen Lass (Chapter 8) provide the initial findings from a massive study of citizen interests and partisan preferences in 1994. They use large weekly surveys to track the dynamics of the election, and then analyze the ability of parties and other political actors to define the agenda of the campaign. Russell Dalton and Wilhelm Bürklin (Chapter 9) describe the social bases of party support in 1994. They find clear evidence of the contrasting electoral constituencies East and West that perpetuate the political divisions that unification causes within the parties. Helmut Noporth and Dieter Roth (Chapter 10) examine the issue beliefs and candidate images that guided Germans' vote choices in 1994. These chapters describe how Westerners and Easterners differ both in their political values and in how these values affect electoral choices.

The third section of this book moves beyond the election to define some of the social forces that divide German society. Manfred Kuechler (Chapter 11) examines the sensitive issue of foreigners in Germany, and how the public and the political parties perceive this issue. He suggests that the fundamental problems in integrating foreigners into German society remain, and the parties have avoided these problems but not solved them. Eva Kolinsky (Chapter 12) describes how gender-related issues were treated differently under the FRG and GDR, and then traces the legacy of these differences for contemporary electoral politics.

The concluding chapter by Max Kaase (Chapter 13) places the 1994 election and current political debates in the context of the broader and more fundamental questions of democracy and the political development of the new Germany. This chapter, along with the other contributions to this volume, provides a useful framework for marking the future course of German union and the German party system.

**Notes**

I want to thank Andrei Markovits for his collaboration in editing a special issue of *German Society and Politics* (April 1995) that provided a preliminary report on the election, and which helped to develop my own thinking about the election's significance for German politics.

1. Ironically, although many people felt betrayed by Kohl reneging on his promise of no new taxes, data from the Forschungsgruppe Wahlen showed that most Westerners doubted the honesty of this promise when it was made in 1990 (Forschungsgruppe Wahlen, 1990).
2. The Federal Republic granted ethnic Germans the right to resettle in Germany and immediately attain citizenship. In addition, the Basic Law (Article 16) guaranteed the right to asylum to individuals persecuted on political grounds. Individuals who claimed asylum were allowed into the Federal Republic, and then supported by the state until their appeal is heard by the courts, which could take two years or more. In 1993 the provisions of Article 16 were amended to restrict the granting of asylum and the citizen rights of ethnic Germans.
3. The German electoral law requires that a party win 5 percent of the second vote (*Zweitstimme*) to share in the proportional representation of parliamentary seats. In the Bundestag election, a party can also share in the PR distribution of seats if it wins a plurality in at least three electoral districts.
4. See the survey results in the monthly reports of the Forschungsgruppe Wahlen, *Politbarometer*. Mannheim: Forschungsgruppe Wahlen; also see Chapter 10.
5. The CDU had, however, taken a number of steps to lessen the problems associated with unification. Massive public and private investments of the East were having a noticeable impact on the economic infrastructure by 1994. A 1993 "Solidarity Pact" restructured the financing of unification and delayed any new taxes until 1995 (after the election). By the end of 1993 the controversial *Treuhand* (trusteeship authority) had largely completed its work and was being phased out. Finally, several leading economic indicators such as capital investment, productivity, and new orders for plants and

equipment, began to move upward in late 1993, possibly signaling an economic recovery.

6. One possibility was that the election for the presidency would signal a potential shift in party alliance preferences, as it had in 1969. The SPD had hoped to attract some support from the FDP. After Hamm-Brücher was eliminated, most FDP representatives switched their support to Herzog.

7. In its western campaign, the CDU revived anti-communist themes from its past. This "red socks" campaign played on Westerners' fears about the PDS and their latent ties to the Stasi and GDR personnel. See Chapters 2 and 6 for more on this aspect of the campaign.

8. The electoral law provides that if a party win more district seats in a Land than it is due based on the proportional distribution of the second votes, it is allowed to keep the additional district seats and the size of the Bundestag is increased.

   In 1994, the CDU received 12 overhang seats: 2 in Baden-Württemberg, 2 in Saxony-Anhalt, 2 in Mecklenburg-Western Pomerania, 3 in Thuringia, and 3 in Saxony; the SPD had 4 overhang seats: 3 in Brandenburg and 1 in Bremen. The total of 16 overhang seats was the largest ever in Bundestag elections, prompting criticisms that the awarding of such seats violated the proportionality principle of the German electoral system.

9. The Forschungsgruppe Wahlen's survey from April 1996 yielded the following national distribution of current vote intentions: 43 percent for the CDU/CSU, 32 percent for the SPD, 12 percent for the Alliance 90/Greens, 6 percent for the FDP, and 4 percent for the PDS. In March 1996 state elections in Baden-Württemberg, Rhineland-Palatinate, and Schleswig-Holstein, the Social Democrats experienced significant losses, with the Greens and the FDP posting consistent gains. SPD losses may affect the composition of the state governments and thus the partisan balance in the Bundesrat.

## References

Bürklin, Wilhelm, and Dieter Roth, eds. 1994. *Das Superwahljahr*. Köln: Bund Verlag.

Dalton, Russell. 1992a. *Politics in Germany*, 2d ed. New York: HarperCollins.

——, 1992b. "Two German Electorates," in Gordon Smith et al. *Developments in German Politics*. London: Macmillan.

——, ed. 1993. *The New Germany Votes: Unification and the Creation of the New German Party System*. New York and Oxford: Berg Publishers.

——, and Wilhelm Bürklin. 1993. The Future of the German Party System," in Russell Dalton, ed. *The New Germany Votes*. Oxford: Berg Publishers.

Forschungsgruppe Wahlen. 1990. *Bundestagswahl 1990*. Mannheim: Forschungsgruppe Wahlen.

Padgett, Stephen, and Tony Burkett. 1986. *Political Parties and Elections in West Germany*. New York: St Martin's Press.

Sinn, Gerlinde and Hans-Werner Sinn. 1992. *Jumpstart: The Economic Unification of Germany*. Cambridge: MIT Press.

Smyser, W.R. 1992. *The Economy of United Germany*. New York: St Martin's Press.

# II The Political Parties

# 2
# The Christian Democrats: Just in Time and Just Enough

## David P. Conradt

The Christian Democrats have been Germany's dominant governing party since the founding of the Federal Republic. In twelve national elections prior to the 1994 poll, it had emerged as the largest party eleven times; only in 1972 did it not win a plurality of the party vote. During this period it led eight of the twelve governments that were formed in the post-election coalition process. In 1994 it attempted, with Chancellor Helmut Kohl again at the helm, to win its fourth straight national election. As in 1990 the interelection period was fraught with problems for the Union, but unlike 1990 when the unification issue brought the party a decisive victory, a weak economy and frustrations over the costs and pace of unification made 1994 a close call.

This chapter describes Kohl's, and the Christian Democrats', rise from the depth of the interelection slump to receive just enough votes to regain government control after the 1994 Bundestagswahl.

### The Interelection Period

The CDU entered the 1994 electoral marathon as a decided underdog. After having profited from the euphoria of unification in 1990 the party suffered from the inevitable discontent that accompanied the complex task of putting Germany back together again (Hofmann and Perger, 1994: 294–296). Throughout most of the 1991–1993 interelection period the party lagged behind the Social Democrats in state elections and public opinion polls. Voters during this period also preferred either of the two Social

Democratic chancellor candidates, Björn Engholm (1991–1993) and Rudolf Scharping (1993–1994), to the veteran Chancellor.

The Union's troubles began shortly after the 1990 election. Reneging on its 1990 campaign pledge of "no new taxes", the Kohl government in February 1991 announced increases in gasoline taxes, social security contributions, and a 7.5 percent surtax on incomes. The Chancellor's explanation for the increase, the unexpectedly high costs of unification and the Gulf War, was not accepted by the voters. Voter backlash was immediate. In February, 1991 the CDU lost power in Hesse. Defeats in the Rhineland-Palatinate, Kohl's home state, and Hamburg followed.

By 1992 it was apparent that poor economic conditions in the East, combined with voter discontent over new taxes in the West, and the asylum issue were causing the Christian Democrats to hemorrhage in both parts of the country. In the East support for the Union in public opinion polls dropped from about 42 percent at the 1990 election to less than 25 percent in July 1992. Likewise the CDU's junior partner, the Free Democrats, saw their support in the East decline from 13 percent to 7 percent during the same time period. In the West the story was much the same although the decline of the CDU was not as severe. (Generally there has been less volatility among Easterners.) The CDU dropped from over 44 percent in 1990 to about 37 percent in the West in mid-1992 polls.

The sharp decline in public opinion polls was mirrored in election results. At the April, 1992 state election in Baden-Württemberg, a traditional CDU stronghold, the party's share of the vote fell by 10 percent and the Union was forced into a Grand Coalition with the SPD. This was the worst electoral performance for the party in this state since 1960. Later in the year more bad news followed in Schleswig-Holstein where the Union failed to dent the SPD's absolute majority. The Union was rapidly losing its base in the states. By 1992, less than two years after the 1990 national victory, the party governed in only two of the ten states (Bavaria and Baden-Württemberg) of the "old" Federal Republic.

A clearer picture of the dynamics of the interelection period for the CDU is provided in Tables 2.1 and 2.2. In two of the three elections in 1991, environmental questions topped voter concerns and the Union lost in both states. In Hesse, the SPD, with substantial assistance from the Greens, regained control of the government. In the Rhineland-Palatinate the Union lost power for the first time since democratic politics were resumed in 1947. Local issues dominated the Hamburg election. At all three elections most of the Union's losses went to the FDP and the SPD (Table 2.2). The far right was not a factor.

In 1992 the asylum issue dominated national politics and cost the CDU dearly at that year's two state elections. As Table 2.2 shows, the Union gave up 9 percent of its 1988 vote in Baden-Württemberg to the Republikaner (REP). This accounted for over 40 percent of the REP's vote at that election (Forschungsgruppe Wahlen, 1992a: 40). The pattern in Schleswig-Holstein was similar. The Union's minority position in this state was further weakened as it lost 7 percent of its 1988 vote to the far right *Deutsche Volksunion* (DVU), the North German cousin of the Republikaner. As in Baden-Württemberg, this loss accounted for about 40 percent of the DVU vote (Forschungsgruppe Wahlen, 1992b: 38). Little wonder that Kohl and the CDU wanted the asylum issue to disappear before the 1994 national election.

By early 1994 and the Lower Saxony election, the unemployment issue had emerged as the top voter concern. The 1993 constitutional amendment limiting asylum rights had effectively eliminated the far right as a political factor. The expected CDU loss in Lower Saxony benefitted above all the SPD and its very popular minister-president, Gerhard Schröder. One of every ten 1990 CDU voters switched to Schröder's SPD.

But more disturbing for the Union than its low standing in the polls and at state elections was its relationship to the Free Democrats. In June, 1992 for the first time since the end of their coalition ten years earlier, the Free Democrats and the Social Democrats cooperated on a major piece of legislation – a postunification pro-choice abortion bill. It was Kohl's first parliamentary defeat since becoming Chancellor in 1982. Polls found that FDP voters were increasingly leaning towards the Social Democrats rather than the CDU as a future coalition partner (*Der Spiegel*, June 1992). On key issues in 1992, such as long-term nursing care insurance and the asylum question, the Union received more support from the Social Democrats than from their coalition partner. If the FDP was planning on switching partners, the CDU would be forced into either opposition or into a Grand Coalition.

Adding to the Chancellor's and his party's difficulties were a wave of cabinet resignations. Between March, 1992 and June,

**Table 2.1** Issues, Candidates and Winners at State Elections*, 1991–1994

| State | Date | Top Issues | Party of Preferred Candidate | Winner |
|---|---|---|---|---|
| Hesse | Jan., 1991 | Environment<br>Housing<br>Schools | CDU | SPD+<br>Greens |
| Rhineland-<br>Palatinate | April, 1991 | Environment<br>Unemployment<br>Transportation | SPD | SPD |
| Hamburg | June, 1991 | Housing<br>Transportation<br>Zoning (*Hafenstraße*) | SPD | SPD |
| Baden-<br>Württemberg | April, 1992 | Asylum<br>Housing<br>Unemployment | CDU | SPD, REP |
| Schleswig-<br>Holstein | April, 1992 | Asylum<br>Environment<br>Unemployment | SPD | SPD, DVU |
| Lower Saxony | March, 1994 | Unemployment<br>Environment<br>Housing | SPD | SPD |

*Source*: Forschungsgruppe Wahlen surveys cited in election reports.
* States where the CDU suffered losses.

**Table 2.2** CDU State Election Losses, 1991–1994

| State | Date | Percentage of Voters at Previous Election Lost: To FDP | To SPD | To Far Right |
|---|---|---|---|---|
| Hesse | Jan., 1991 | 8 | 5 | 1 |
| Rhineland-<br>Palatinate | April, 1991 | 5 | 13 | 1 |
| Hamburg | June, 1991 | 3 | 7 | 1 |
| Baden-<br>Württemberg | April, 1992 | 3 | 8 | 9 |
| Schleswig-<br>Holstein | April, 1992 | 3 | 6 | 7 |
| Lower Saxony | March, 1994 | 3 | 10 | 3 |

*Source*: Forschungsgruppe Wahlen surveys cited in election reports.

1993 eight cabinet ministers resigned including a key architect of the coalition, Foreign Minister Genscher. Genscher's departure was entirely voluntary, but that was not the case for most of the other departures. In March 1992, Kohl's Defense Minister was forced to resign after a scandal over illegal arms shipments to Turkey. The German weapons were used by the Turks in their attacks on rebel Kurds. The Transportation Minister, Günter Krause, one of the few eastern politicians to achieve national prominence, was dismissed over an alleged misuse of public funds for private purposes. The Interior Minister was forced to resign when security police used excessive force in arresting fugitive members of the Red Army terrorist gang.

More bad news was yet to come. In November, 1993 Kohl was dealt one of the worst defeats in his eleven-year Chancellorship when he had to withdraw the candidacy of his hand-picked choice for the position of Federal President, the East German, Steffen Heitmann. While there was widespread support for an Easterner as the next person to occupy the largely symbolic post of President, Heitmann's nomination drew heavy criticism even from his own party. His remarks that women should spend more time in the home and that Germans should not be singled out for special blame because of the Third Reich drew praise from the far right, but damaged both Kohl and the Christian Democrats. The collapse of the CDU-led government in Saxony-Anhalt because of the alleged misuse of public funds by leading (western) members of the government, including the minister-president, who was also hand-picked by Kohl, was an additional blow to the Union. Kohl had now suffered defeats in two areas where he was considered invulnerable, in personnel matters and intraparty politics. By December, 1993, with the national election only ten months away, even the pro-CDU press saw the Chancellor as "wounded" and "physically and psychologically over-extended" (Feldmayer, 1993: 3).

Amidst all the prophecies of defeat the Chancellor remained outwardly, at least, serenely confident and with some reason. Prior to the final phase of the campaign the political decks had been cleared of several potential damaging obstacles. A 1993 "Solidarity Pact," passed with the support of the Social Democrats, restructured the financing of unification and delayed any new taxes until 1995, that is, until after the election. The controversial asylum question, which had fueled the resurgence of the radical right, had been resolved by the May, 1993 constitutional amendment which restricted the right of asylum to terms satisfactory to most voters. By late 1993 it was apparent that the Union would face no threat from the right. In the East the controversial *Treuhand* (trusteeship authority), the agency charged with privatizing the state-owned economy, had largely completed its work and was to be phased out. It would not be a campaign issue. In the waning days of the last parliamentary session, another addition was made to the already generous welfare state. Again with the support of the Social Democrats, parliament passed a program of long-term nursing care insurance (*Pflegeversicherung*). Voters would not begin paying for this benefit until after the election. Finally, toward the end of 1993 several leading economic indicators such as capital investment, productivity, and new orders for plants and equipment, began to move upward. It would still take several months for the public to perceive an economic upturn, but the end of the recession was in sight.

## The Campaign

### Helmut Kohl: The Last Heavyweight

As in 1990, the Christian Democrats' campaign focused almost exclusively on Helmut Kohl, the last heavyweight of postwar German politics (Gennrich, 1994: 3). With Willy Brandt and Franz-Josef Strauß gone from the scene, Kohl is the only major political leader who experienced both the war and the entire history of the Federal Republic. Kohl sought to become the first Chancellor to escape relatively unscathed from a major recession. The 1965–1967 recession, the first in the Republic's postwar history, brought down the Erhard government, which was replaced by a Grand Coalition. The 1974–1976 recession played a major role in the collapse of Willy Brandt's government and the 1981–1982 recession ended the government of Helmut Schmidt.

The Chancellor's popularity, it was hoped, would compensate for the weakness of regional CDU organizations and leaders. After 12 years as Chancellor, only Bismarck and Adenauer had served longer, and as the leader of the Christian Democrats he projected the image of practical experience, confidence, and optimism that German voters have always found appealing.

For party campaign planners the turning point in 1994 was the February Parteitag in Hamburg and specifically Kohl's final speech (Gauly, 1994: 9). The speech had little if any immediate effect on the Union's standing in the polls, which continued to decline; it did the party little good in the Lower Saxony state election a few weeks later where it suffered an expected defeat as the SPD secured an absolute majority of parliamentary seats. However, the speech did rejuvenate and energize the party's activists, the foot soldiers who would do the campaigning in the months ahead (Interviews with Hans-Joachim Reck, Thomas M. Gauly, CDU Headquarters, Bonn, 12 October 1994).

The speech, according to CDU officials, had to be heard to be appreciated. In it Kohl reminded the party faithful of the great achievement of unification and the coming challenges of building the European Union. But it was his emotional, Reaganesque peroration that brought the house down. Kohl cited an excerpt from former USA Ambassador Vernon Walters' recent memoir which recalled a visit that Walters and Averill Harriman made to a bombed-out German family in 1948. The family resided in the cellar of a destroyed house. After the visit Walters asked Harriman if they would ever experience a fully recovered Germany in their lifetime. Harriman replied that they certainly would and in relatively short order. When asked to explain, Harriman reminded Walters of the bowl of flowers on the kitchen table. People who in this sea of destruction can gather flowers and put them on the table, he observed, are also capable of rebuilding.

With his voice breaking, Kohl declared:

> that was the generation of our parents and grandparents. Flowers are a good symbol for this second great postwar challenge that we are now confronting. Let's make sure that the flowers stay on the table as a symbol of a peaceful, a free Germany, a tolerant, hospitable Germany, a Germany in which hatred of Germans or foreigners can find no home. Then this Germany will become what we have always wished: our beautiful fatherland. This is certainly something worth working for.

The most widely distributed campaign poster contained no text or slogan, not even the initials of the party, but simply a picture of Kohl in the middle of an admiring crowd. For campaign planners the basic issue was simply a decision for or against the Chancellor (Stock, 1994a: 5). The Union's television spots continued the highly personalized theme. With the Tina Turner melody, "Simply the Best," as background, voters, mainly from the East, praised the Chancellor, who was shown with world leaders such as Clinton, Yeltsin, Mitterrand, and Major. After the June, 1994 European election, in which the CDU and Kohl had a stable lead in the polls, the Union also rejected any television debate with Scharping.

The Chancellor's standard speech, which was echoed by lesser party luminaries, focused on the accomplishments of his governments since 1983: at home, 3 million new jobs between 1983 and 1990, a decline in government spending (until unification) relative to the total economy, and an 18 percent gain in real income. In foreign policy, the Chancellor pointed to Germany's leadership in the European Union and its support for the postcommunist systems in Eastern Europe and the former Soviet Union.

With the economy in the East improving, Kohl increased his forays into the new states where he conceded that his 1990 prediction of "flowering landscapes" within five years had been a bit premature. Nonetheless, he reminded Easterners that his government had done far more for their economy since 1990 than the communists had achieved in forty years of socialism. His favorite statistic was the 4 million new telephone connections installed since 1990 as compared to only 1.8 million under the communists. Another crowd-pleaser in the East was the Chancellor's statement that since unification the average pension for Easterners had increased almost 300 percent, from DM 500 to more than DM 1,400 per month.

The CDU in the West reverted to traditional communist-bashing after the SPD's Saxony-Anhalt gambit, which is discussed on pp. 34–6; in the East the party crafted its position toward the former GDR's communist past to conform to the opinion of most Easterners. When he was in the East, Kohl repeatedly stated that he wished the Stasi documents and the background checks associated with the files would "go the devil." (Since 1990 the proportion of Easterners who want to forget about (*Schlußstrich ziehen*) the forty years of communist misrule has increased from 23 percent to 54 percent (*Der Spiegel*, 3 July, 1995: 49).) Crowds fell silent when the Chancellor asked himself rhetorically how he would have behaved had he been born in the East. Would he have sought his own private niche, or have opportunistically cooperated with the communist regime? Kohl always answered: "I don't know" (Stock, 1994b: 3).

CDU planners were also very proud of their telemarketing. Following each television spot, viewers were asked to call the party for more information (it was not a free call). Up to 15,000 calls were received each evening at party headquarters. Most calls were followed up with mailings and in some cases return calls by local organizations. In contrast to the past campaigns, the party reduced greatly its output of printed material and made few major buys in the print media. By 1994 the private cable and satellite television stations had coverage and ratings that equalled and in some cases exceeded the public stations. Given this information-saturated electorate, many regional and local organizations reduced the number of traditional election meetings and rallies. In spite of this emphasis on electronic media, Kohl still made 102 campaign appearances from the end of August until the election.

*The Improving Economy*

Not long after the Hamburg convention, public perceptions of an improving economy jumped sharply. In the West, between February and March, 1994 the proportion of voters who viewed the economy as "moving forwards" increased from 27 percent to 42 percent, one of the largest 1 month gains ever reported by the polling organization (Forschungsgruppe Wahlen, 1994a: 3). The trend was similar, although somewhat muted, in the East.

The Chancellor and the CDU were the major beneficiaries of this perceived economic *Aufschwung*. By April 1994 Kohl, who had trailed Scharping in polls since the SPD leader became the party's chancellor candidate in mid-1993, was within four points of the challenger. Two months later the Chancellor had a ten-point advantage that he never relinquished (see Chapter 10).

In the East, Scharping held a 62–30 advantage over the Chancellor in February which disappeared by August. Support for the CDU also increased from only 30 percent in March to 42 percent by June, a level which then remained fairly constant until the October election. In February only 29 percent of the electorate expected the government to win the election, by June 1994 about

70 percent expected the coalition's reelection.

Most of this Kohl comeback occurred between March and the June 1994 European election. In late summer the Social Democrats stopped the hemorrhaging. Their new team approach helped to stabilize the SPD's support at about the 36 percent mark it maintained until the election.

After the European Parliament election there was little doubt that the CDU would remain the largest party and that Helmut Kohl would be preferred over Scharping as the next Chancellor by a wide margin. It was also apparent that the Union could lose its junior partner, the Free Democrats, if it fell below the 5 percent hurdle – and hence its position as the dominant coalition partner. Without the Free Democrats the Union would be forced into a Grand Coalition with the Social Democrats, or even worse find itself thrown into opposition by a tripartite alignment of Social Democrats, Greens and Free Democrats. Finally, there was the possibility that the PDS could return to the parliament either by surmounting the 5 percent mark or by winning three direct district elections. A strong PDS showing could reduce the combined CDU–FDP seat total from a majority to a plurality. The CDU thus faced a dilemma. It could not continue to govern without the FDP, yet the FDP could not clear the 5 percent barrier without substantial help from CDU voters, which would cut into its own vote total.

## The Red Stockings: A Mid-Campaign Pick-Me-Up

Following the decisive victory at the European parliament election (see Chapter 1), the Union was concerned that the campaign had peaked too soon. With the national election still four months away, campaign strategists worried that the CDU's message would become stale and tired. The party searched for a new campaign theme to carry it through to the October election.

What campaign planners called "a gift from Heaven" came in late June when the Social Democrats in the eastern state of Saxony-Anhalt formed a minority government with the Greens that was "tolerated" by the former communists, the Party of Democratic Socialism. With their own campaign strategy in a shambles, the Social Democrats were desperate for a win and a media-assisted shift in momentum. In 1994 the numerous state elections that preceded the October vote were somewhat similar to the functions of presidential primary elections in the United States. The outcomes of these elections could either rejuvenate or depress the party faithful.

At the Saxony-Anhalt state election the Social Democrats and the Greens fell 9 seats short of a majority to replace the existing CDU–FDP government. Instead of forming a Grand Coalition with the CDU, the SPD decided to govern with the Greens and accepted PDS assurances that it would not use its 21 seats to support the CDU and bring down the government.

The Union now had what it considered was a gripping theme to counter the SPD's "its time for a change" campaign. The CDU, of course, was well-trained and experienced in Cold War-style anticommunism and an entire media campaign was prepared linking the Social Democrats with the PDS. A poster with a red sock on a wash line with the slogan "On to the future, but not in red socks!" was quickly produced and distributed.

The so-called "Rote Socken" (red socks) message was not limited to the West, as some party strategists proposed, but its major purpose was to divide the western Social Democrats. Kohl and other CDU leaders never tired of citing Kurt Schumacher, the first postwar leader of the SPD, who after 1945 termed the Communists "rotlackierten Faschisten" (red-lacquered Fascists). In their standard campaign speeches, CDU speakers asked rhetorically: How could this old and honorable democratic party, the Social Democrats, cooperate with this discredited band of ex-communists? The CDU ran a series of TV spots arguing that the new SPD leadership had betrayed the party's rank-and-file electorate by the decision to cooperate with the ex-communists.

Publicly, the SPD responded to CDU attacks on its Saxony-Anhalt decision by questioning the democratic commitment of the Christian Democrats in the eastern state. As a "bloc party" in the communist-dominated National Front, it was hardly an integral part of the communist system. The only unblemished democratic parties in the East, according to the SPD, were the Social Democrats and the Greens, the new parties founded during the Revolution of 1989–1990. They, therefore, should build the government. SPD partisans claimed that the Christian Democrats could further its own "democratic maturation process" by accepting this new government and becoming a loyal opposition. Privately, SPD strategists argued that the party had little choice but to form a government with the Greens, since a Grand Coalition so close to a national election would have undercut the party's entire strategy. Yet some in Bonn were hesitant. The drive for the alignment came from Saxony-Anhalt, not Bonn, and above all from the Alliance 90 group.

There is some question as to whether the "red socks" campaign had any positive impact for the Union, especially in the East. Almost three-fourths of the eastern electorate did not see the PDS as a "danger to democracy" (Basis Poll, September 1994). Even most Christian Democratic supporters in the East (55 percent) did not view the PDS as a "danger". Western opinion on this question was more evenly divided, but only 41 percent of western voters saw the PDS as a danger while 49 percent did not. These data suggest that the entire campaign was a wash: the CDU lost as many voters, particularly in the East, with this issue as it gained. Indeed, the CDU in the new states downplayed the whole campaign. Many party members in the East had cooperated and profited from their relationship with the communist regime. Also the big CDU gains took place *before* the "Red Socks" campaign. The proportion of voters who expected the CDU to win did *not* change significantly between June and October.

Nonetheless, the red-stockings theme gave the party faithful a mid-campaign pick-me-up and brought some life into an otherwise dull campaign. While it did little to mobilize the undecided voter, it probably did serve to energize CDU activists.

The final campaign surprise occurred about a week before the vote when Kohl announced in a television interview that the current campaign would be his last. At some point in the new legislative period he would step down from the Chancellorship, but still remain a parliamentary deputy. Although he later seemed to hedge on whether and when he actually would retire, most observers do not expect him to lead the CDU in the next election.

## The Results

It was not until the early morning hours of 17 October that the CDU was certain that it would return to power. The economic upturn had come just in time, but it was a quirk in Germany's complicated electoral law that produced just enough of a majority, ten seats, to insure Kohl's reelection. The initial computer projections and the final raw vote totals gave the CDU–FDP coalition a majority of only two seats. But after the calculation of the "overhang mandates" the size of the parliament increased by sixteen seats and the Kohl government's majority by an additional eight seats.[1]

Shortly after the polls had closed and the first projections, which gave the government at best a two seat majority, were broadcast, Chancellor Kohl appeared at CDU headquarters and claimed victory. To the bewilderment of journalists and pollsters he cited a probable working majority of *ten* seats for his coalition. This prediction was not based on any advanced district-level calculations of his election staff, but was simply an educated guess by the Chancellor after briefly eyeballing the raw vote. He was mindful of election night in 1969 when Willy Brandt (SPD) and Walter Scheel (FDP) seized the initiative to form a new government even though the CDU remained the largest party. Kohl with his early victory claim wanted to head off any possible approach by the SPD and the Greens to the FDP. A tripartite SPD–Green–FDP (traffic light) coalition with 348 seats would have had a majority of 24 seats. His fears were unfounded. The SPD leadership never made any attempt to construct such a government. About seven hours later, after all the votes had been counted and the overhang mandates distributed, Kohl's prediction of a 10-seat majority proved to be absolutely correct.

The high number of excess mandates in 1994 can be traced to specific state-level factors. In Brandenburg, for example, where the SPD was awarded three additional seats, the party won all twelve of the district contests as compared to only five district victories in 1990. This unexpectedly good showing was due to the weakness and divisions of the CDU in this state and the popularity of the SPD minister-president Manfred Stolpe. Generally, however, the SPD's grassroots organization in the East is very weak; the party had difficulty finding good local candidates to run against the better-known CDU entries. In the four other eastern states the CDU won 10 excess mandates. An added factor favoring the CDU in the East was the strong showing of the PDS, which generally took more votes from the SPD than the CDU and turned many districts into three-cornered contests where the CDU was able to win a plurality.

The CDU was able to carry the nearly moribund FDP across

the 5 percent line, but it did so at the expense of its own vote total. Fully 60 percent of the FDP's second ballot vote of 7 percent, or about 4 percent, came from CDU voters (Forschungs-gruppe Wahlen, 1994b: 16). It could be argued, of course, that these ballot splitters were not CDU voters, but rather "coalition" voters using the two-ballot system to maximize the return for the governing parties. They could also be practicing what one pollster has called "political polygamy"; over 40 percent of the German electorate "feels close" to more than one political party and favors government by coalition (Köcher, 1994: 5).

This combined CDU–FDP total would have yielded a majority of about twenty-five seats had it not been for the return of the PDS to the parliament, which was the result of yet another quirk in the electoral law: the waiver of the 5 percent rule if a party wins at least three district seats. With four district victories the PDS, with only 4.4 percent of the second-ballot vote, shared fully in the proportional pay-out and received a total of 30 mandates.

## The Aftermath: The CDU in the Post-Kohl Era

As expected, the CDU offered few initiatives in its new government program. Social Democratic control of the Bundesrat means that the country is governed by a *de facto* Grand Coalition. No major government program can be passed without the support of the Social Democrats. With the loss of its comfortable majority, the continued decline of its junior partner and the foreseeable exit of Helmut Kohl from the political stage, the Union is now in a state of transition which corresponds to its condition after Adenauer's departure in 1963. The party's most glaring weakness is the lack of a successor generation either in the Bundestag or the states which could assume leadership positions in the near term. Within the Bundestag, Wolfgang Schäuble, the heir apparent and probable Chancellor candidate in 1998, remains a question mark because of his health. He has been confined to a wheelchair since an October, 1990 assas-sination attempt. Schäuble also has little campaign experience at the national or state level. Even in his home state of Baden-Württemberg he has never led the ticket. It is not known if he can become the *Wahllocomotive* (electoral locomotive) that the CDU has always had in winning national campaigns.

At the state level the leadership picture is also bleak. In the western states, only the Bavarian CSU governs with an absolute majority. In two other Länder, Baden-Württemberg and Bremen, the party is in a Grand Coalition with the Social Democrats. In the East, the Union enjoys an absolute majority only in Saxony where the government is led by Kohl's old nemesis, Kurt Biedenkopf. In three other eastern states, Berlin, Mecklenburg-Western Pomerania and Thuringia, it governs in coalition with the SPD. None of the three CDU minister-presidents has shown any potential for national leadership. Most of the CDU opposition leaders in the states are young unknowns who have yet to make their mark at the state level.

Although the Union has held its own in post-election polls and state elections, the FDP has continued to decline. In three state elections in 1995 the FDP surmounted the 5 percent barrier only once. It is now represented in only five of sixteen state parliaments and participates in only one state government (Rhineland-Palatinate). It has also practically vanished from many local governments. If this trend continues the Union will need a new junior partner. Some observers even speculate that a collapse of the FDP before 1998 could cause Kohl to reassess his retirement plans and run again. Only Kohl, it is argued, could bring the Union an absolute majority of seats, which would be necessary in the absence of a coalition partner. Given the electoral system, if neither the FDP nor the PDS returned to the Bundestag the CDU could secure an absolute majority of seats with less than 50 percent (some estimate as little as 45 percent) of the popular vote (Gennrich, 1995: 3).

The weakness of the FDP has also prompted a lively discussion within the CDU about a possible new relationship with the Greens, whom the Union once denounced as a dangerous, anti-democratic left-wing sect (also see Chapter 5). Following the 1994 disappearance of the FDP from local government in North Rhine-Westphalia, the CDU at the local level formed alliances with the Greens in several small towns and cities. The alternative in most cases would been opposition or a Grand Coalition with the SPD. A few CDU prominents, most notably former General Secretary, Heiner Geißler, publicly advocated a rethinking of the Union's relationship to the Greens. Even Chancellor Kohl found a few kind words for the party, and the CDU in the Bundestag voted against the SPD and awarded the Greens one of the chamber's vice-presidencies at the beginning of the new legislative term. Most party leaders, including Kohl, however, avoid any public speculations about a future Black-Green alignment, citing the differences between the parties especially on economic and defense policies, and for fear of upsetting an already very nervous FDP.

Kohl's apparent "last hurrah" in 1994 was thus a muted victory. The Christian Democrats were the prototype of the so-called "catch-all" parties that emerged in postwar Western Europe and Japan. Unlike its counterparts, especially in Italy and Japan, it has prospered even in the 1990s. But with no leader of Kohl's stature in sight it will be difficult for the Union to maintain its hegemony as the changing German party system enters the next century.

**Note**

1. For information on this aspect of the electoral system, see Chapter 1.

**References**

Feldmayer, Karl. 1993. "Das Undenkbare Denken. Untergangsstimmung in der CDU," *Frankfurter Allgemeine Zeitung* (1 December).

Forschungsgruppe Wahlen. 1992a. *Wahl in Baden-Württemberg. Eine Analyse der Landtagswahl vom 5. April 1992.* Mannheim: Forschungsgruppe Wahlen.

———. 1992b. *Wahl in Schleswig-Holstein. Eine Analyse der Landtagswahl vom 5. April 1992.* Mannheim: Forschungsgruppe Wahlen.

———. 1994a. *Politbarometer* (March). Mannheim: Forschungsgruppe Wahlen.

———. 1994b. *Bundestagswahl 1994. Eine Analyse der Wahl zum 13.*

*Deutschen Bundestag*. Mannheim: Forschungsgruppe Wahlen.

Gauly, Thomas M. 1994. "Das Jahr 1994. Strategie und Planung im Superwahljahr," unpublished manuscript, CDU Campaign Staff, Bonn.

Gennrich, Klaus. 1994. "Die Union setzt auf Kohl, das letzte Schwergewicht," *Frankfurter Allgemeine Zeitung* (25 June).

——. 1995. "Der Kanzler braucht wenig Durchschlagskraft. Weg und Ziel der Union heißt Kohl," *Frankfurter Allgemeine Zeitung* (18 July).

Hofmann, Gunter and Werner A. Perger. 1994. "Ohnmächtige Riesen. Die strategische Basis der Volksparteien im Superwahljahr," in Wilhelm Bürklin and Dieter Roth, eds. *Das Superwahljahr*. Cologne: Bund Verlag.

Köcher Renate. 1994. "Der Phönix unter der Asche," *Frankfurter Allgemeine Zeitung* (23 November).

Stock, Wolfgang. 1994a. "Kohl allein ist das Thema," *Frankfurter Allgemeine Zeitung* (25 August).

——, 1994b. "Die Namen der Gegner kommen kaum vor," *Frankfurter Allgemeine Zeitung* (12 October).

# 3
# The Social Democrats: From Offense to Defense

## Gerard Braunthal

If the German voters had followed the example of dissatisfied voters in other advanced industrial countries who have recently ousted the parties in power in a national election, then on 16 October 1994 the Germans should have cast their ballots for the SPD and other opposition parties in record numbers. Many did, but not enough to give the SPD a mandate to form a new government.

The SPD shortfall was the more painful coming on top of similar losses in the 1983, 1987, and 1990 elections. In each instance, the party could not convince enough voters to oust Kohl's conservative–liberal government. In the 1983 and 1987 elections, most voters thought the CDU/CSU–FDP government was more competent than the SPD to deal with the key economic issues of prime importance to them. In the 1990 election, Kohl's swift endorsement of German unification and the SPD's hesitancy on unification (based primarily on fears that the financial burden would be too high) was the decisive factor explaining the party's smashing defeat.

There were, of course, other reasons the SPD had difficulties in mobilizing electoral support since 1983. Among them were its numerous leadership changes and divisions among members of its top policy-making bodies, partially caused by feuds among its factions. These problems led to doubts among voters about the SPD's competence to govern the country again, as it had done in coalition with the FDP from 1969 to 1982. But at the beginning of the electoral cycle for the 1994 Bundestagswahl, the SPD thought it could be different this time.

## Leading up to the Superwahljahr

When the patriarchal Willy Brandt resigned as chairperson in 1987, after twenty-three years in office, Hans-Jochen Vogel (the SPD chancellor candidate in 1983) led the party until 1991. Then the young Björn Engholm, minister-president of Schleswig-Holstein, assumed the chairmanship. However, Engholm resigned in May 1993 after admitting that he had lied to an investigative commission probing a CDU election scandal in his Land.

Johannes Rau, minister-president of North Rhine-Westphalia and chancellor candidate in 1987, took over as acting chairperson until the party elected Rudolf Scharping as chairperson at a convention in June 1993. Scharping was the 45-year-old minister-president of Rhineland-Palatinate. Before the election, SPD leaders had decided to inject more intraparty democracy into the organization, following years of membership discontent with the oligarchical decision-making process (Braunthal, 1994: 24–5) In an unprecedented referendum among SPD members about their candidate preference for the post, Scharping triumphed over Gerhard Schröder, minister-president of Lower Saxony and former Young Socialist (Juso) chairperson, and Heidi Wieczorek-Zeul, Bundestag deputy and former Juso chairperson.

Scharping had studied political science, law, and sociology at Bonn University in the late 1960s and early 1970s. He had risen swiftly in the party. One of the favorites of Brandt's "grandchildren," he headed the SPD Land organization in Lower Saxony from 1985 to 1993 and became minister-president in 1991. Although lacking the colorful personality of his rivals Schröder and Oskar Lafontaine (minister-president of the Saar and chancellor candidate in 1990), party activists respected Scharping for his diligence, honesty, reliability, and unassuming manners (Rosenbaum, 1993; Leif and Raschke, 1994). He is a pragmatist rather than ideologue, but feels politically at home in the party's center and right wings. He had worked closely with other party presidium members, who included the deputy chairpersons Rau, Lafontaine, Wieczorek-Zeul, Herta Däubler-Gmelin, and Wolfgang Thierse (the former SPD-GDR leader); the party treasurer Inge Wettig-Danielmeier; and the party secretary Günter Verheugen.

Among Scharping's immediate tasks was to gain consensus among presidium members on major policy recommendations and to dampen the fratricidal feuds between the party's left and right wings that had long divided the party on domestic and foreign-policy issues. The left wing consisted of a shrinking group of Old Left working-class members, a minority of SPD deputies, and a large group of New Left members clustered in the Jusos. To coordinate their positions, the leftist groups formed the Frankfurt Circle. The right wing consisted of conservative and pragmatic leaders and deputies, strongly anticommunist and antileftist, who formed the Seeheim Circle. To keep peace between the two wings, a loosely knit center bloc emerged, whose spokespersons included many former left-wing leaders and moderate politicians. When the SPD factions failed to achieve consensus on policy issues, the media exploited the intraparty division, which in turn damaged the party's image, especially during an election year.

Scharping and his associates also had to confront the SPD's slumping membership, which declined from a peak of more than 1 million in 1976, to 865,000 in 1993. Among the members in 1993, less than 30 percent were women and only 4 percent were under age 25 (*Der Spiegel*, 17 May 1993). Party leaders were especially concerned about youth opting out of politics altogether or supporting the Greens and the Party of Democratic Socialism (PDS), the successor to the ruling Socialist Unity party (SED) in the GDR. The party also wondered about the low number (25,000) of SPD members living in eastern Germany.

The new eastern SPD, founded in October 1989 when the SED was still in power, also had its growing pains. In the March 1990 elections of the GDR parliament, it failed to reach a hoped for plurality. The votes it received from well-educated, middle-class, urban and left intellectual voters could not overcome the low support it received from blue-collar workers who, dissatisfied by decades of "real existing socialism," eagerly endorsed the CDU's promises to raise their standard of living. Despite the East German SPD's merger with the West German SPD in September 1990, party officials have been unable to build up an effective organization in an area that was paradoxically the stronghold of the party before 1933.

The SPD in the West has become more "new" middle class, with a rising percentage of salaried employees and civil servants and a declining percentage of blue-collar workers among its supporters. Its young members have become interested in the

"New Politics" themes of participatory democracy, the quality of life, and other postbourgeois (or postmaterialist) values, while the SPD's older members have retained acquisitive (or materialist) values related to such "Old Politics" issues as job security and adequate income. Scharping and his fellow leaders continued to face the dilemma of how to reconcile these conflicting values within the party and narrow the gap between the New Politics members and the primarily Old Politics voters.

Thus, on the eve of "Super Election Year 1994," in which nineteen local, Land, European, and national elections were to be held, the SPD leaders faced several challenges. This chapter deals with the party's campaign strategy and actions in the 1994 national election. It inquires into the SPD programs and issues, the mobilization of social groups, and the long-term implications of the election for the party. Such an inquiry must be set within the parameter of coalition politics, which turned out to be crucial in the election.

## The Campaign: Phase One

Party managers must plan early to win an election. In mid-1993, Scharping formed a commission, and in early 1994 a kitchen cabinet, to draft details of the SPD campaign. At the party convention in Wiesbaden in November 1993, Scharping and Lafontaine, the party's spokesperson on economic and financial affairs, presented the central themes of the SPD electoral program. They tried to gain the support of most left and right faction members in order to present to the public a united party capable of beating the weakened Kohl government.

In their convention speeches, the two leaders dealt primarily with ways in which an SPD-led government would make improvements in employment, the economy, finances, and the social welfare system – the problems that public opinion polls found were of greatest concern to voters (see Chapter 10). To raise more revenue to help eastern Germany, the SPD proposals included a 10 percent tax surcharge on incomes of more than DM 50,000 for singles and more than DM 100,000 for married couples (changed later to 60,000 DM and 120,000 DM respectively because too many SPD adherents would have fallen into the higher tax-paying bracket). The SPD chiefs reasoned that such a proposal, which exempted 80 percent of taxpayers, was fairer than Kohl's plan to reimpose a 7.5 percent solidarity surcharge on all taxpayers.

Scharping and Lafontaine called for cuts in government expenditures, including welfare programs; and a meshing of the government budget with improvements in the economy that were linked to increases in productivity. Only then, so ran the argument, could the economy become more competitive with that of other countries and could unemployment be reduced. The two SPD leaders also called for job sharing and reduced working hours, more apprenticeship training, state help for financially weak firms that hired unemployed workers, state help for eastern firms for three to five years, greater support for families with children, the imposition of an energy tax that would pay for mass transit, the building of 100,000 apartments per year to ease the shortage of affordable apartments, and ecological modernization.

In the party's campaign strategy, Scharping, imitating President Clinton, planned to win over the larger group of undecided centrist voters rather than the small percentage of Green voters on the SPD's left flank. He asked the Wiesbaden convention delegates to make further retreats on controversial domestic policies, such as political asylum, on which the party had already made important concessions to the CDU/CSU, and civil liberties, on which the CDU/CSU has normally taken a tougher law-and-order stance than the SPD. He convinced a slim majority of delegates to support, with conditions, the Kohl government's bill allowing security agencies to put eavesdropping devices in apartments where criminal activities were suspected. (In 1994, Scharping agreed to the privatization of the postal service over the objection of the postal workers' union.)

At Wiesbaden, Scharping relegated disputed foreign policy planks to the sideline, knowing that their discussion would produce damaging debates. He won support, after years of intraparty discussion, for his proposal that German troops be allowed to participate in United Nations peacekeeping operations if they were not to be involved in combat and the Bundestag gave prior approval. Thereby, his foreign policy hardly differed from that of Kohl.

In early 1994, SPD leaders were optimistic that they would win the national election. The party had done well in most Land elections during the 1990–1993 period. It was a member of 11 out of 16 Land coalition governments and held the minister-presidency in 9 of them. For a brief period in 1990 and since April 1991 the SPD-governed Länder held a majority in the Bundesrat, which gave the party the power to block CDU/CSU–FDP legislation affecting the Länder. However, such veto power can only be effective if the SPD minister-presidents, who are pledged to serve the interests of their states, agree to take a common position. This is normally the case, but there have been exceptions.[1] The SPD has to live with such divergences and schisms, but they accentuate its problems in an election year (Sturm, 1993: 123–4; Braunthal, 1994: 274–6).

The SPD leaders' optimism in early 1994 also was caused by public opinion polls which showed that the SPD would win if an election were held then (see Chapter 8). Polls indicated that the SPD would capture 38 to 41 percent of the vote; the CDU/CSU, 32 to 37 percent; the Alliance 90/Greens, 9 percent; the FDP, 6 percent; and the PDS, a few direct district seats. The SPD ranked high because voters characterized the party as the most competent to deal with the key issues facing the nation and because the voters had more confidence in Scharping than in Kohl.

The SPD expected to make a strong showing in the October election because of the mounting dissatisfaction with the Kohl government's inability to improve the economy. Voters in western Germany were tired of huge budget deficits, high unemployment, and the costs of rebuilding the eastern German economy. Voters in eastern Germany felt betrayed by Kohl's "blooming landscape" promises that unification would bring the benefits of capitalism at little cost. The SPD leaders' optimism was reinforced by the March 1994 election in Lower Saxony where the party captured an unprecedented absolute majority of seats in the Landtag. Minister-president Schröder no longer had to govern with a coalition partner.

However, the favorable signals forecasting an SPD victory in the October national election did not last. The economy began to improve in spring 1994, rebounding to the benefit of the citizens – and to the CDU/CSU–FDP government. Beginning in May 1994, polls found that respondents believed that the CDU/CSU was more competent than the SPD to solve economic problems (see Chapter 10). In addition, Scharping committed a series of errors that did not help the party. When he unveiled the new SPD election program shortly before Easter, he confused gross income with net income in describing which citizens would have to pay higher taxes. Critics consequently questioned his knowledge of economic affairs. Moreover, Scharping was unable to avoid internal party disputes over the issue of imposing a speed limit on the *Autobahnen* and revisions in abortion legislation. By overreacting to the election in May of Roman Herzog (CDU) to the federal presidency, Scharping was viewed as a poor loser.[2] These image problems contributed to the poor showing of the SPD in the European Parliament election in June. The party mustered only 32.2 percent of the vote, a drop of more than 5 percent since the previous election of 1989 (see Table 1.1).

In the meantime, the SPD managers worked on details of the national election campaign after the leadership had agreed on fundamental strategies. The managers emphasized the themes of employment, housing, and taxation; they drafted slogans ("security instead of fear" (*Sicherheit statt Angst*), "jobs, jobs, jobs" (*Arbeit, Arbeit, Arbeit*), and "the time had come for change") and chose photos for street placards, including one showing a grandmother saying: "Kohl? I am for someone younger." They targeted, among others, the blue-collar workers, who no longer vote automatically for the party, and the large group of undecided voters. The party told these groups that only an SPD-led government would strengthen their economic and social position, and produce a new political start in the country. The specialists also planned the various phases of the costly (nearly DM 90 million) campaign, including the "hot" one in the six weeks before the election. Scharping was to travel throughout Germany in a special train and deliver about 120 speeches.

The SPD domestic and foreign policy proposals, first presented at the 1993 Wiesbaden convention, were incorporated into an "SPD government program" that the party unveiled in March 1994 and affirmed at a special election convention in Halle on 22 June. The program, sketched above, substantially narrowed the party's differences with the CDU/CSU, although the SPD remained to the left of the CDU/CSU in maintaining its commitment to expanding social justice and siding with the growing underclass in both parts of Germany (SPD, 1994). At the June convention, the party formally elected Scharping as its candidate for the chancellor's post.

Scharping's attempt to unify the party and to minimize internal criticisms of his policies during the campaign were not entirely successful. Schröder, in an interview with the weekly *Der Spiegel*, assailed Scharping's electoral strategy. The SPD, Schröder argued, should not make unemployment and crime, with their negative connotation, the principal themes to win the centrist voters. He also argued that the party should not focus on Scharping as the top candidate. Rather, the SPD should emphasize its team of highly skilled minister-presidents who had legislative successes in their Länder (*Der Spiegel*, 20 June 1994).

The SPD left wing warned Scharping that the party would not win if its program hardly differed from that of the CDU/CSU, omitted any vision of the future (including the ecological renewal of industrial society), and hewed closely to the status quo (*Neue Ruhr Zeitung*, 18 February 1994). In numerous appearances at party meetings, Scharping tried to defuse these criticisms. Only half in jest, he told leftists that if they needed visions, they should visit a doctor.

To offset internal party criticisms, Scharping looked for allies elsewhere. He announced to delegates at a meeting of the Federation of German Industry (BDI) in May that if the SPD won the election, it was willing in 1995 to conclude a solidarity pact with business, limit wage increases, lower the costs of fringe benefits, and promote investments. German Trade Union Federation (DGB) officials, most of whom are Social Democrats, were miffed by Scharping's position, but they did not want to assail publicly his plan for fear of weakening the party's chance in the October election.

As part of the campaign ritual, major German politicians met with foreign government officials to increase their own standing in the country. In April 1994, Scharping visited the United States to convince President Clinton and Congressional leaders that an SPD-led German government would not veer away from the basic German foreign policies, including support for NATO. Scharping said that the SPD backed German participation in UN blue-helmet peacekeeping activities if they did not violate the German Basic Law and if they received Parliamentary approval in each instance (*New York Times*, 10 April 1994).

In late August, Scharping, who until then had run the campaign almost single-handedly, finally announced the members of his shadow cabinet, who would assist him in the campaign and become ministers if the SPD won the election. However, unless the SPD gained the nearly impossible goal of an absolute majority of votes, Scharping would have to appoint some ministers from another party. Thus, the list was interesting primarily as an indicator of the ranking of leaders within the SPD. The fifteen members consisted of eight men, including Scharping's two main rivals, Lafontaine (to become Minister of Finance), Schröder (to become Minister of Economics, Transportation, and Energy), and seven women. Party officials promptly printed 150,000 copies of a placard showing the three male minister-presidents as the troika that could produce an SPD victory. Some women members in the shadow cabinet were displeased that not one among them was chosen as being worthy of troika status (*Der Spiegel*, 5 September 1994).

### The Campaign: Phase Two

Early September marked the beginning of the "hot phase" of the campaign, during which the party scheduled the last round of rallies, citizens' meetings, the distribution of leaflets, and an avalanche of advertisements. At a mass rally of 100,000 SPD members in Dortmund on 4 September, SPD leaders unveiled the party's "first 100-day program" should it gain political power in the new Bundestag. The program set priorities on issues, which had been spelled out in more detail in the SPD government program.

In planning the timetable of the campaign, SPD strategists did not foresee the tepid SPD–CDU debate on policy issues. This lack of action partly occurred because there was a general consensus among the major parties, especially on foreign policy. The strategists realized that their earlier campaign picturing the SPD as the organization ready to fight vigorously the ills of society had been ineffective. The CDU/CSU had used the SPD message as an argument that the Social Democrats were merely an alarmist party, which worried about a nonexistent misery in the country. Thus, the SPD strategists, shifting tactics, portrayed their party as one that strove for a greater sense of community among the population. The placards and media advertisements now read, among others, "More money for children" and "Affordable apartments." Scharping was shown as a family man who excelled at bicycling, tennis, and other sports (*Der Spiegel*, 25 July 1994). However, the attractiveness of placards and advertisements could not compensate for Scharping's lack of emotion and charisma in his campaign speeches laden with dry facts.

## Coalition Disputes

One theme that existed throughout the Superwahljahr concerned the coalition possibilities after the election. The question of which party would join a coalition with the SPD, should it win a plurality of votes, greatly interested the media, the public, and SPD members. The CDU/CSU chiefs queried Scharping repeatedly about his choice of a coalition partner to make him acknowledge that he might form a "red (SPD)–green" coalition (or a red (SPD)–red (PDS)–green coalition, see next section). Because a red–green coalition was acceptable to only 40 percent of SPD members, the CDU/CSU hoped to benefit from a backlash against a potential alliance of two "leftist" parties. Knowing that any prior commitment was bound to lose the SPD numerous votes, Scharping said that the SPD would not decide on a coalition until after the election. According to one press report, Scharping told colleagues privately that he was willing to form a coalition with the reformist Greens, but with the understanding that he would not make a public announcement before the election (*Die Zeit*, 17 June 1994). Yet, a few SPD leaders (Verheugen, Schröder, and Wieczorek-Zeul) endorsed such a coalition publicly during the campaign, although they disagreed with the Greens on some key issues. They opposed the Greens' demand for a DM 5 per liter tax hike on gasoline (it would hurt the lower-income groups especially) and for the eventual abolition of the NATO alliance and the German armed forces. However, they knew that these were maximum demands subject to compromise.

Scharping's initial strategy of avoiding conflict with the CDU/CSU led some observers to conclude that, despite his denials, he and some other top SPD chiefs favored a grand coalition with the governing party after the October election. Yet the signals were not that clear. In August, Scharping launched a summer offensive, denouncing CDU/CSU *Fraktion* leader Wolfgang Schäuble for his nationalist speeches and Kohl for failing to reduce un-

employment. Most SPD leaders officially rejected a grand
coalition for ideological reasons and for fear that it would create
a small and weak legislative opposition of minor parties.

The media also speculated on the possibility of a "traffic light"
coalition of red, green, and yellow (FDP). Both the FDP,
committed to its alliance with the CDU/CSU, and the SPD ruled
out such a possibility. Wieczorek-Zeul, expressing the SPD's
hostility to the FDP, said that one cannot ally with a party that
shared responsibility with the CDU/CSU for the misery in
Germany. Observers also predicted that a traffic light coalition
would be too unstable and not last the four-year legislative term.
The Greens recalled ruefully that Scharping as minister-president
of Rhineland-Palatinate had formed a coalition with the FDP
rather than with them.

### SPD and PDS

The CDU, playing on the citizens' fear of communism, had
demanded early in 1994 that the SPD distance itself completely
from the PDS. Scharping retorted that the SPD had no intention
of ever forming a political alliance with the PDS. He reminded
the CDU chiefs that many of their politicians in Brandenburg had
come to an understanding with PDS leaders not to compete with
one another for certain offices in order to defeat rival SPD
candidates (*Die Welt*, 17 January 1994). Scharping also urged the
CDU to tell its voters in those East Berlin districts where the PDS
candidates had a chance to gain a Bundestag seat to vote for the
SPD candidate, who was second strongest, and thereby prevent a
PDS victory. Not surprisingly, the CDU refused to make such an
appeal.

After the 26 June Landtag election in Saxony-Anhalt (in the
former GDR), the coalition issue took on a new dimension. The
CDU and SPD could have formed a grand coalition, but SPD
leaders in Bonn did not want to give voters throughout Germany
the impression that such an alternative could serve as the model
for a national government after the Bundestagswahl. Therefore,
SPD and Greens, as they had done in a few other Länder, formed
a coalition government. However, as the two parties did not have
a majority in the Land parliament, their minority government
needed the legislative support of another party; in this instance,

the PDS. The new Land government's dependence on the PDS for survival changed the nature of the national election campaign.

The CDU knew immediately that it had the perfect election issue to assail the leftist parties (SPD, Greens, and PDS). It cleverly resuscitated the dormant anticommunist feelings among many citizens. Inaugurating a "red sock" (the symbol of the PDS) campaign, it denounced the unholy leftist alliance in Saxony-Anhalt. Implicit in this denunciation was the message that the SPD and the Greens – already a dangerous alliance – were sympathetic to the PDS and had sold out to it. The CDU issued posters with the slogan "Into the future, but not with red socks." Kohl characterized the Saxony-Anhalt "left front" as "a scandal on an enormous scale" and a "treasonous act," which if replicated in Bonn would lead to a "change of system in our republic" (*Boston Globe*, 29 August 1994).

In response, the SPD printed posters showing a photo of Kohl meeting the GDR chief Erich Honecker, with the caption that 63 percent of CDU deputies from the new Länder had been members of the communist National Front before unification (*Die Zeit*, 29 July 1994; *Der Spiegel*, 25 July 1994). To minimize the CDU propaganda, eastern SPD leaders supported Scharping in a sharp anti-PDS declaration at a Dresden meeting in August. Scharping's demonizing of the PDS did not find unanimity among SPD adherents, however. For example, Schröder said it was more important to integrate the PDS into the democratic system than to try to keep it out.

**The Election**

Public opinion polls had predicted correctly that the SPD would not supplant the CDU/CSU as the governing party. The SPD gained 36.4 percent of the votes, but remained 5 percent behind the CDU/CSU (see Table 1.2). Although the SPD had received 2.9 percent more votes than in 1990, it was still disappointed by the result. It did well in many of its traditional bastions in western Germany, mustering 50 percent of the workers' votes and 60 percent of those organized in trade unions, but trailed the CDU in the other occupational categories. In western Germany, the SPD did best in the Saar, Bremen, North Rhine-Westphalia, and

Lower Saxony, but in some areas lost votes compared to the 1990 election. In eastern Germany, where the SPD emphasized its plans to cut unemployment, it gained the most votes in Brandenburg and Saxony-Anhalt, and less in other areas. Its worst showing was in Saxony, where it barely received 25 percent of the total vote.

In recent elections, many voters, disgruntled by public policy failures and scandals, have increasingly switched parties or have not voted. In the 1994 election, the SPD total vote of more than 17 million voters included 700,000 former CDU voters, 600,000 former FDP voters, and 600,000 former non-voters. However, the SPD lost 200,000 previous voters to the PDS and more to the other parties (*Frankfurter Rundschau*, 18 October 1994). Among voters between the ages of 25 and 34 the SPD gained the most votes (39 percent), ahead of the CDU/CSU (32 percent) and the Greens (13 percent). The SPD mustered relatively few votes (33 percent) among men under 24. It received more support from Protestants than from Catholics and more from urban than rural dwellers (see Chapter 9).

The SPD lost the election for many reasons. First and probably foremost, the economic upswing in mid-1994 redounded to the benefit of the governing parties. Second, a colorless Scharping, although known for his intraparty management skills, kept making tactical and strategic mistakes. He failed to communicate his views to the public, and alienated many voters by his refusal to talk about the coalition question. Third, many potential SPD voters feared an SPD coalition with the Greens, especially if it was dependent on PDS toleration. Others viewed the party's program as an imitation of the CDU/CSU program. Fourth, the SPD allowed the CDU/CSU to set the agenda for nearly all campaign issues instead of offering its own agenda (Seifert 1994: 1449; Raschke, 1994a).

Yet, the SPD's gains in votes and Bundestag seats over 1990 made the defeat less painful. Party members, having lost their lethargy during the many years of SPD opposition, knew that Scharping had produced more intraparty unity than his predecessors. Thus, they hoped that he would strengthen the party in the new legislative period.

## Prospects for the Future

Forecasts in the political realm are fraught with dangers, given the many unpredictable variables. If the CDU/CSU–FDP government holds power for its full term until 1998, the SPD will remain the chief opposition party in uneasy tandem with the Greens and the PDS. What are the SPD's prospects of forming the next government, given the continuing realignment of parties and dealignment of voters (Dalton and Bürklin, 1993: 233–56)?

The answer depends, first, on how voters will judge the SPD's legislative position and competence in domestic and foreign policies from 1994 to 1998. The party's policy positions will be shaped by its top leaders. If they fail to present challenging alternatives to the governing coalition (known in Bonn circles as the "KoKo [Kohl Koalition] system"), then the SPD's chance of electoral success in 1998 remains slim, unless an economic recession or other political crisis coincides with the next election.

The legislative position and the SPD's competence on issues also will be shaped by its minister-presidents, who have a majority in the Bundesrat. They have opportunities to influence and, more important, block government-initiated legislation that directly affects the Länder. Thus, the CDU/CSU–FDP majority in the Bundestag cannot expect to receive automatic approval for their legislation in the Bundesrat. As a consequence, the parliamentary mediation committee (*Vermittlungsausschuß*), in which Bundesrat and Bundestag representatives have an equal number of seats, becomes a crucial organ to reconcile differences between the parties. In effect, the SPD and CDU/CSU members of the committee, which Lafontaine has headed since late 1994, serve as an informal grand coalition.

Second, future SPD prospects of victory depend on the voters' judgment of the new SPD leadership. In 1995, the SPD was beset by a fratricidal leadership struggle between Scharping and Schröder, who accused the chairman of not consulting him and other top leaders during and since the 1994 campaign. Other critics denounced Scharping's pragmatic and conservative positions and his lethargic leadership style. As a consequence of the infighting, the party's ranking in the polls plummeted to a dangerous low. Delegates at the November 1995 convention, partly blaming Scharping for the disaster, did not support his renewed candidacy as chairman. Instead, they voted for the left-leaning Lafontaine to succeed him. The new SPD chairman is likely to pursue a more confrontational course against Kohl's policies than had Scharping. As a consequence, the gap between the two parties will widen.

The upheaval in the SPD in 1995 created new uncertainties within the party. Although Scharping remained head of the SPD *Fraktion* in the Bundestag, Lafontaine's chairmanship of the party does not mean that he will be nominated automatically as chancellor candidate in 1998. Schröder remains a serious rival. Either of the two leaders are more willing than Scharping to form a national red–green coalition should the SPD gain a plurality.

Third, future SPD prospects depend on its organizational strength in eastern Germany and its tortured relationship with the PDS. After five years, the party still faces major obstacles in recruiting eastern German workers and students, who are wary of supporting a "Wessi" (West German)-dominated organization. Moreover, the SPD has not come to a consensus on admitting disillusioned SED (currently PDS) members into its ranks. Practice among eastern German local SPD branches varies widely from rejection to acceptance, although all reject PDS members who have been found guilty of human rights violations during the GDR era.

This divisive SPD–PDS issue at the local level was paralleled by a dispute between SPD chiefs in the new Länder and Scharping (then still party chairman) in Bonn. The dispute concerned the talks between SPD and PDS chiefs in Mecklenburg-Western Pomerania and Thuringia after the October 1994 Land elections; the talks concerned the PDS' willingness to tolerate a possible all-SPD minority government as they had in Saxony-Anhalt. Because of the failure of the Greens and the FDP to overcome the 5 percent barrier in the two elections, the SPD had only the choice of being tolerated by the PDS or becoming the junior coalition partner with the CDU. In both instances, it chose the latter alternative.

Scharping felt that such SPD–PDS talks, although they were fruitless, played into the hands of the Kohl government, which would renew its charge that the SPD cannot be trusted to avoid links with the PDS. Therefore, in December 1994, Scharping prepared the draft of a new declaration on quarantining the PDS. Scharping did not get approval from Schröder, Lafontaine, and top eastern SPD politicians. They felt it was the wrong approach to deal with a party that many Easterners see as their milieu. Eastern SPD politicians also reminded Scharping that they, as well as officials from other parties, worked continuously with PDS members in the new Länder's executive and legislative bodies. Scharping tabled the draft (*Der Spiegel*, 7 November and 12 December 1994; Raschke, 1994b).

Within the SPD, a compromise between the two positions on the PDS question may emerge. Thierse, an SPD deputy chairperson and deputy from East Berlin, might facilitate such a compromise. He sharply criticized the PDS for harboring many unreformed communists, but nevertheless called for a new approach: "We must produce a climate in Germany that does not demand of the East Germans that they hold everything wrong concerning their earlier life (under the GDR). If the Social Democrats do not take the initiative, the people's basic feeling of depreciation of their own life will drive them to the PDS" (*Der Spiegel*, 7 Nov. 1994).

When Lafontaine became the SPD's new chairman, he held a well-publicized talk in November 1995 with the FDS *Fraktion* chairman, Gregor Gysi. According to CDU/CSU critics, Lafontaine, sharing Thierse's conciliatory position, wanted to make the PDS "presentable" in order to tolerate its support for a red–green coalition in 1998 or, a more unlikely eventuality, to form a "red–green–red" governing coalition (*Kölner Stadt-Anzeiger*, 20 November 1995). A strong conservative wing within the SPD will bitterly oppose any rapprochement with the PDS at the national level.

Fourth, future SPD prospects depend on its ability to attract key voter groups. Among them are a politically alienated youth in both parts of Germany. The Jusos have warned their elders that unless political initiatives are introduced that speak to youth's economic, social, and cultural concerns, the party's future will be cloudy. SPD leaders are also worried about the party's sagging strength in its former city strongholds, such as Frankfurt, whose employees work increasingly in the service sector (Schacht, 1994: 999–1000). Whether the SPD's pragmatic course suffices to gain the electoral support of these groups is debatable. Brandt was successful from 1969 to 1972 because he offered an imaginative reform program to the citizenry. The SPD's chancellor candidates since then, partly because of financial constraints and partly because of a politically conservative climate, have not provided this imagination.

Granted, a true reformist program might not stop the high popular discontent with all parties; the erosion of social milieus among the population; the increasing fragmentation of society, especially in eastern Germany, in which a distinct political culture is developing; and the process of dealignment, in which voters are no longer bound to a particular party. Yet if the SPD were to move back to left center, where it was under Brandt, then the negative trends will be offset by increased electoral support from apolitical youth and other non-voters, the middle class, moderate PDS voters in the new Länder, and other switch voters. Thus, in 1998, the SPD might have a chance to top the vote for the CDU/CSU if Kohl is no longer the party's chancellor candidate. Should the SPD and the Greens assume the reins of government, it will be the first time in the history of the Federal Republic that opposition parties will replace the government in a regularly scheduled election and the first time in the history of Europe that a red–green coalition governs.

**Notes**

1. May 1991, the SPD and FDP ministers in the Rhineland-Palatinate cabinet abstained in the Bundesrat from voting on a bill because they could not agree on whether to support it or not. In 1992, the Kohl government introduced a bill in the Bundesrat increasing value-added tax, which was supported by SPD-governed Brandenburg but opposed by other SPD-governed Länder.
2. The party had hoped that its candidate, Johannes Rau, would receive the support of enough FDP delegates to the federal convention to win. However, the FDP delegates voted for Herzog in the third round, after their candidate for the presidency had lost out in the earlier rounds (Busche, 1994: 996–7).

## References

Braunthal, Gerard. 1994. *The German Social Democrats Since 1969: A Party in Power and Opposition*. Boulder: Westview Press.

Busche, Jürgen, 1994. "Die verpasste Chance," *Die Neue Gesellschaft-Frankfurter Hefte* 41 (November).

Dalton, Russell, and Wilhelm Bürklin. 1993. "The German Party System and the Future," in Russell Dalton, ed. *The New Germany Votes*. Oxford and New York: Berg.

Forschungsgruppe Wahlen. 1994. *Bundestagswahl 1994: Eine Analyse der Wahl zum 13. Deutschen Bundestag am 16. Oktober 1994*. Mannheim.

Konrad-Adenauer-Stiftung. 1994. *Die Bundestagswahl vom 16. Oktober 1994 – eine erste Analyse*. Sankt Augustin.

Leif, Thomas and Joachim Raschke. 1994. *Rudolf Scharping: Die SPD und die Macht*. Reinbek: Rowohlt.

Raschke, Joachim. 1994a. "BPA-Nachrichtenabteilung," *Fernseh-Hörfunkspiegel* I (August 22).

——. 1994b. "SPD und PDS: Selbstblockade oder Opposition?" *Blätter für deutsche und internationale Politik* 12.

Rosenbaum, Ulrich. 1993. *Rudolf Scharping: Biographie*. Berlin: Ullstein.

Schacht, Konrad. 1994. "Vorspiel zum Wechsel: Sieben wahlsoziologische Thesen zur Bundestagswahl," *Die Neue Gesellschaft-Frankfurter Hefte* 41 (November).

Seifert, Jürgen. 1994. "Kräfteverhältnisse und Optionen im neuen Bundestag," *Blätter für deutsche und internationale Politik* 12.

SPD. 1994. "Das Regierungsprogramm '94," *Politik*. Bonn.

Sturm, Roland. 1993. "The Territorial Dimension of the New Party System," in Stephen Padgett, ed., *Parties and Party Systems in the New Germany*. Aldershot: Dartmouth.

# 4
# The "Great Escape": The FDP and the Superwahljahr

## Geoffrey K. Roberts

"Klausi! Klausi!" – the staffers and supporters gathered at the Bonn headquarters of the FDP had every reason to greet the entrance of their leader, Klaus Kinkel, to the election night party with such cries. They were, though, cries of relief more than of jubilation. After nine successive Land elections (including the three on 16 October 1994, the date of the Bundestag election) and a European Parliament election in which the FDP had repeatedly failed to reach the 5 percent required to obtain parliamentary representation, the Free Democrats managed to secure 6.9 percent in the Bundestag election. This was enough for the FDP once again to be present in the Bundestag and to participate in yet another federal coalition government. As well as being the first celebration of a Bundestag election in the new headquarters in Bonn, it was Kinkel's first and last Bundestag election as party leader. Whether the FDP could consolidate, revive, and reassert itself in the German party system by the next Bundestag election in 1998, are questions that will be taken up in the final section of this chapter.

Certainly there was a poignant contrast between election night on 2 December 1990 and on 16 October 1994. In the former election the FDP secured levels of voting support in western and eastern Germany that surpassed even the most optimistic forecasts for the party (11 percent overall; 13.4 percent and a constituency victory in the new Länder). In the latter election pessimistic forecasts had suggested that the FDP might lose its Bundestag representation, as it had done in every Land election since September 1993. So cheers greeted the first prognoses from the television studios that projected that the party would scramble over the 5 percent hurdle. The party's re-entry into the

Bundestag staved off what otherwise would have been the almost inevitable disappearance of the party. However, this success did nothing to alleviate problems concerning the party's leadership, programmatic identity, or role in the party system that the run of elections in 1993–1994 had so uncompromisingly exposed.

This chapter considers the political events that impinged on the FDP in the four-year period since the first all-German Bundestag election in 1990. The chapter examines the fortunes of the FDP in other elections in Superwahljahr 1994, the campaign strategy devised by the party, the way in which the party implemented that strategy, and the outcome of the Bundestag election in relation to the future of the party.

## The Fortunes of the FDP: 1990–1994

In 1990 the FDP began its new period as government partner to the Christian Democrats with confidence and optimism. Opinion polls continued to reflect relatively high levels of support in both eastern and western Germany,[1] and in Land elections in 1991–1992 the FDP did reasonably well (see pp.64–5).

Membership of the FDP, though, was in decline after 1990. In 1991 only 92,000 members were in eastern Germany (compared to a nominal 138,000 at the time of the fusion in August 1990); there were 70,000 members in western Germany. At the end of 1992 total membership (East and West) had declined to 103,000, and at the end of 1993 was barely 94,000. The membership paid less dues – just over DM 13 million – than the larger membership of the PDS or the much smaller membership of Alliance 90/ Greens (*Woche im Bundestag*, 22 February 1995: 6). The decline in party membership in the East – a phenomenon other parties were also experiencing – was partially due to financial reasons and partially to political reasons. For instance, some members were discouraged by the dominance of ex-"bloc party" members in leading positions in the eastern party organizations (*Der Spiegel*, 12 August 1991: 75). More generally, there was an eastern rejection of party politics after forty years of near-compulsory membership by those who had entered the FDP (and CDU and PDS) at the time of the *Wende*. These individuals initially had been members of parties of the Democratic Bloc, and now they wanted to detach themselves from such associations (*Frankfurter Allgemeine Zeitung*, 2 October 1991). The party also suffered from the loss of a popular leader. Hans-Dietrich Genscher had been the most popular politician in Germany after the 1990 election (*Der Spiegel*, 27 April 1992: 58; *Süddeutsche Zeitung*, 28/29 September 1991). His resignation as Foreign Minister in April 1992 removed from active politics the FDP's principal asset, in eastern as well as in western Germany.

Otto von Lambsdorff took over the helm of the FDP, but his leadership came increasingly into question. In 1991 he was re-elected as FDP leader at the Suhl party congress, but with only 67 percent of delegate votes. Lack of any obvious successor who could command majority support in the party helped Lambsdorff to retain his post. In 1992, some party activists called for him to resign ahead of his planned retirement in 1993, but he rejected them. In 1993 he was succeeded by Klaus Kinkel, the Foreign Minister, who was elected unopposed.[2]

Kinkel's leadership was criticized even before he was elected. Some criticized his style and his unproven talents as a politician rather than as a civil servant, while others expected that the double burden of being Foreign Minister and party leader would mean that at least one of these functions would not be fulfilled satisfactorily. Even the legendary Genscher sometimes had difficulty in combining the two posts (*Der Spiegel*, 17 May 1993: 40). Möllemann and other prominent members of the North Rhine-Westphalia Land party were especially vocal in their criticisms of Kinkel (*Der Spiegel*, 6 December 1993: 25–6). Many critics thought that Kinkel was too close to the Chancellor, too ready to compromise, and too unable to define a clear and independent profile for the FDP. His ability to discipline and control his party colleagues was also criticized.

In addition, the FDP had to manage three ministerial changes in the cabinet that created strains within the party. Genscher's resignation led to Kinkel moving from his post as Justice Minister to become Foreign Minister. He defeated Irmgard Schwaetzer in a ballot of the party Executive and the parliamentary group (*Fraktion*), after premature and embarrassing publication of Schwaetzer's appointment. Sabine Leutheusser-Schnarrenberger succeeded Kinkel as Justice Minister, defeating the left-liberal Burkhard Hirsch by 56 votes to 27. When Möllemann resigned as Minister of Economics, he was replaced by Günter Rexrodt (who

defeated two other candidates in a ballot of the FDP *Fraktion* and
party executive). The resignation in February 1994 of Rainer
Ortleb as Minister of Education led again to a ballot by the
*Fraktion* and party Executive; Karl-Hans Laermann was the
successful candidate, defeating Gerhardt by 41 votes to 37.[3]

The FDP also had several important organizational problems
that required its attention. The party had to adjust to two changes
of General Secretary in this period. Lambsdorff selected Uwe
Lühr (who had won a direct constituency seat in Halle in the 1990
election: the first for the FDP since 1961). When Kinkel became
party leader, he chose Werner Hoyer as his General Secretary, a
member of the North Rhine-Westphalia FDP. Hoyer provided a
regional balance to Kinkel's own Baden-Württemberg affiliation.[4]
Bringing the eastern Länder and local party structures up to the
standard of those in the West was another urgent task. The party
provided a special budget of DM 3 million for the improvement
and consolidation of eastern party organizations. The national
party appointed regional agents to assist local party officials in
improving membership services, the organization of meetings,
party finances, and other matters.[5] The FDP head office
established a branch in Berlin to coordinate matters relating to
the eastern FDP. This office dealt with redundancies of staff of the
former Liberal Democratic (LDPD) and National Democratic
(NDPD) parties of the GDR which had been merged into the FDP.
The office also negotiated with the Treuhand concerning
property claimed by the party, as well as dealt with the Berlin
press and organized any Berlin meetings of the Praesidium or
Executive.[6] The saga of determining the rightful ownership of
property and financial balances of the former LDPD and NDPD
continued into 1994, and left the FDP's finances in a state of
uncertainty up to the time of the Bundestag election (*Der Spiegel*,
7 September 1992: 126; *Frankfurter Allgemeine Zeitung*, 4 May
1994).

## The Electoral Fortunes of the FDP: 1991 to September 1994

Following the surprisingly good results in the Bundestag election
of 1990, the FDP hoped that it could match that performance in
Land elections. In the spring of 1991, it secured 7.4 percent in the
Hesse election and 6.9 percent in Rhineland Palatinate (where it

entered a coalition with the SPD under Scharping). The FDP managed only 5.4 percent in the June 1991 Hamburg election, but in September that same year, it won 9.5 percent of the vote in Bremen, and joined a "traffic-light" coalition with the SPD and Greens (the first in the West). On 5 April 1992 it secured only 5.9 percent in Baden-Württemberg and 5.6 percent in Schleswig-Holstein.

A re-run of the Hamburg election in September 1993 brought the first of a long series of Länder elections that left the FDP below the crucial 5 percent level. The FDP received only 4.2 percent in the Hamburg election, losing votes especially to the new anti-establishment Statt party, as well as to the CDU and SPD. In the March 1994 Lower Saxony election (the start of the electoral marathon that was the Superwahljahr) the FDP received only 4.4 percent. In the June Saxony-Anhalt Land election the party won only 3.6 percent. A "double election" on 11 September left the FDP with only 2.2 percent in Brandenburg and 1.7 percent in Saxony. The Bavarian election completed the pre-Bundestag election series: the FDP got 2.8 percent. Only in the 1992 Schleswig-Holstein election (a gain of 1.2 percent) did the FDP improve on the previous Land election result. In Baden-Württemberg it managed to equal its 1988 result. In all the others there were losses ranging from under 1 percent (the three 1991 elections) to 9.9 percent (Saxony-Anhalt). This dismal performance was confirmed by a failure to retain seats in the European Parliament in the June 1994 election: the FDP received 4.1 percent.

What explained these poor results? The FDP failed to establish a clear and independent profile in many of the Länder, especially where it had not been needed for government. Indecisive or ambiguous statements of coalition intention also gave the party a poor image and left voters confused about what supporting the FDP would mean for the next government coalition (Forschungsgruppe Wahlen, 1993: 49; Fliszar, 1994: 9). The party's inadequate organization in the eastern Länder also weakened the party, as did conflicts within Land party organizations (especially in Saxony-Anhalt). Hoyer (the FDP General Secretary) blamed the eastern Land parties for these defeats, although he also acknowledged the personal attraction of Stolpe (Brandenburg) and Biedenkopf (Saxony).

In the European election, the FDP could not present itself as necessary for the formation of a coalition because no government was going to result from that election. This outweighed the FDP's publicity emphasizing its strong European credentials. But even its support for Europe was not clearly presented to the voters. An advertisement in the *Frankfurter Allgemeine Zeitung* on 9 June 1994 gave a rather heterogeneous set of reasons by which the FDP sought to attract votes. It claimed to have five women among its top ten candidates without employing any quota rules; it boasted of the good attendance records of its members of the European Parliament; and it pointed out that it needed 5 percent to get any seats, whereas 1 percent fewer votes for the larger parties only slightly reduced their representation. "Whoever wants effective representation of German interests in Europe will vote FDP," it concluded. The FDP's television campaign "spot" seemed to be as much propaganda for the European Union as publicity for the FDP: referring to the economic advantages of Europe, its role in combatting nationalism and its benefits for Germany in trading terms. "Germany needs Europe; Europe needs the Liberals; and we need you" was Kinkel's message (Free Democratic Party, 1994). A poster (directed as much at the Euroskeptical *Bund freier Bürger* as at other party rivals) said: "Don't relinquish Europe to those who don't want it: vote FDP." Lambsdorff found the European result traumatic: he was reported as saying that it endangered the very existence of the party (*Frankfurter Allgemeine Zeitung*, 14 June 1994).

The local council elections repeated the pattern of disheartening results. Of the local elections held in 1994, the FDP won less than 5 percent in Baden-Württemberg, Saarland, and Rhineland-Palatinate. The Free Democrats gained over the 5 percent level in Saxony, Saxony-Anhalt, Mecklenburg-Western Pomerania, and Thuringia but the results in those Länder were not encouraging with the Bundestag election on the horizon.

Another rather different kind of election also played a role in the build-up to the Bundestag election campaign. In 1969, the FDP's choice between the two candidates for the federal president – Gustav Heinemann (SPD) and Gerhard Schröder (CDU) – indicated the party's likely coalition choice after the Bundestag election that year. The FDP's support of Heinemann signaled that an SPD–FDP coalition would not be ruled out if the electoral arithmetic permitted its creation. In 1994, a very similar situation existed. Once again there were two electable candidates: Johannes Rau (minister-president of North Rhine-Westphalia and former SPD chancellor candidate) and Roman Herzog (president of the constitutional court and the Christian Democrats' candidate). Once again, support within the FDP existed for both candidates: Möllemann vocally supported Rau, and other prominent FDP politicians expressed a preference for the SPD's candidate. The differences, though, were twofold compared to 1969. First, the FDP had its own candidate: Hildegard Hamm-Brücher. The FDP had put her forward after Kohl had produced his original candidate, Steffen Heitmann, without consultation with the FDP. She was not likely to be elected, but the FDP would vote for her on the first two rounds of balloting, and then discuss which candidate to support in the decisive third round, when a simple majority would elect. Kinkel was adamant that he would try to produce a united FDP vote to maximize its weight in the election. This would prove the validity of Solms' remark (leader of the FDP parliamentary party in the Bundestag): "The FDP decides who will be the federal president; nobody else." The other difference, though, was that the FDP leadership had already settled on a coalition strategy for the Bundestag election: a continuation of the existing coalition (see p.68). The vote in the presidential election therefore would not be a portent of post-October coalition possibilities.

In the end, Herzog was elected with most, though not all, the FDP votes in the electoral college. Kinkel had demonstrated his ability to give direction to his party while confirming his loyalty to the coalition. "The callousness with which Kinkel manipulated the decisive debate in the FDP delegation and thus prevented the mood from after all inclining towards Rau, can be flourished in front of Kohl. The master himself could not have done it better" (Perger, 1994).

**Campaign Strategy: 1994[7]**

The FDP considered its campaign strategy for 1994 at a meeting of its Executive in April 1993. Against a background of rumor about a possible grand coalition forming before or after the Bundestag election, the party discussed the themes and tactics for the campaign. The need to conduct its campaign in a period when numerous other elections would precede the Bundestag election meant that an early campaign scheme and "flexible response capability" were both essential.

Before analyzing the campaign strategy that emerged, we must first describe the process that led to the FDP's decision on its coalitional preferences. In the early months of 1994, there was much heated debate within the FDP about the timing of a coalition decision. Some wanted a decision as early as possible, to allow the party to concentrate on substantive issues and to reassure the CDU/CSU; others wanted the decision delayed until the Nürnberg congress in September. Several leading politicians in the party – including Möllemann – were dubious about the advisability of a decision in favor of the Christian Democrats.[8] After pressure both from prominent politicians such as Weng (the deputy leader of the FDP *Fraktion*) and Rexrodt (Minister for Economics), and from the party's "grass-roots," the leadership decided to bring the decision forward to the Rostock party congress in June. The Praesidium voted unanimously on 11 April to recommend that the FDP should seek a continuation of the coalition with the Christian Democrats after the Bundestag election; the FDP Executive agreed to this recommendation on 2 May. The party congress at Rostock in June then confirmed this coalition decision. Indeed, at the Rostock Congress, Kinkel left no room for possible negotiations with the SPD, if by any chance the post-election arithmetic made a coalition with the Christian Democrats impossible. Later in the summer, Kinkel and Solms, and indeed the whole Praesidium, repeatedly ruled out FDP participation in a traffic-light coalition with the SPD and the Greens, although the opinion polls suggested that such a coalition might be the only alternative to a grand coalition if the PDS won seats again in the Bundestag.

The organization and the methods of communication used in the FDP's campaign strategy were fairly orthodox and similar to those used in other recent Bundestag elections (Soe, 1993). Campaign strategy was the concern of an election committee, whose members included the General Secretary (Hoyer), the party's business manager (Rolf Berndt), representatives of the public relations agency and media firm responsible for implementation of campaign publicity decisions, the director of the Friedrich-Naumann Foundation, and the staff of the FDP head office, together with additional members as necessary. It reported to the party Executive. Regular meetings with the party's business managers of the Land organizations enabled the party to monitor the progress of the campaign, and adjust to changing local circumstances. Because of changes in the law concerning party financing from public funds and the expenses of other elections in Superwahljahr, the FDP had less money available than in 1990. Of a total central budget of about DM 20 million, DM 6 million was set aside for the European Parliament election, and DM 9–10 million for the Bundestag election.

FDP strategists divided the Bundestag election campaign into three phases. The first, building on the European Parliament election, was to focus on mobilization of party activists, culminating in the Nürnberg party congress in September. Then came a short period when the FDP would communicate its substantive policy themes to the public, such as reductions of taxes and subsidies, an emphasis on social tolerance, promotion of technical and societal innovation, and protection of civil liberties. This phase was to end with the Bavarian Land election. The final phase of the campaign, the closing weeks before election day, was to press home the functional arguments for voting FDP: to use second votes to preserve the presence of the FDP in the Bundestag and to re-elect Kohl as chancellor of a Christian Democrat–FDP coalition. Without the FDP, the Free Democrats claimed that the CDU/CSU would not have a majority.

The campaign had to respond to the other elections that occurred in 1994. Because these outcomes were almost uniformly dismal for the FDP, this proved to be a particularly challenging task. There was also the problem of fighting several elections simultaneously. This involved offering differentiated messages to the voters, and even in a few cases different coalition strategies. The Saarland election, rescheduled to occur on the same day as the Bundestag election, was an especially awkward case. The FDP Land organization at first wanted to make a statement favoring a post-election coalition with the SPD (accepting the realities of party strength in the Land). The Land committee (*Hauptausschuß*) stated this intention on 13 September. The Bonn party leadership intervened and influenced the decision of a special Land party congress, which on 22 September decided by a narrow majority not to make any pre-election coalition decision.

How was the FDP to reach the electorate? Although the intention was to have a homogeneous campaign image for the party, the Land parties (responsible for much of the conduct of the campaign on the ground) wanted to emphasize their own themes and use their own publicity materials. The most blatant example was North Rhine-Westphalia. Here the differences of view and personal rivalries between the federal party leader (Kinkel) and the Land party chairman (Möllemann) resulted in the Land party using its own posters that focused on Möllemann, Genscher, and Lambsdorff (all members of that Land party organization), and excluding Kinkel. Kinkel did, of course, appear on posters rented by the federal party in North Rhine-Westphalia. One of these Land posters had Genscher facing a chess-board accompanied by the slogan "a clever move" and calling for the second vote to be given to the FDP. This was so popular that other Land party organizations asked for copies to use locally. It was especially popular among FDP local organizations in eastern Germany.

The media mix communicating the FDP message was, like the campaign organization, fairly orthodox in conception. The party rented 24,500 poster sites from 30 September until polling day. The FDP produced a range of leaflets and posters, and made these available to Land and local party organizations (each constituency was given vouchers worth DM 1500 with which to order publicity materials from party headquarters). A coordinated press campaign placed advertisements first in the weeklies (*Der Spiegel*, *Focus*, and *Die Zeit*), then in nationally distributed daily papers, and then in regional newspapers during the closing days of the campaign.

A variety of other efforts complemented the central party activities. Earlier in the year the FDP *Fraktion* had placed a series of advertisements in newspapers presaging themes of the Bundestag election campaign. One, for example, read: "The economy needs less than one thinks. Less taxation. Less bureaucracy. Less state" (*Die Zeit*, 11 March 1994). Local parties were encouraged to supplement centrally placed press advertising with their own local publicity. As in earlier Bundestag elections, "Liberal Initiatives" (groups of well-known individuals not generally members of the party) placed advertisements on behalf of the FDP. One said: "We know what the Liberal party has achieved for this country . . . Germany needs the Liberals" and was signed by sportsmen, actors, scientists, businessmen and others (*Frankfurter Allgemeine Zeitung*, 13 October 1994). Another, produced by a Berlin group, tried to persuade voters that a second vote for the FDP would not be wasted, because recent opinion polls indicated that the FDP was above the crucial 5 percent level (*Frankfurter Allgemeine Zeitung*, 15 October 1994). The party used direct mailings to target groups (such as members of the professions), and invited representatives of those groups to attend special meetings with FDP politicians.

The FDP bought time for short advertising "spots" on commercial radio, but commercial television advertising was too expensive for the party. Of course, the FDP used its allocation of "free" party political broadcasts on public television and radio. A novelty in publicizing the party was the use of cinema advertising (in about 800 cinemas in the end-phase of the campaign), although in the Adenauer period cinema advertising had been used extensively.

Campaign headquarters in Bonn organized the schedule of the eleven most prominent FDP politicians, as it had done in previous campaigns. Unlike those earlier campaigns, however, in 1994 the traditional party rally was used hardly at all. The party decided that the time and resources involved in organizing a mass rally were unlikely to be balanced in persuading voters to support the FDP or persuading the media to publicize such meetings. A rally was held in Bad Durkheim in mid-September to mark the formal start of the campaign, at which Kinkel, Genscher and other top names were among the speakers, but otherwise the emphasis was placed on photo-opportunities and dialogue meetings with the public or journalists. One such dialogue meeting with Kinkel took place in Hof, where a variety of themes from plutonium smuggling to opportunities for women re-entering the workforce were discussed. Kinkel used this occasion to stress the functional role of the FDP in relation to the coalition. However, crowds at FDP events were generally disappointing. Even Genscher could attract nothing like the numbers who came to hear him in 1990. Schwaetzer, the Minister for Construction, reportedly drew groups of the party faithful about as large as those attending meetings of the Natural Law party (*taz*, 8 October 1994)!

All this planning depended on the successful mobilization of local party activists. This mobilization began before the European parliamentary election campaign. The June issue of the magazine for party members (*Die Liberale Depesche*: 12–3) made an appeal: "Your conversations with neighbors, members of your family and colleagues at the workplace have greater effect than all the leaflets, TV party broadcasts and election rallies. What you can attain through personal conversation, the party never can achieve by spending money." This appeal suggested that members use phone conversations and private correspondence to add an appeal for FDP votes. It recommended using centrally produced posters and leaflets to contain locally devised messages. FDP headquarters made a hot line available to answer queries about the campaign.

What was the content of all this publicity? The party decided to highlight Kinkel in all phases and aspects of the campaign. There was concern that he was not sufficiently well known, and that he might be squeezed out of the news by media emphasis on Kohl and Scharping. The campaign strategists wanted to stress Kinkel's role as Foreign Minister (and his continuation of the work of Genscher) and his achievements as party leader. There was to be no differentiation of the campaign in eastern Germany, except where themes relevant to eastern problems could be emphasized to the FDP's advantage.

The detailed content of the FDP electoral program appeared in the manifesto entitled: *Liberal denken. Leistung wählen* (Think Liberal. Vote for achievement). A preamble set out the past achievements of the FDP, its principal policy themes, its opposition to a red–green or *immobiliste* grand coalition, and its opposition to extremism of the left or the right. There followed ten chapters of detailed policy proposals, commencing with "market economy renewal for Germany" and the "ecological market economy," and concluding with "foreign and European policy." An index helped the reader to find specific proposals ranging from the subsidiarity principle to "promotion of compost making." Of course, few voters would obtain the full version of the manifesto; fewer still would ever read it. It existed for other reasons: to answer any challenges that the party had too few concrete policy proposals and to prove that any and every interest had been given its entry (hence the items on refuges for women, bird protection, university construction and the disabled, for instance). The program also served as the basis for future coalition negotiations and a defense when other parties pressed the FDP to agree to policies at odds with those in the manifesto.

Effective communication of the FDP program and policies to

voters came through other means. The FDP distributed a two-page version of the manifesto: "Twelve key themes of liberal policy." More effective were leaflets that focused on a small selection of points. These usually employed the principal slogan of the FDP campaign: "This time everything's at stake" (*Diesmal geht's um alles*). The leaflets emphasized themes such as the reduction of bureaucracy, improved prospects for the *Mittelstand* including restrictions on subsidies and reductions in income tax, respect for minorities, and radical reform of the social services. The party also emphasized the functional arguments for voting FDP: continuation of the existing coalition, and prevention of a red–green coalition (with or without the PDS), a grand coalition, or single-party government of the CDU/CSU. Most prominent of all was the ubiquitous plea for "second vote, FDP."[9]

The principal television spot for the FDP used a surrealistic boccia-type game with colored balls representing the parties and combinations of parties for coalitions to emphasize the positive benefits of voting FDP. Other television spots stressed the stability of the Kohl–Kinkel government; the special role of the FDP ("A Germany without the FDP, that would be a different Republic"); and the danger of a single-party CDU/CSU government "without the Liberals to control and correct them" (Free Democratic Party, 1994). These themes of the continuity of the coalition and the undesirability of any of the possible alternatives were repeated in the press advertising of the final few days of the campaign. These themes also appeared in the numerous discussion programs on television and radio in which party representatives put their case. CDU/CSU supporters were the target of a message that, without the FDP in the Bundestag, only a red–green or a grand coalition would be feasible.

Research found that only about 4 percent of voters were core FDP voters, but 16 percent shared liberal values and ideas and thus might be persuaded to vote FDP. The electorate also supported the FDP's functional role in providing majorities for one of the major parties and then acting as a "Liberal corrective" within the coalition, ensuring a centrist tendency in government (Beerfelz, 1993: 28–30). The party hoped again to persuade those with higher incomes and those concerned about tax increases and preserving private enterprise to vote FDP.[10] However, an early version of the manifesto ran into trouble when it used the term "party of the better-off" (*Partei der Besserverdienenden*). After protest from the party grass-roots and criticism in the press, the Praesidium decided in May to drop that reference from the draft election program.

In national terms: on large poster sites, in the national press, in advertising, in news reports and commentaries, on television and radio, in party "spots" and on talk shows and commentaries, the FDP retained a campaign presence suited to its status as junior partner in the coalition. On the streets, it was a very different matter. Even the most prominent FDP politicians could no longer attract crowds as they had done in 1990 and in earlier Bundestag campaigns. In the run-up to the European election, Kinkel, Lambsdorff, and Genscher could not draw crowds to open-air meetings in eastern Germany. In some towns, the party was less visible than many of the smaller parties: the STATT party or Natural Law party, for instance, and certainly could not match the visibility of the Greens, the SPD, or CDU/CSU (and in eastern Germany the PDS). Even where Land elections had just taken place or were about to take place, the FDP seemed almost invisible. In Dresden just after the Land election, one could see more posters of the DSU (an almost forgotten party now) than FDP posters. No FDP posters were visible in central Munich a few days before the Bavarian Land election, yet there were plenty for other parties (including the *Bund freier Bürger*). This pattern held true for Thuringia and the Saarland as well. Other parties, even small parties, established greater presence on the streets and in market squares with their information-stands than did the FDP. Compared to previous Bundestag elections, the FDP had a serious problem in mobilizing its members to assist with the campaign.[11]

Small wonder, then, that in September 57 percent of respondents in a survey thought that the FDP would not return to the Bundestag (37 percent thought that it would). Only 19 percent said they would welcome the absence of the FDP, though; 42 percent would regret it (*Der Spiegel*, 19 September 1994).

## The Bundestag Election Results

The FDP's 6.9 percent share of the vote in the 1994 Bundestag election was a respectable result for Kinkel and his team, especially in view of the FDP's other results during the Superwahljahr

The FDP and the Superwahljahr

(see Table 1.2). Indeed, the party had worse results in the Land elections that took place simultaneously with the Bundestag election: Thuringia 3.2 percent; Mecklenburg-Western Pomerania 3.8 percent; Saarland 2.1 percent; and in local council elections in North Rhine-Westphalia 3.8 percent (and the loss of two-thirds of its local council seats).

Eastern Germany, the stronger of the two parts of Germany for the FDP in 1990, was the weaker this time. In the former GDR the FDP obtained only 3.5 percent of the vote (a decline of 8.9 percent). In the West, it secured 7.7 percent (a 3.2 percent drop from 1990). Overall, the party lost 4.1 percent: its largest decline ever for a Bundestag election. The first vote results (for constituency candidates) were far worse: only 3.4 percent in the West and 3 percent in the East. The FDP had only forty-seven seats in parliament instead of the seventy-nine won in 1990. It thus gave up second place in the coalition to the CSU and third place in the Bundestag to the Greens.

One opinion research institute (Infas) explained the loss of nearly 2 million FDP votes as follows: about 600,000 votes went to the Christian Democrats (net of votes won from the CDU/CSU); over half a million lost to the SPD; half a million lost to non-voters; and 120,000 lost on balance to the Greens (*Focus*, "Wahl-Spezial," 18 October 1994).

The FDP had relied heavily since 1969 on split-ticket voting (gaining party list votes from voters giving their first votes to a candidate of some other party) (Roberts, 1988). They again benefited from such split voting in 1994, though almost exclusively in the West, where the surplus of second votes over first votes was 3 percent (in the East it was only 1 percent). This is close to the outcome in 1990: a surplus of 3.8 percent in the West and a surplus of 1.2 percent in the East. Estimates indicate that the FDP profited especially from Christian Democratic voters. Of all who gave the FDP a second vote, 54 percent had given first votes to the CDU or CSU. This is congruent with other estimates that nearly two-thirds of those voting for FDP party lists were really CDU/CSU sympathizers (Forschungsgruppe Wahlen, 1994: 72).[12] Nearly 10 percent of FDP second votes came from those who gave their first votes to the SPD. Only 32 percent of the FDP second votes had also supported the FDP with their *first* votes. To keep this in perspective, it must be noted that only 8.2 percent of those giving Christian Democratic candidates their

The Political Parties

first vote then gave the FDP their second vote, and among these would have been FDP sympathizers anxious not to waste their first vote by voting for an FDP constituency candidate (Forschungsgruppe Wahlen, 1994: 16).[13]

The best results for the FDP came, as so often before, from towns that contained universities or else areas – many of them in Baden-Württemberg – containing high proportions of prosperous voters. Eight of the FDP's best twelve results were among their best twelve in 1990 also. All the FDP's worst FDP results were in eastern Germany, especially in East Berlin where three constituencies produced under 2 percent for the FDP. Only 14 constituencies in all of the West produced FDP vote shares below 4.4 percent; only 10 in the East were above 4.4 percent (Forschungsgruppe Wahlen, 1994: B100, B106). The best Land results were in Baden-Württemberg (9.9 percent) and Hesse (8.1 percent). The worst were all in the East, ranging from 2.6 percent (Brandenburg) to 3.8 percent (Thuringia).

Many factors can explain the collapse of the FDP vote. First, there was an enormous loss of votes in the East: in 8 constituencies the FDP lost more than 15 percent of the 1990 vote. In Saxony-Anhalt as a whole the Free Democrats lost 15.6 percent. Had the FDP limited its losses in the East to the percentage loss in the West, the party would have received nearly 10 percent in eastern Germany and a more respectable 8 percent overall. The failure of the FDP to establish effective Land and local party structures in the new Länder, the precipitous decline in party membership in the former GDR, internal party conflicts, especially in Saxony-Anhalt, Genscher's departure from the FDP team, and poor results in local and Land elections (demonstrating the weakness of the FDP) all contributed to this situation in the new Länder. But there were more general reasons, applicable to western as well as eastern Germany.

Klaus Kinkel failed to establish himself as a forceful and determined leader. His responsibilities as Foreign Minister (intensified by Germany's six-month period of presidency of the EU Council of Ministers) and his inexperience in the moods and workings of the FDP (he only joined the party in January 1991) left him at a disadvantage compared to the leaders of the other parties or to his FDP predecessors. His popularity rating (a mean of 0.4, on a scale ranging from plus 5 to minus 5) was the lowest of all the party leaders, and even among FDP supporters only reached 1.4 (Forschungsgruppe Wahlen, 1994). The rating for the FDP itself was negative (-0.5), whereas the public had a better regard for the SPD at 1.6, the CDU at 1.4, and even the Greens at 0.5. Nor could the FDP convince voters that its contribution to the Bonn coalition should be acknowledged. Voters rated the coalition as a whole at 0.5, the contribution of the Christian Democrats at 0.7, and the FDP contribution at -0.5 (Forschungsgruppe Wahlen, 1994: 49, 65–6).

## Consequences of the Election

> The Liberals on Sunday celebrated their exhumation from the tomb of statistics as a resurrection.
>
> (*Süddeutsche Zeitung*, 18 October 1994)

The immediate consequences of the Bundestag election involved three things for the FDP: coalition negotiations; diagnosis of reasons for the party's desolate situation; and a scheme for the revival of the FDP's fortunes.

On election night, Kinkel agreed with Kohl and Waigel that coalition negotiations should be conducted swiftly, avoiding the drawn-out procedure of 1990. The FDP settled on its coalition team and decided its strategy concerning both personnel and policy aspects.[14] The FDP would not keep the five posts that it had held in the prior cabinet. Its weaker position in the coalition and an agreement to reduce the number of ministerial posts ensured this outcome. So the party was content with retention of its three most senior positions, and the incumbents retained their posts: Kinkel (Foreign Minister), Rexrodt (Economics Minister), and Leutheusser-Schnarrenberger (Justice Minister). The FDP managed to have some influence on the coalition's program; for example, in granting temporary German nationality to children born in Germany of non-German nationals who could decide whether to retain or renounce German citizenship at age 18. However, the FDP could not get its hoped-for termination date for the solidarity supplement on taxes.

A diagnosis of what had gone wrong for the FDP necessarily involved ideas concerning ways to restore the party's fortunes. One immediate issue was the status of Jürgen Möllemann. He had feuded with Kinkel from the time of Kinkel's election as party leader, and had linked that feud to an alternative strategy for the FDP. Well before the votes were cast he had blamed Kinkel and his associates for the parlous state of the party and its disastrous election results. Möllemann had passed up the opportunity to return to the cabinet as Education Minister when Ortleb had resigned by imposing conditions that Kinkel could not and would not fulfill. Party leaders dissuaded him from being a candidate for a vacant place on the Praesidium in June 1994, and he was pointedly excluded from the coalition negotiating team after the election. His lack of loyalty to Kinkel led to his Land Executive resigning *en masse* on 24 October as a way of forcing Möllemann from office. In the election for a leader of the North Rhine-Westphalia party in December, Möllemann was defeated. This seemed to be the end of his political career.

To analyze the situation of the FDP, an extraordinary party congress (the third congress of 1994) was held at Gera. The outcome was not especially inspiring. Kinkel did not correct the impression of being a leader whose time had run out: except no obvious challenger was available.

Proposals for a new orientation for the party were not lacking: but they pointed in different directions. A group in Berlin, including Alexander von Stahl (a former public prosecutor), pressed the party to adopt a more right-leaning orientation. The party's leadership feared infiltration by radicals if they followed this course (*Der Spiegel*, 26 December 1994: 24–5; 9 January 1995: 18–21). There were others who saw room for the FDP only to the right of the CDU/CSU, and who wanted a more national liberal stance (Walter, 1994: 1100). On the left, a group including Gerhart Baum (the former Minister of the Interior), held a meeting in Hanover to call for a return to social liberalism. The lack of sympathy for this course among the party's elites suggested that this, too, would enjoy little support as a strategy for renewal. Left, right, and center apparently agreed on one thing: that the FDP must return to being a programmatic party, and not be merely a functional provider of majorities. This theme was discussed in the party's journal, for instance, where the author recognized that a liberal program would carry with it the danger of alienating those whose interests the FDP had protected within the coalition (Rohde, 1991: 23). The call, then, was for a second Freiburg Theses.[15] But there is no agreement concerning the content and direction of such a new basic program. It would not be easy to combine traditional liberal principles of civic rights and constitutional protection with the market economy priorities of many members, donors, and clients so influential in the party today. As Ulrich Wildermuth states, "Today's liberalism once again needs an ideologically delimited rationale, which can dispute with Conservatives to the right and yes, but with whom, though, with whom? to the left" (Wildermuth, 1991: 41).

## Longer-term Perspectives

> The FDP has survived, but it will not be discharged from the intensive care ward.
>
> (*Focus*, "Wahl-Spezial", 18 October 1994: 4)

The FDP has been here before. Political analysts and Cassandras by the score have predicted the imminent demise of the party ever since it was founded in 1948. However, it is overly sanguine to imagine that recovery now will be automatic. The special conditions in eastern Germany make it especially hard for the FDP to identify, attract and retain levels of loyal (or even just self-interested) supporters. The electorate there is too volatile, the party system more complex, the social structure still too unsettled for that. The election results – at all levels – have demonstrated that the FDP still has to operate in two different electoral and party contexts in East and West Germany. That will complicate the search for an integrative program from the party.

Oddly enough, the weaker position of the FDP in the Bundestag is simultaneously a stronger position regarding coalition opportunities – in theory. A "traffic-light" coalition of the FDP with the SPD and Greens is arithmetically possible, though politically it is extremely unlikely. Coalition loyalty and political incompatibility between the FDP and the left parties ensure that. And yet, so many within and outside the FDP have complained that Kinkel's FDP is indistinguishable from the CDU/CSU. How better to remind the electorate of the FDP's independent profile than a coalition switch? It is, after all, now thirteen years since the FDP last undertook a change of coalition partner in Bonn: equal to the period of partnership with Brandt and Schmidt. Perhaps Kohl's self-signaled departure sometime in 1997 will provide the FDP with the excuse it needs for a change, just in time for the 1998 Bundestag election?

The FDP has very little time in which to revive its fortunes. It managed to retain its place in the Hesse parliament in the Land election of February 1995 with 7.4 percent of the vote. However, that was apparently a flash in the pan. In May the FDP lost its representation in the Bremen Land parliament (3.4 percent, compared to around 10 percent in the previous two Land elections) and in North Rhine-Westphalia (4 percent). In October 1995 it only obtained 2.5 percent in the Berlin Land election. In opinion polls, the party rarely received the 5 percent of support that would be necessary for its survival in the Bundestag in the 1998 election; for example, in December 1995 one survey put support for the FDP at 3 percent in western Germany, and only 1 percent in eastern Germany (Forschungsgruppe Wahlen, 1995).[16]

These results compelled the party to seek a new leader. Though Kinkel had secured a vote of confidence at the extraordinary party congress in Gera in December 1994 (see above, p. 78), he announced his intention in May not to seek reelection as party chairman at the Mainz congress in June. Wolfgang Gerhardt was elected as Kinkel's successor.[17] Gerhardt promised to make integration within the party a priority. Integration of the different wings and regional interests in the FDP is just one of the many challenges which still face the party. It must restore grassroots activism and morale, and especially in eastern Germany, where the party is seen as arrogant and unfeeling, and neglectful of the needs of its eastern German membership and potential voters. It must at all costs regain representation in local councils and Länder parliaments; the coming Länder elections in Rhineland-Palatinate and Baden-Württemburg provide the party's most favorable opportunities. It must urgently improve its organization, at Land and federal levels. Above all, it must respond to changes in an electorate and a party system which are no longer, and never again can be, the safe and predictable environment within which the FDP has operated since the days of Adenauer.

**Notes**

The author acknowledges with gratitude financial assistance from the University of Manchester for his research visit to Germany in September–October 1994 and is grateful to the DAAD for their generous support of the visit of members of the Association for the Study of German Politics to Bonn at the end of the election campaign.

1. For example, an Allensbach opinion poll published in May 1992 placed the FDP on 11.6 percent for the Federal Republic as a whole, and 13.9 percent in the East (*Frankfurter Allgemeine Zeitung*, 8 May 1992).
2. Jürgen Möllemann had made no secret of his ambition to become leader and had counted on support from Genscher and Lambsdorff (both, like Möllemann, members of the North Rhine-Westphalia Land party). However, Möllemann destroyed his chances of succeeding Lambsdorff by resigning as Minister of Economics as a consequence of impropriety in the business interests of family members in January 1993 (*Der Spiegel*, 4 January 1993: 18–26). In any case, Möllemann probably had too many enemies in the party to have won the leadership (*Der Spiegel*, 8 June 1992: 28–30).
3. Again there was embarrassment, as had been the case with Irmgard Schwaetzer, caused by the premature announcement that Gerhardt was the successor, based on overconfidence that the candidate favored by the party Praesidium would be acceptable to the party's *Fraktion*.
4. The office of General Secretary is filled by a nominee of the party chairman, but that nomination must be confirmed by a vote of the delegates at a party congress.
5. Information provided by staff of the FDP head office in Bonn, 17 October 1991.
6. Information provided in interview with staff in Berlin FDP Office, 6 November 1991.
7. I acknowledge with gratitude the assistance given to me by members of the staff of the FDP head office in Bonn (some of whom were members of the election committee) in gathering information about the campaign, and by party staff and politicians in the Länder. Many of the details in this section are

derived from interviews and discussions with those staff members and politicians.

8. Möllemann's criticism of Kinkel's coalition strategy was one reason for the decline in support for his re-election as chairman of the North Rhine-Westphalia Land party (he obtained only 59.6 percent, compared to 82.2 percent in 1990 and 73.5 percent in 1992). Several of his colleagues from the North Rhine-Westphalia party offered assurances that Möllemann's criticisms of the coalition decision were not those of the Land party as a whole (e.g., Schwaetzer: *Frankfurter Allgemeine Zeitung*, 16 April 1994).

9. Color also played an unusual role in the FDP's publicity materials. For example, a postcard and sticker had the intriguing message: "Profeel" in blue on a yellow background (a pun on "profile" but intended to associate the FDP with being "pro-feelings"); another asked, "Do you want a government: or an attempt at one?" and used the blue and yellow of the FDP for the first line and the red and green of the opposition for the second line. An advertisement in *Focus* (10 October 1994) also used this split color scheme: "Next Monday you must reckon on anything in Germany [on a black and red background] . . . Unless you are calculating. And vote for us . . . Therefore the second vote for the FDP [on a yellow and blue background]."

10. A poll in May indicated that members of the free professions were again likely to vote strongly for the FDP: 23 percent of those surveyed said that they would vote for the FDP, 48.5 percent for the Christian Democrats, 14 percent for the SPD and only 8 percent for the Greens (Survey by Nürnberg Institute for the Free Professions, *Frankfurter Allgemeine Zeitung*, 26 May 1994).

11. This paragraph is based on personal observation of the campaign from mid-September, which included visits to villages, towns, and cities in eleven of the sixteen Länder.

12. Another estimate based on surveys of the electorate suggested that 59 percent of FDP second votes came from voters who described themselves as CDU supporters: *Der Spiegel*, 17 October 1994: 6–7.

13. It is interesting, though, to note that of those who did vote for FDP candidates with their first vote, only 69 percent also voted for FDP party lists with their second votes; 18.6 percent

voted for Christian Democrat lists and 8 percent for SPD lists! (Forschungsgruppe Wahlen, 1994: 16).

14. As well as Kinkel, the team consisted of Solms (leader of the FDP Bundestag *Fraktion*); Gollert (Mecklenburg-Western Pomerania, representing the new Länder); Frau Schwaetzer (as deputy leader of the party and representative of North Rhine-Westphalia); and Hoyer (the General Secretary, also from North Rhine-Westphalia). Hoyer later announced his resignation as General Secretary, but continued in office until Kinkel's new nominee, Guido Westerwelle (a former chairman of the Young Liberals), was elected as Hoyer's successor at the Gera congress on 11 December 1994.

15. The Freiburg Theses defined the principles of social liberalism, were accepted by the FDP party congress at Freiburg in 1971, and became a symbol of liberal renewal for the period of the SPD–FDP coalition (Haussmann, 1989).

16. FDP fortunes improved in the three 1996 Land elections (see p. 21).

17. Gerhardt secured only 57 percent of the votes; Jürgen Möllemann obtained 33 percent, (*Das Parlament*, 16/23 June 1995).

## References

Beerfelz, Hans-Jürgen. 1993. "Strategy and Perspectives of the FDP in the Information Society," paper presented at the annual meeting of the German Studies Association, Bethesda, Maryland, 9 October 1993.

Fliszar, Fritz. 1994. "Noch eine Chance für die FDP?" *Liberal* 36: 8–9.

Forschungsgruppe Wahlen. 1993. *Wahl im Hamburg*. Mannheim: Forschungsgruppe Wahlen.

——. 1994. *Bundestagswahl 1994*. Mannheim: Forschungsgruppe Wahlen.

——. 1995. *Politbarometer 12/95*. Mannheim: Forschungsgruppe Wahlen.

Free Democratic Party. 1994. *Die FDP im TV Spots. 25 Jahre Werbe-*

*Spots der FDP zu Bundestags – und Europawahlen von 1969* (Video) St Augustin: liberal-Verlag.

Haussmann, Hartmut. 1989. "Die Freiburger Thesen," in Wolfgang Mischnick, ed., *Verantwortung für die Freiheit. 40 Jahre FDP*. Stuttgart: Deutsche Verlagsanstalt.

Perger, Werner A. 1994. "Unverkrampft die Macht behauptet," *Die Zeit*, 27 May.

Roberts, Geoffrey K. 1988. "The 'Second-Vote' Strategy of the West German Free Democratic Party," *European Journal of Political Research* 16: 317–37.

Rohde, Friedrich. 1991. "Besitzstand. Anmerkungen zur liberalen Programmatik," *Liberal* 33 (February): 18–23.

Soe, Christian. 1993. "Unity and Victory for the German Liberals: Little Party, what now?" in Russell J. Dalton, ed., *The New Germany Votes*. Providence and Oxford: Berg.

Walter, Franz. 1994. "Partei der Besserverkleideten. Die FDP auf dem Weg zurück in die Zukunft," *Blätter für deutsche und internationale Politik* 9: 1091–100.

Wildermuth, Ulrich. 1991. "Die FDP – eine schwierige Partei," *Die politische Meinung* 264: 39–43.

# 5
# The Greens' Comeback in 1994: The Third Party of Germany

## E. Gene Frankland

*Bündnis 90/Die Grünen* (the Greens) set out in the Superwahljahr to reestablish themselves in the Bundestag and to replace Helmut Kohl with a *rot–grün* coalition.[1] The consensus of opinion, inside and outside of the party, was that the Greens would clear the 5 percent threshold. Their defeat on 2 December 1990 stemmed from a unique convergence of negative factors: the inability to adapt to the post-unification policy agenda, the New Left appeal of SPD Chancellor candidate Oskar Lafontaine, continuous factional wrangling, and the amateurism of their campaign. During 1991–1993 the situation changed. The Greens united with the eastern *Bündnis 90* (Alliance 90); centrist Rudolf Scharping became SPD party leader; the *Fundis* (fundamentalists) left the Greens; and the party became more professionalized. In late 1993, polls indicated that the Greens were running ahead of the FDP and a SPD–Green Bundestag majority was possible (Forschungsgruppe Wahlen, 1993).

"Quite fantastic," party co-speaker Ludger Volmer gushed in the evening of 16 October 1994 when *Deutsche Welle* asked about the projected results: the Greens had become the first party ever to stage a comeback in the Bundestag after losing its *Fraktion*! Although they had not displaced Kohl, the government's new majority seemed so thin that Volmer foresaw its disappearance during the legislative period. Federal election results confirmed those of the European election of 12 June: the Greens ranked as Germany's third party. However, as western Greens relished victory, eastern Greens pondered their own survival. The Bundestag votes confirmed the negative trends of eastern Land elections of 1994. Of those parties winning seats in the thirteenth Bundestag, only the Greens saw their electoral share go up in the

West and down in the East.[2]

We begin by reviewing the Greens' recovery during 1991–1993. Then we consider intraparty politics prior to the Mannheim conference in 1994, the electoral program and strategy adopted in Mannheim, and subsequent interactions with other parties. After assessing the "second-order" elections of the summer, we focus on the characteristics of the Greens' federal campaign. Lastly, we discuss the implications of the results of the Bundestagswahl and the Land elections of February and May 1995 for the future of the Greens.

## Reform and Recovery 1991–1993[3]

The unexpected defeat of the Greens in the first all-German election shook the party from top to bottom. Joschka Fischer and Antje Vollmer of the *Realo* (realist) and *Aufbruch* (awakening) factions respectively seized the initiative by proposing structural changes. At the Neumünster conference in April 1991, two-thirds majorities approved reforms, such as replacing the federal steering committee of activists with a federal council (*Länderrat*) of party and parliamentary leaders as well as eliminating term limits for members of the Federal Executive (*Bundesvorstand*). However, the proposal to abandon the grassroots-democratic rule that forbids simultaneous holding of party executive office and parliamentary mandate failed narrowly. The tumultuous exit of Jutta Ditfurth, the last prominent *Fundi*, from the conference – and the party – sharpened the reformist image of the Greens. Yet, as *Bundesvorstand* elections indicated, the majority of delegates still favored a leftist leadership, albeit one which was "pragmatic and open to coalitions" (Poguntke and Schmitt-Beck, 1994: 97). In the following months, *Aufbruch* dissolved and *Realos* avoided confrontations with the *Bundesvorstand* (Bruns, 1994: 29).

The Greens' increasing pragmatism correlated with success in Land elections. In January 1991 they won 8.8 percent of the votes in Hesse and formed a coalition with the SPD. In April, the Rhineland-Palatinate Greens won 6.4 percent (better than in 1987). In June, the Hamburg Greens won 7.2 percent while the (*Fundi*-backed) Alternative List managed only 0.5 percent. In September, the Bremen Greens increased their electoral share to 11.4 percent and joined an *Ampelkoalition* ("traffic-light" coalition) with the SPD and the FDP. The Baden-Württemberg Greens won 9.5 percent and the Schleswig-Holstein Greens won 4.97 percent (the best ever for both) in April 1992 Land elections. Lastly, in September 1993, the Hamburg Greens polled 13.5 percent – the highest percentage of Landtag votes ever won anywhere by the party.

However, without a "marriage of convenience" with Alliance 90 (Schoonmaker, 1992), the odds were stacked against the Greens clearing the national 5 percent threshold. Although the Greens and Alliance 90 shared many policy views, the Easterners were more likely to favor "roundtable" dialogue (Jahn, 1994: 13); to oppose constraints on individuals, such as gender quotas; and to see themselves as neither left nor right. Alliance 90 activists did not want to be swallowed up by the larger and more aggressive Greens, but they were realistic about electoral arithmetic.[4]

In mid-1992, a joint commission, *equally* representing 37,000 Green party members and 3,000 Alliance 90 members, began work on an association agreement. Easterners came out ahead in the dispute about the fused party's official name (*Bündnis 90/Die Grünen*). The commission proposed amendments of the Green party charter to protect the special interests of Easterners. For example, they may form an intraparty association, and they are overrepresented on the *Bundesvorstand*.[5] In the membership ballot of April 1993, 91.8 percent of the Greens and 85.7 percent of Alliance 90 approved the association agreement (Raschke, 1993: 927).

## The Logic of Electoral Competition

On the eve of 2 December 1990, one still found Green activists who boasted that the party had never used marketing research or pollsters (Schoonmaker and Frankland 1993: 159). A leopard may not be able to change its spots, but after being gored, it reviews its techniques. After the 1990 election the Greens organized seminars with political scientist Joachim Raschke, who prescribed large doses of professionalization (1991). The *Bundesvorstand* reviewed survey analysis (Schmitt-Beck, 1994) that indicated the Greens' "core" voters constituted 4 percent of the electorate; their "potential" voters were another 8 percent. In

1993 the electoral commission recommended something unprecedented: hiring a professional advertising agency to market the Green party. The *Länderrat* approved a "full-service" contract with the TRUST agency of Frankfurt to create a "corporate design" for the Greens with attractive script, emblems, and layouts for campaign materials, and to work with the commission across the full range of projects (Selzer, 1994: 8). Even the party's sunflower logo from 1980 was to be redesigned.

Since the mid-1980s, *Realos* have sought to recast the Greens as a party fit for governmental responsibility. A perennial obstacle was the Left's propensity for verbal radicalism, which other parties welcomed as evidence of the Greens' irresponsibility. Ideologues have been overrepresented among the delegates to federal conferences. At the October 1992 Bonn conference, when speakers argued that in flagrant cases of human rights abuse (such as Bosnia) military force should be an option, they found themselves labeled "war-mongers" by many conference participants. Despite Fischer's advocacy of a more realistic foreign policy, 90 percent of the delegates voted for total pacifism. However, at the November 1993 Aachen conference, the Greens conveyed idealism and realism. The conference approved the 1994 Euro-program, endorsing European integration as the best defense against the resurgence of nationalism. Its slogan was "Better Europe Widened Than Democracy Limited." The program wanted an enlarging European Union to become more democratic, multicultural, and ecological. Widely known and experienced candidates prevailed in the voting for promising positions on the party list. Fischer and Volmer found common ground at Aachen in sharply criticizing the SPD.

This strategy debate continued into early 1994. One perspective was that the Greens should await socioeconomic conditions more favorable for a successful alliance with the SPD. Raschke warned that the Greens lacked the competence and consensus to be part of a federal government that must tackle massive economic problems (*Der Spiegel*, 7 February 1994: 42–4). He maintained that during four years of grand coalition, the Greens could expand their electoral base and increase their organizational capacities. The Baden-Württemberg Greens' Fritz Kuhn argued that a grand coalition would be a "potential catastrophe" for Germany. He advocated targeting mainstream voters by moving economic policy into the center of the Greens' campaign (*die tageszeitung*, 3 December 1993: 10). In contrast, Friedrich O. Wolf urged party policies corresponding to the interests of the left-alternative milieu, rather than generalized appeals to an "imaginary middle-class clientele" (*die tageszeitung*, 10 January 1994: 10).

At the January 1994 Berlin strategy conference, *Realo* and Left prominents reached a consensus that rather than wait for better times, the Greens should campaign to share governmental responsibility now. The Left had advanced no alternative, but were concerned about *Realo* overaccommodation to SPD positions. On the eve of the Mannheim conference, Volmer advocated negotiating with the SPD *and* sharpening the Green programmatic profile (*die tageszeitung*, 24 February 1994: 10).

## The Mannheim Conference

Adorned with the new planet earth-with-sunflower petals symbol, the Mannheim conference banner proclaimed: "Shorten worktime, create jobs, and ecologically run the economy." In contrast to 1990, the Greens' leadership sought to align the party with the top concerns of the electorate. February 1994 polls indicated that unemployment was easily the number one concern of Westerners (62 percent) and Easterners (81 percent); if one added related problems, economic concerns registered above 80 percent (West) and 90 percent (East). Environmental protection ranked fifth among problems cited in the West (8 percent) but failed to make the list in the East (Forschungsgruppe Wahlen, 1994e).

The *Programm zur Bundestagswahl 1994* devoted almost as many pages to its first chapter, integrating economic, ecological, and social policies, as to its other three chapters. Its preamble stressed the difficulty of problems, stated the need for a "new beginning," and declared party readiness for a coalition of "serious" reform politics with the SPD.

The Mannheim program outlined an "ecological offensive" to transform society, requiring economic growth in some sectors and contraction in others. It sought to steer the economy toward eco-capitalism. Noteworthy among the Greens' proposals was raising gasoline taxes immediately by 50 Pfennig per liter and annually by 30 Pfennig for fifteen years. Delegates debated how the additional revenues should be used. The majority rejected the *Bundesvorstand* proposal to offset eco-taxes by lowering other taxes for less affluent citizens. They favored applying new revenues toward the development of environment-friendly technologies. The conference declined the "opportunity" to tackle massive state debts with a Green austerity program.

As at earlier conferences, Green delegates sought to reiterate long-standing commitments. The Mannheim program declared that it is legally, technically, and economically possible to shut down nuclear energy plants within two years. Fischer (Hesse Environment Minister) had argued vainly against setting a deadline. The delegates voted against leftist Hans-Christian Ströbele's motion for unrestricted freedom of immigration. However, the Left prevailed in maintaining the Greens' anti-militarist profile. The program called for dissolving NATO, rejected German participation in UN peacekeeping forces, and advocated dismantling of the Bundeswehr.

Thus, the Mannheim conference resulted in a consensus to participate in federal government and a program whose policies included some that (if adhered to) could block governmental participation. Delegates had reaffirmed the party's *Anderssein*. Green prominents immediately turned to damage control in the press. For example, Antje Vollmer remarked, "The people know, that our party conferences are always a bit off the wall" (*Der Spiegel*, 7 March 1995: 29). Ludger Volmer (1994: 20) reminded supporters that there would always a discrepancy between a program's positions and what is doable in four years of coalition.

### *Wer rot–grün will, muß grün wählen*

"Whoever wants red–green, must vote green" was a slogan that came out of Mannheim. February polls indicated that Scharping was more popular than Kohl and that the CDU–SPD option was the most popular coalition in the West and the East (*Die Zeit*, 18 March 1994: 4). Scharping, who declined to speculate about coalition partners, criticized the radical provisions of the Mannheim program. Yet, SPD manager Günter Verheugen left the door open for post-election talks with the Greens. Just as Fischer had feared, the conservative press headlined the Greens' radical foreign policies. Kohl declared that a federal SPD–Green coalition would have disastrous consequences for Germany.

Polls indicated that an *Ampelkoalition* was the second most popular combination in the East, but it trailed far behind in the West (*Die Zeit*, 18 March 1994: 4). At the Mannheim conference, the Greens had chosen neither to support nor to oppose this option. Governing experiences in Bremen had led proponents of an *Ampelkoalition* to doubt the reform commitment of the FDP. If a grand coalition looked possible after the Bundestagswahl, the Greens did not exclude negotiations on an *Ampelkoalition*. Scharping's first preference was a coalition with the FDP, but the polls had indicated that this coalition would lack a majority of Bundestag seats.

During 1985–1990, Land coalitions between the SPD and the Greens had been rocky experiences. Observers questioned whether there could be win-win electoral outcomes for both partners. However, a willingness to compromise had prevailed since 1990 in Lower Saxony and its *rot–grün* coalition became the first to survive an entire legislative period.[6] SPD Minister-President Gerhard Schröder and Green leaders were favorable toward a renewed partnership. "Red–green passed its test . . . a triumph for both parties" editorialized the *Frankfurter Rundschau* (14 March 1994) in the aftermath of the Land election. The Greens won 7.4 percent of the votes (+1.9), and the SPD won 44.3 percent (+0.1). However, because of the FDP's failure to win seats, the electoral system produced a one-seat majority for the SPD.

The SPD leadership welcomed the Lower Saxony victory, but national polls indicated that an absolute majority was not in sight for the party. In Lower Saxony, Schröder had cast the SPD as a modernizing pro-industry party of the middle, while the Greens had run as the "red–green reform motor" (Raschke, 1994: 3). According to Kitschelt's analysis (1993: 106–7), whenever the SPD shelves the "left-libertarian" strategy, a political space to the left of the SPD opens up for the Greens in western Germany. The risk of such an implicit division of labor was that SPD success with a centrist strategy could result in a grand coalition in Bonn. Fischer urged on proponents of ecological renewal in the SPD: "[T]ogether we are going to make a real eco-social reform coalition" (*die tageszeitung*, 19 March 1994: 14). On 20 March, the Schleswig-Holstein Greens won 10.3 percent (+4.2) of local votes, and SPD–Green majorities emerged in Kiel and other localities.

West and East Greens agreed that an SPD–Green alliance was

necessary to halt the rightward drift of national politics. However, among Alliance 90 veterans there was no consensus about the "natural" coalition partner at the subnational level. With a membership of 1,000, the Saxony Green party was the largest in the new eastern Länder.[7] Its most notable figure, Bundestag deputy Werner Schulz advocated a *schwarz–grün* coalition in Dresden, which other Green activists vocally opposed. More disconcerting for federal party leaders, Wolfgang Templin, former speaker of Alliance 90, expressed sympathy with nationalists' concerns in interviews with right-wing publications. As in 1990, the federal leadership distanced the Greens from the PDS. However, some *Bundesvorstand* members left the door open to *ad hoc* cooperation with PDS parliamentarians. Ludger Volmer and Christiane Ziller articulated the official party line: "[E]ach vote for the PDS is, in fact, a vote against a red–green reform government in Bonn" (1994: 17). Their widely shared view was that if the SPD had to choose, it would opt for a grand coalition, rather than a SPD–Green minority government tolerated by ex-communists.

### Second-Order Elections of Summer 1994

After the indirect election of the federal president in May,[8] the rhythm of Superwahljahr picked up with the European Parliament election and local elections in seven Länder on 12 June. Although Euro-elections are national events, because power in Brussels is *not* at stake, they fall into the "second-order" category with local and Land elections (Reif, 1984). This time, however, the Euro-election was occurring four months before the Bundestag election, so it was widely perceived as the test run.

In 1993, the Greens challenged the Maastricht Treaty in the federal constitutional court; in 1994, they ran on a pro-European Union platform. Claudia Roth, who headed the Greens' Euro-list, observed that her party was the only one taking the European election serious for its own sake (*die tageszeitung*, 11 June 1994: 5). The Greens favored opening the EU to Eastern Europe, democratizing the EU, and prioritizing ecology in EU politics. Their campaign was low key, confident, and multifaceted. Brochures communicated the party's concerns for work and solidarity as well as for the environment. In the final days of the campaign, the author observed Green posters printed in various foreign languages along Berlin streets. As the multicultural party, the Greens appealed to non-Germans, who for the first time could vote for Germany's MEPs.[9]

On 12 June, the green side of *rot–grün* scored a big success, winning 10.1 percent of Euro-votes (+1.7 compared to 1989) (see Table 1.1). On the other side, the SPD's votes declined 3 percent while the CDU saw its votes increase by 1 percent. With the FDP, the PDS, and the Republikaner failing to clear the 5 percent threshold, the Greens claimed to be the third party of Germany. Heide Rühle of the Greens' electoral commission attributed success to a campaign of "firm opposition and doable alternative concepts" (1994: 4-5). INFAS data indicated that over 660,000 SPD voters switched to the Greens. Several left-wing Social Democrats urged a declaration supporting a *rot–grün* alliance. Scharping responded by renewing his criticism of the Greens' "illusionary" program.

The Greens won 11.0 percent of Euro-votes in the West. However, their eastern support reached only 5.5 percent; in Brandenburg and Mecklenburg-West Pomerania, they failed to clear 5 percent. The regional pattern of Green results was also apparent in the local elections of 12 June. In Baden-Württemberg, Rhineland-Palatinate, and Saarland council elections, and in Munich city elections, the Greens' shares averaged around 8 percent. In Saxony, Saxony-Anhalt, Thuringia, and Mecklenburg-West Pomerania, the Greens averaged around 6 percent. Small eastern gains for the Greens were overshadowed by the PDS big gains, which solidified its position as the third party in the East.[10] The PDS dual appeal as the home of former SED activists and as the protest party of eastern voters was more than local Green parties could hope to handle with small memberships, sparse funds, and weak networks.

On 26 June, the Saxony-Anhalt Greens just made it back into the Landtag with 5.1 percent of list votes. In addition, they won 6.8 percent of district votes, which suggests that voters tended to see the party sympathetically, but also tangentially to power in Magdeburg.[11] The Saxony-Anhalt Greens joined a minority government with the SPD tolerated by the PDS. SPD leaders, confronting the options of sharing power with a scandal-ridden CDU or governing with the Greens and (issue by issue) with the PDS, chose the "adventure" of a *de facto* left majority. Scharping stressed that the Magdeburg model did *not* pertain to Bonn. Green prominents welcomed Scharping's "signal" that any *Wende* (turn) required working with the Greens. SPD deputy leader Wolfgang Thierse observed that it was time to show what was possible with a *rot–grün* coalition in Magdeburg. The Saxony-Anhalt Green leader Hans-Jochen Tschiche saw ample grounds for cooperation with the PDS, but not all eastern Greens were positive about the new model. Marianne Birthler, federal party co-speaker, and Werner Schulz opposed any dependence on the SED-successor party and foresaw a media campaign against a *rot–grün* alliance. During the rest of the summer, CDU federal managers targeted the "Left Front" (see Chapter 2).

The second-order elections of summer 1994 had demonstrated that right-wing radicals and new protest parties were out of the picture; the FDP was in a precarious position; the Greens and the PDS were likely to reenter the Bundestag; and the SPD was short of a parliamentary majority with the Greens (or the FDP).[12] Yet electoral turnouts had been low by German standards, so surprises were possible during the "hot" phase of the campaign.

## The Fall Campaign

"Ein Land reformieren" became the slogan of the Greens' fall campaign. Its managers targeted special groups – women, youth, the handicapped, and homosexuals – and urban centers of potential support. They contrasted the substance of the Greens' campaign with the shallowness of those of the other parties. The party commissioned a series of placards, headlining the reform theme, with specific subtitles and composite imagery. For example, one placard stated, "Ein Land reformieren: Die schwarzen Tage sind gezählt" (A country to reform: The black days are numbered). It showed Germany outlined as if it were a window and a hand raising a dark shade that was decorated with pears (a reference to Kohl); in the lower right corner was the party logo. The other placards shared the slogan, the logo, and the map of Germany, but focused on specific issue areas.[13]

The electoral commission organized a fall series of policy events, for example, a women's conference in Berlin. The party's quota system had already put women up front; women headed fourteen of sixteen Land lists for the Bundestag. The federal campaign also featured some innovations. The Greens sponsored a Rock CD ("Der Grosse Lauschangriff") with music from a number of contemporary groups and a catalogue of environmentally friendly products. They also staged an independent competition for video spots against right-wing extremism to air during their free TV broadcast slots. Thus, the Greens reminded sympathizers that they were still *not* a party like the others.

Since 1993, the party had planned to run an all-German campaign, addressing eastern problems within a national framework. However, after eastern setbacks in June, the federal party sponsored special activities (e.g., Green info-bus tours and private radio spots) to supplement the eastern parties' Land campaigns. Compared to 1990, there was more coordination between federal and Land campaign managers. According to surveys (Forschungsgruppe Wahlen, 1994a; 1994b), the Saxony and Brandenburg Greens enjoyed a relatively positive image. However, by September, the parties were at such a structural disadvantage that it is hard to visualize how different campaign tactics would have altered the negative outcome in the Landtag elections. The overarching issue of both turned out to be the leadership of a popular minister-president, navigating a sea of post-unification storms.

As the Superwahljahr began, some polls placed the Saxony Greens as high as 15 percent. Because of the weakness of the Saxony SPD, however, the numbers never indicated a majority for *rot–grün*. Therefore, Schulz argued for a *schwarz–grün* alliance as an alternative to a grand coalition in Dresden; others found insufficient commonality of policies to sustain an alliance with the CDU. On 11 September, the Saxony Greens received only 4.1 percent of the list votes; their press secretary attributed the defeat mainly to the party's inability to mobilize its own clientele (Turnowsky, 1994: 20).

The Brandenburg Greens had been plagued by disunity. The *Ampelkoalition* and the Green parliamentary group in Potsdam (unaffiliated with *Bündnis 90/Die Grünen*) had fallen apart over the controversy about the past connections between SPD Minister-President Manfred Stolpe and the Stasi. Despite the fact that Stolpe was likely to lead the SPD again, the Brandenburg Greens strongly favored a *rot–grün* alliance. On 11 September, they won only 2.9 percent of the list votes; a splinter group, *Bürgerbündnis*, which received 1 percent, could not be blamed for their debacle.

The elections in Saxony and Brandenburg were hardly test runs for the Bundestag; an absolute majority for incumbent Kohl was clearly not in the federal picture. Nevertheless, interpretations of the results provoked conflicts among Green prominents. In Saxony, they squabbled over whether the party's profile was obscured by debates about relations with the CDU in the context of a federal campaign seeking partnership with the SPD. Ludger Volmer and Heide Rühle of the federal leadership criticized the eastern Greens' preoccupation with the past. This generated heated replies from veterans of the citizen movements, notably Konrad Weiss. Fischer, whom the press has long labeled the "secret chairman," intervened to dampen the East–West conflict. He attributed eastern setbacks to: the weakness of the Green milieu, the protest voting for the PDS, and the "monarchical" principle (*die tageszeitung*, 13 September 1994: 3).

Compared to 1990 Landtage results, the PDS scored big on 11 September in Saxony and Brandenburg. This result, coupled with polls indicating a possible majority of Bundestag seats to the left of the CDU, reignited the debate among Green activists about relations with the PDS. Preferences among the Green voters were clear – only 7 percent favored coalition or toleration of the PDS (*Der Spiegel*, 29 August 1994: 32). Nevertheless, the Saxony-Anhalt Green leader Tschiche spoke favorably of joint lists with the PDS. Three former Alternative List officers argued that the Greens should seek a Berlin alliance with the SPD *and* the PDS, which veteran citizen activists immediately pronounced "unacceptable." The *Länderrat* unanimously resolved: "The PDS is our political opponent. He who makes its politics presentable, stabilizes Kohl and prevents change" (*Frankfurter Allgemeine Zeitung*, 19 September 1994: 1).

In Bavaria, where environmental protection was an issue, the Greens faced conservative competition from the Ecological Democratic Party (ÖDP), which ended up with 2.1 percent of Land votes on 25 September.[14] The Greens won 6.1 percent. Some votes were lost to the SPD, whose party leader, Renate Schmidt, appealed to young women. A *rot–grün* government was never really possible because of the SPD's weakness. Bavarian results confirmed that Green defeats in Saxony and Brandenburg had no contagious effect in western Germany (Forschungsgruppe Wahlen, 1994c: 45).

For the "hot" phase of the federal campaign, Green party leaders distilled from the Mannheim program an action program of ten reform projects for four years of governmental participation. The number one project was "ökologisch wirtschaften" (to "ecologize" the economy). Reforms included exiting from nuclear power (no time table), highway speed limits, controls on genetic technology, and stiff energy taxes. Polls during the fall indicated that most of the electorate correctly associated these policies with the Greens, although none of them enjoyed majority support.[15] The second project was to fight mass unemployment; the third, to develop eastern Germany and undo the damage done by Kohl's policies. The anti-NATO provisions of the Mannheim program, which had generated the most press coverage, appeared in a moderated form within the ninth project, *"Die Außenpolitikzivilisieren"* (to civilize foreign policy). Since the Mannheim conference, Green leaders had signaled that long-term foreign policy differences with the SPD would not be an obstacle to coalition negotiations for 1994–1998.

In mid-September, the *Länderrat* selected the Greens' negotiation commission, whose "heavy duty" membership included prominent figures from the Left (e.g., Jürgen Trittin), the center (e.g., Helmut Lippelt), the *Realos* (e.g., Joschka Fischer), and the East (e.g., Werner Schulz). Collectively it was a group with years of experience in party executives, parliamentary groups, and Land governments – a group that communicated the political competence to deliver upon campaign promises.

Since 1990, the Greens have moved toward an acceptance of the role of personalities in simplifying policy complexities and in providing emotional handles for average citizens in an age of media politics. During the 1994 campaign, Joschka Fischer came as close as anyone since Petra Kelly to be being *the* superstar of the Greens. Many Green activists had resented Kelly's media prominence in the 1980s. Indeed, a decade later, Fischer surmised that "85 percent of Greens consider me an asshole" (*Frankfurter Allgemeine Zeitung*, 7 October 1994: 4), but an indispensable one, he implied. Fischer campaigned nationally, drawing good crowds and press coverage. Although the middle-aging Fischer did not look particularly "radical" anymore, journalists still saw him as good copy, compared to the likes of Scharping.

*The Political Parties*

**Electoral Outcomes**

In contrast to the December 1990 "surprise," the Greens' results in 1994 were in the anticipated range. The party won 7.3 percent of list votes, which was 2.2 more than the combined shares of Western Greens and *Alliance 90* in 1990 (see Table 1.2). In 1994 they won 7.8 percent of the votes (+3.1 since 1990) in the West. They received 4.3 percent (-1.9) in the East, losing votes in all five Länder and East Berlin. The Greens were the only contending party whose electoral share went up in one part of Germany and down in the other. Only 5 of 49 Greens elected to the Bundestag came from the former GDR, 3 less than during 1990–1994. In the Mecklenburg-West Pomerania and Thuringia elections on 16 October, the Greens won no Landtag seats, with 3.7 and 4.5 percent of list votes respectively.

The Greens gained votes in all western Länder in 1994, ranging from +1.7 percent of list votes in Bavaria to +6.8 percent in Hamburg. In Berlin, Bremen, and Hamburg, the party won 10.2 to 12.6 percent. Its 5.8 percent in Saarland was the weakest performance, but this represented a gain of 3.5 percent since 1990. The Greens won 7.1 percent of western district votes (compared to 3.8 of eastern district votes). Their first district win did not materialize in Berlin Kreuzburg/Schöneberg, where Ströbele captured 28 percent of the votes (4.2 percent less than the SPD's winner).

Saarland's Land election and North Rhine-Westphalia local elections coincided with the federal election. For the first time, the Greens won seats in Saarland's Landtag, with 5.5 percent of the votes. Thus, at the end of Superwahljahr, the Greens held seats in eleven of sixteen Landtage, compared to seven for the FDP. In contrast to the FDP, the Greens scored big gains in the local elections of North Rhine-Westphalia. Their 10.2 percent overall made them the third force in many councils within Germany's most populated Land.

The demographics of federal voting suggested that the Greens' comeback is unlikely to be short-lived. They drew disproportionate support from the 18–44 age groups. The high for western Greens was 15 percent among 18–24-year-olds; in the East, it was 10 percent. In both parts of Germany, the Greens did the best with young women, which indicated that the major parties' recent feminist appeals have not made the Greens *passé*.

As in the past, the Green electorate overrepresented the more educated, the more urban, and white-collar employees or civil servants. There were East–West differences, such as greater support in the East among farmers and greater support among the unemployed in the West. Overall, however, the demographic correlates of Green voting in the West also showed up in the East but with less strength (Forschungsgruppe Wahlen, 1994d: 68). Optimists would foresee eastern sympathy for the Greens translating into more votes as economic conditions improve and "postmaterialist" issues develop more salience. Yet, the PDS has borrowed wholesale from the Greens' program and has made headway among young voters in the East.

### Intraparty and Interparty Implications

It is hard to exaggerate the significance of these electoral outcomes for the Greens. During 1990–1994, although they had a (thin) presence in the Bundestag and their federal leadership performed in an integrative manner, the Greens still lacked a "power center" (Raschke and Schmitt-Beck, 1994: 176). After the Bundestagswahl, the situation changed quantitatively and qualitatively. It will be hard for the media to ignore forty-nine Green MPs, the third largest *Fraktion*. The new roster includes a "critical mass" of talented and telegenic politicos, who will not have to worry about being rotated, as had earlier Green MPs. The new *Fraktion* retained collective leadership, but loosened grassroots-democratic rules by electing leaders for two-year terms (instead of one year) and by closing its meetings to outsiders. The forty-nine Green MPs are supported by more than 150 parliamentary staffers (whose salary schedules are more differentiated by level of expertise than previously). The Green "think tank" on the Rhine, which the voters dismissed on 2 December 1990, is back in business, under what promises to be a more professional and less chaotic management.

Green delegates to the November 1994 party conference in Cologne, however, were concerned that the tilt of power back to the *Fraktion* might go too far. They rejected a proposal to loosen the long-standing rule that forbids the simultaneous holding of a parliamentary mandate and a federal party office. Proponents argued that some overlap between parliamentary and party bodies would facilitate coordination. The Greens' sister party in Austria, the Green-Alternatives, had the same incompatibility rule, but abolished it in October 1992. German Greens have viewed the rule as more central to their "alternative" identity.

The party's organizational resources grew as a result of its federal electoral performance. The Greens qualified for DM 15.5 million to reimburse campaign expenses.[16] Some of these monies can offset the loss of *Fraktion* funds in eastern Landtage. Bundestag Greens set up a new working group for eastern issues to provide programmatic assistance to the struggling eastern parties. Of the party's 43,000 members, only about 3,000 are in the East. At the November 1994 conference, outgoing co-speaker Volmer (who had been elected to the Bundestag) recommended opening the party to former SED members, but keeping the Greens' distance from the PDS as a party. Saxony's Schulz responded, "There were not thousands of Gorbachevs in the SED, who are now going to knock on our door" (*die tageszeitung*, 7 November 1994: 4). He observed that the party's eastern weakness would not be overcome by western patent solutions.

Although eastern interests have been more carefully considered in the Greens – who did not rapidly annex their eastern allies – than in the major parties, East–West tensions will remain troublesome, as was evident at the time of the December 1994 party conference in Potsdam. Green delegates elected two western Greens as federal co-speakers: Jürgen Trittin from the Left and Krista Sager from the *Realos*. Fischer, the newly elected co-speaker of the Bundestag Greens, supported this (ideology and gender-balanced) dynamic duo; Trittin had been a Green minister in the Lower Saxony government and Sager had been the parliamentary leader of the Hamburg Greens. The 1993 association agreement did not mandate an East–West quota for the co-speakerships. Yet Easterners argued that one speaker should come from the East, as had previously been the case. The majority of delegates agreed to their demand to speed up the movement of the party headquarters to Berlin.

Although the Greens and the SPD both scored gains in the Bundestagswahl, their totals fell short of what was needed for a majority of seats in a five party Bundestag. The Greens found themselves back in their role of "alternative" opposition, but there had been a change in interparty relationships. Local elections in North Rhine-Westphalia fueled a debate about a *schwarz–grün* alliance. Previously there had been isolated cases of the Greens and the CDU sharing local council power in Hesse and Baden-Württemberg After the Bundestagswahl, CDU–Green alliances emerged in a dozen local councils of North Rhine-Westphalia, despite reservations expressed by federal and Land Green party leaders. In late 1994 there were ten times as many SPD–Green local alliances as CDU–Green. Yet the novelty of the CDU working with the Greens, whom conservatives had portrayed until recently as a radical leftist party, seized the imagination of many journalists. Was the CDU opening its options in case of the FDP's demise?

Although there have been Green vice-presidents in the Landtage, since 1983 the major parties have blocked the Greens from this largely symbolic office in the Bundestag. In November 1994, the Greens' Antje Vollmer was elected to one of the vice-presidencies with the support of the CDU leadership (over SPD opposition), which signified its acceptance of the Greens as an *established* party. Green leaders welcomed the opportunity to send the SPD a message that they should not be taken for granted. However, the consensus among Green prominents remains that there are not sufficient policy commonalities beyond the local level to support CDU–Green alliances in the near future.

In the Land elections of February and May 1995, the Greens continued to make electoral gains. In Hesse they won 11.2 percent of the votes (+2.4 percent) and offset the SPD's losses to preserve a narrow *rot–grün* majority. Coalition negotiations yielded significant enhancements of the policy domains of the two Green ministers. The FDP stayed in the picture in Wiesbaden by winning 7.5 percent of the votes. But it fared poorly in the Bremen and North Rhine-Westphalia elections on 14 May, losing its seats in both Landtage. The FDP's post-Kinkel leadership appears to be seeking a niche for the party by emphasizing economic and national liberalism. However, young success-oriented professionals seem to be more attracted to the Greens as the rising "new" middle class party (Walter, 1995).

On 14 May 1995, the Bremen Greens raised their share of the city-state's votes to 13.1 percent. The SPD, losing votes to a right-of-center protest initiative, received only 33.4 percent. SPD leaders, confronting the options of governing with a one-seat majority with the Greens (resisted by right-wing Social

Democrats) or sharing power with the CDU, chose the latter. In contrast to the 1980s, this was a case where the stability of a *rot–grün* government appeared to be threatened by disunity within the SPD, not within the Greens. The Bremen results are also noteworthy because, despite vigorous efforts, the PDS failed to stage its first breakthrough in a western Land (see Chapter 6). The PDS won only 2.4 percent of the votes. Observers had speculated that it might have a future as a protest party where the Greens have become oriented toward governmental responsibility. Bremen voters relegated the PDS to a regional status.

The results of the North Rhine-Westphalia Land elections were a moderate earthquake. The heavy industrial economy of North Rhine-Westphalia as well as Green disunity had long been obstacles for the party, which belatedly entered its Landtag in 1990. On 14 May 1995, they *doubled* their share of the votes to 10 percent, and the SPD lost its absolute majority. Minister-President Johannes Rau, who has long opposed a *rot–grün* coalition, suddenly confronted the choice of a majority with the Greens or with the CDU. An SPD–Green coalition in Düsseldorf emerged over the resistance of right-wing Social Democrats. Green leaders portrayed it as the test run for 1998.

In Bonn, SPD leaders dismissed Fischer's proposal of a joint opposition strategy in the Bundestag. Cooperation in national politics ultimately would be more difficult in opposition (or government) because of the divergencies of SPD and Green foreign and defense policies. Mainstream observers now see greater realism at the top of the Green party, but fear that radicalism still lurks in its ranks. Co-speaker Sager favors updating the (basic) federal program of 1980 to reflect the post-Cold War era. Critics fear that this might undermine party unity. Proponents reply that the program itself envisages politics as a learning process. In any case, after the electoral outcomes of 1994–1995, it will be impossible for the major parties to ignore the Greens as a variable in the national power equation.

## Conclusion

In fifteen years, the Greens have risen, fallen, and comeback as Germany's third party. Electoral shock therapy in 1990 facilitated the clarification of the party's identity and the consolidation of its organization. Intraparty changes were followed by a series of successes in Land elections in 1991–1993. In 1990, the Greens dodged *the* issue of the first all-German election, unification (Schoonmaker and Frankland, 1993: 148). In 1994, they tackled *the* issue of the second all-German election, economic revival. Compared to 1990, their 1994 campaign was professionally planned and executed to showcase reform policies and competent leaders. During 1994, the debate about relations with the PDS disrupted party harmony, but it was a far cry from the factional wrangling that sapped their 1990 campaign. The Greens did not "comeback" in the East, but they were able to offset losses there by mobilizing potential voters in the West. In the aftermath of the 1994 Bundestagswahl, pundits were speculating about the Greens' prospects for assuming the FDP's pivotal role in the party system. It was not a theoretical question anymore after May 1995 Land elections in Bremen and North Rhine-Westphalia.

A decade ago the Greens were split over how they should relate to government: fundamental opposition, toleration, or coalition. The question quickly boiled down to how to relate to the SPD. This was a sensitive point for Green activists who had negative experiences as past members of the SPD, and especially for radical leftists, who saw the SPD as the historical obstacle to socioeconomic transformation. At Mannheim in 1994, the Greens united behind a *rot–grün* strategy to bring about ecological and social reforms. To floating voters between the Greens and the SPD, the message was that the SPD could not be counted upon to stick to its reform promises without Green partners. Scharping's centrist strategy lent credibility to their slogan: "Wer rot–grün will, muß grün wählen".

Despite speculations about coalitions with the CDU, the immediate future of the Greens depends significantly on the SPD. A partial swing back to Lafontaine's New Left strategy could cut into the Greens' 1994 votes. A party whose core vote has been around 4 percent would seem too vulnerable to short-term forces to assume the historic role of the FDP. However, since 1994 the Greens have made headway by winning 10–3 percent of the votes in Hesse, Bremen, and North Rhine-Westphalia.

The big problem lies in the East, where "postmaterialist" issues still have limited resonance. The eastern Greens' active member-ship was tiny before the 1994 elections and now seems likely to be overwhelmed by the task of rebuilding. Furthermore, Easterners are split on how to deal with the PDS. The early (western) Greens shared a negative consensus toward the Bonn party cartel and appealed to those protesting against its policies. In 1994, the protest vote in the East went to the "outsider" PDS, which inherited the SED's "insider" organizational resources that allow it to help Easterners with everyday difficulties in a uniting Germany (Chapter 6). Although the PDS has borrowed heavily from Green programs, its dubious democratic legitimacy in the eyes of veterans of the citizen movements – and Westerners – will make Green–PDS alliances beyond local politics difficult in the near future. Despite PDS reformers' efforts to recast their party as a "postmaterialist" democratic socialist party, the mass membership PDS is hardly a "new politics" party in the sense of the Greens of the 1980s.

But what kind of party are the Greens after the electoral outcomes of 1994–1995? Systemic imperatives have steadily pushed them in the direction of being more of an electoral-professional and less of a movementist-amateur party. Veen and Hoffmann's study (1992) described the Greens as "an almost established" party. Today one should delete the "almost" after the CDU has voted a Green MP into the Bundestag vice-presidency and CDU prominents have begun to debate whether there is a future for a *schwarz–grün* alliance. Yet the Green party has retained a profile more regionally diverse, decentralized, participatory and elite-challenging than the major parties. The new *Fraktion* modified its grassroots-democratic rules, but the Cologne conference's support of the incompatibility rule showed that activists are still not prepared to risk full parliamentarization of leadership. The Greens' social base of the "new" middle class of educated individuals tends to reject mass organization and to be motivated by specific causes rather than party loyalty. Thus, the Greens have to balance vote- and office-seeking goals with policy and democracy-seeking goals. According to Raschke (1991), they should develop as a projects-oriented framework party of competence, plurality, and civility. Lower Saxony CDU leader Christian Wulff has described the Greens as a "holding company" with diverse interests under its roof, an "interesting" model in an increasingly heterogeneous society (*die tageszeitung*, 22 May 1995: 10).

During the 1980s, political scientists pondered the question of whether the Greens were a "short-term cyclical protest or indicator of transformation" (Müller-Rommel, 1989). Today we can dismiss the first possibility, but still cannot confirm the second. We do know that in 1983 the Greens entered the Bundestag as the anti-party of youthful protesters – in 1994 they came back as the postmodern party of reform professionals.

**Notes**

1. After 1990, the Greens were represented in the Bundestag by two eastern Greens of the *Bündnis 90/Grüne* parliamentary group, whose eight members were not enough for full *Fraktion* powers and funding. After spring 1993, the parliamentary group was officially linked to the (united) Green party.
2. The CDU and the FDP lost votes in the West and the East; the SPD and the PDS won votes in both. The PDS's western gains were only 0.7 percent since 1990. See Table 1.2.
3. For more discussion of the Greens' reform and recovery during 1991–1993, see Frankland, 1995: 37–9.
4. The 1990 special electoral law applied the 5 percent threshold separately to the East and the West. *Bündnis 90/Grüne* won seats with 6 percent of eastern votes, which was 1.2 percent of total votes. The Greens won no seats with 4.8 percent of western votes, 3.9 percent of total list votes. There were no separate East–West zones in 1994.
5. As Poguntke and Schmitt-Beck (1994: 89) observed, there is no guarantee of the special privileges of Easterners – unless more join the party – because Westerners have the two-thirds majority of votes necessary to amend the party charter.
6. The SPD–Green coalition in Hesse (1991–1995) became the second to survive a legislative period. The SPD–Green coalition in Hesse (1985–1987) and the SPD–Alternative List coalition in Berlin (1989–1990) broke up prematurely.
7. *Die tageszeitung* (29 April 1994: 12) also reports: 400 party members in Brandenburg, 350 in Thuringia, 300 in Mecklenburg-Western Pomerania, and 450 in Saxony-Anhalt; in Berlin, the Alternative List had 2,000 mostly western

members and *Bündnis 90*, 300 mostly eastern members.

8. The Greens supported prominent eastern citizen movement activist and scientist Jens Reich for the federal presidency. After trailing the major parties' candidates on the first ballot at the federal convention, he withdrew.

9. The evidence is that few non-German EU residents took advantage of the opportunity to vote for German members of the European Parliament.

10. Eastern 1990–1994 comparisons are complicated by varied sets of competing and coalescing Green and citizen movements on the 1990 local ballots. However, western Greens clearly increased their local percentages in the 12 June elections.

11. In the 1994 Land elections of Saxony, Brandenburg, and Thuringia, the Greens also received larger shares of the district votes than the list votes. The Mecklenburg-West Pomerania Greens received slightly more list votes than district votes.

12. The PDS was well positioned in East Berlin to win three district seats and thereby to qualify for Bundestag representation proportional to its list votes. On 16 October, it won four district seats and 26 list seats without clearing 5 percent of the votes.

13. See Selzer (1994) for an insider's preliminary assessment of the Greens' 1994 campaign techniques.

14. The ÖDP was founded in 1981 by Herbert Gruhl, who had resigned from the Greens because of the leftist slant of the 1980 program. On 16 October 1994, it won only 0.4 percent of the national votes, about the same as on 2 December 1990.

15. The Allensbach poll indicated that even the Greens' supporters disagreed with their proposal to raise fuel taxes significantly (*Frankfurter Allgemeine Zeitung*, 5 October 1994: 5).

16. The SPD qualified for DM 88.8 million in state funding; the CDU/CSU, DM 91.8 million; the FDP, 14.4 million; and the PDS, 10.6 million (German Information Center, *The Week in Germany*, 20 January 1995: 2). Parties winning sufficient seats to qualify for *Fraktion* status also receive generous grants for parliamentary activities.

# References

Bruns, Tissy. 1994. "Bündnis 90/Die Grünen: Oppositions- oder Regierungspartei?" *Aus Politik und Zeitgeschichte* B1 (7 January): 27–31.

Forschungsgruppe Wahlen. 1993. *Politbarometer*, 12 (December). Mannheim: Forschungsgruppe Wahlen.

——. 1994a. *Wahl in Sachsen: Eine Analyse der Landtagswahl vom 11 September 1994.* No. 73, Mannheim: Forschungsgruppe Wahlen.

——. 1994b. *Wahl in Brandenburg: Eine Analyse der Landtagswahl vom 11. September 1994.* No. 74, Mannheim: Forschungsgruppe Wahlen.

——. 1994c. *Wahl in Bayern: Eine Analyse der Landtagswahl vom 25. September 1994.* No. 75, Mannheim: Forschungsgruppe Wahlen.

——. 1994d. *Bundestagswahl 1994: Eine Analyse der Wahl zum 13. Deutschen Bundestag am 16. Oktober 1994.* No. 76 (2nd Edition), Mannheim: Forschungsgruppe Wahlen.

——. 1994e. *Politbarometer*, 2 (February). Mannheim: Forschungsgruppe Wahlen.

Frankland, E. Gene. 1995. "Germany: The Rise, Fall and Recovery of *Die Grünen*," in Dick Richardson and Chris Rootes, eds. *The Green Challenge: The Development of Green Parties in Europe.* London: Routledge.

Jahn, Detlef. 1994. "Unifying the Greens in a United Germany," *Environmental Politics* 3 (Summer): 312–18.

Kitschelt, Herbert. 1993. "The Green Phenomenon in Western Party Systems," in Sheldon Kamieniecki, ed. *Environmental Politics in the International Arena.* Albany: State University of New York.

Müller-Rommel, Ferdinand. 1989. "The German Greens in the 1980s: Short-term Cyclical Protest or Indicator of Transformation?" *Political Studies* 38 (March): 114–22.

Poguntke, Thomas and Rüdiger Schmitt-Beck. 1994. "Still the Same with a New Name? Bündnis 90/Die Grünen after the Fusion," *German Politics* 3 (April): 91–113.

Raschke, Joachim. 1991. *Krise der Grünen: Bilanz und Neubeginn.* Frankfurt/Main: Schüren.

——. 1993. *Die Grünen: Wie sie wurden, was sie sind.* Cologne: Bund-Verlag.

——. 1994. "Formschwäche ist noch kein Machtwechsel in Bonn," *die tageszeitung* (15 March): 3.

—— and Rüdiger Schmitt-Beck. 1994. "Die Grünen: Stabilisierung nur durch den Niedergang der Etablierten?" in Wilhelm Bürklin and Dieter Roth, eds. *Das Superwahljahr*. Cologne: Bund-Verlag.

Reif, Karlheinz. 1984. "National Electoral Cycles and European Elections 1979 and 1984," *Election Studies* 3: 244–55.

Rühle, Heide. 1994. "Auf dem Weg von Strassburg nach Bonn," *Schrägstrich: Zeitschrift für bündnisgrüne Politik* (Bornheim) 7–8: 4–5.

Schmitt-Beck, Rüdiger. 1994. "Wählerpotentials von Bündnis 90/ Grünen im Ost–West-Vergleich: Umfang, Struktur, politische Orientierungen," *Journal für Sozialforschung* 34: 45–70.

Schoonmaker, Donald. 1992. "The Green Alliance: A Marriage of Convenience." Paper presented at annual meeting of the German Studies Association, Minneapolis, Minnesota, October 1–4.

—— and E. Gene, Frankland. 1993. "Disunited Greens in a United Germany," in Russell J. Dalton, ed. *The New Germany Votes*. Oxford: Berg.

Selzer, Henry. 1994. "Der bündnisgrüne Wahlkampf," *Schrägstrich: Zeitschrift für bündnisgrüne Politik* (Bornheim) 11: 8–10.

Turnowsky, Walter. 1994. "Der König und sein Volk," *Schrägstrich: Zeitschrift für bündnisgrüne Politik* (Bornheim) 10: 20–1.

Veen, Hans-Joachim and Jürgen Hoffmann. 1992. *Die Grünen zu Beginn der neunziger Jahre*. Bonn: Bouvier.

Volmer, Ludger. 1994. "Kompetent und verantwortungsbereit," *Schrägstrich: Zeitschrift für bündnisgrüne Politik* (Bornheim) 4: 19–20.

—— and Ziller, Christiane. 1994. "Neue politische Offensive im Osten," *Schrägstrich: Zeitschrift für bündnisgrüne Politik* (Bornheim) 6: 16–18.

Walter, Franz. 1995. "Rechts ist noch reichlich Platz frei: Eine Überlebenschance für die FDP?" *die tageszeitung* (Berlin), 19 May.

# 6
# The Party of Democratic Socialism: Left and East

## *Henry Krisch*

Three years ago, this author speculated about the future of the Party of Democratic Socialism (PDS) and came to the mistaken conclusion that there was only a small chance of the party repeating its 1990 achievement of securing seats in the Bundestag (Krisch, 1993: 182; Bortfeldt, 1994).[1] It is not only the electoral success of the PDS – in addition to returning to the Bundestag, it increased its representation from seventeen to thirty members – that needs to be explained. Its success raises important questions about the party's place in the German political process and the role of parties within that process.

For at least the immediate future, moreover, the elections consolidated the PDS' role as a major force in the regional politics of eastern Germany. In this perspective the PDS (seen as a successor-party of the GDR's ruling party, the SED) has made a place for itself comparable to analogous parties in other postcommunist states (Phillips, 1994).[2]

### The Basis of the PDS Campaign

The success of the PDS was due in large measure to an astute analysis of the (especially eastern) German political situation that shaped the party's electoral tactics. The PDS' particular strengths determined its focus on significant features of the electoral system, including the electoral calendar of the Superwahljahr 1994 and the provision (not invoked since the early 1950s) that a party could share in the proportional representation of Bundestag seats by winning at least three direct mandates without winning 5 percent of the vote.

Karl Schmitt's detailed exposition of the electoral scene in eastern Germany at the end of 1993 demonstrates how PDS strategy was shaped by the party's position a year before the federal elections (Schmitt, 1994). In the three years following the 1990 Bundestag election, the PDS seemed preoccupied with its own affairs. Much of its energy was consumed by doctrinal debates involving the adoption of a party program in early 1993 (Pfahl-Traughber, 1995). The party's financial and organizational affairs suffered from unresolved issues concerning the disposition of SED property – a matter that still dogged the party after the 1994 elections (Gehrmann and Kurbjuweit, 1994)![3] Its deputy chairman and head of the PDS organization in Berlin, André Brie, was forced to resign after disclosures that he had been an informant of the political police for two decades.[4]

Nevertheless, the party's own strengths and, even more, the conditions of eastern German life, contrived to make the PDS a potentially effective political force. Party membership stabilized at 130,000 (of whom about 95 percent formerly belonged to the SED). Saxony, East Berlin, Brandenburg, and Saxony-Anhalt were the party's main strongholds; there were only about 1700 members in the all ten western Länder combined (Table 6.1). The peculiar social composition of the party's membership supported its political effectiveness. In the eastern Länder some 40 percent of the membership had at least some college or university training; about two-thirds were either already retired or scheduled for early retirement (*Vorruheständler*). Thus throughout 1994 in the eastern Länder the PDS had a skilled force of electoral troops at its disposal (Gohde and Harnach, 1994).

Moreover, the PDS profited from the troubled economic situation of eastern Germany throughout 1992 and 1993 (Moreau, 1994a).[5] The economy's very slow recovery from the shock of unification, widespread dissatisfaction with regulations on the disposal of property once held by the GDR regime, and persisting high levels of unemployment – especially among members of the administrative strata of the GDR – all led to a steep decline in the Kohl government's standing in the new Länder. Crucial to the fortunes of the PDS, this rejection of the incumbents brought little profit to the national opposition, the SPD (Hartung, 1994). This point was frequently bemoaned by writers sympathetic to the SPD (Kuhlwein, 1994; Meckel, 1994). Moreover, the strength of the PDS over the electoral cycle of 1994 showed that it, and not

**Table 6.1** PDS Membership in Late 1994

| Land | Membership |
| --- | --- |
| Berlin | 21,726 |
| Brandenburg | 18,258 |
| Mecklenburg-Western Pomerania | 14,154 |
| Saxony | 32,813 |
| Saxony-Anhalt | 18,270 |
| Thuringia | 16,137 |
| Western Länder (combined) | 1,716 |
| Total | 123,173 |

*Source*: Gohde and Harnach, 1994. At the end of 1993, total membership was 131,406.

the heirs of the autumn of 1989 (Alliance 90), had become the chosen instrument of expressing eastern German political consciousness.

Throughout 1994, surveys showed that unemployment was regarded in the East as the most important political issue (Forschungsgruppe Wahlen, 1994b). This was especially so in early 1994, when the PDS established itself in public awareness as a political factor and as a party that was more likely to deal effectively with the eastern economic situation. Throughout most of 1994, the same surveys showed that most people considered the general economic situation in the East as "bad," or (after April) "so-so."

These economic woes were perhaps more important in engendering feelings of insecurity and lack of autonomy than as a reflection of actual economic need. In the six months prior to the elections, the number of survey respondents who felt their own economic situation was "bad" never exceeded 14 percent. There was, however, a widespread feeling that a PDS presence in state and national legislatures was needed to represent eastern interests neglected by the traditional parties. So strong was this feeling that it often overrode another widely held belief, namely, that the PDS had not completely broken with its GDR past. For those Easterners (76 percent in a poll in September 1994) who regarded themselves as "second-class citizens," implications that the PDS was undemocratic were presumably not as important as its capacity to represent their interests (Gibowski, 1994). Another September 1994 poll found that the reason most often cited for voting PDS (88 percent) was to get Bonn to take eastern problems seriously (Hilmer and Müller-Hilmer, 1994).[6]

## The PDS Campaign: Strategy, Tactics, Program

These objective conditions were perhaps necessary for a good PDS showing at the polls, but clearly they would not have been sufficient if the PDS had not organized an effective campaign. In 1993, the party settled on a strategy and centralized its execution. It created a visually uniform campaign with common themes (although not the same themes in eastern and western states). It tailored its appeal both for *Zweitstimmen* in the hope of surpassing the 5 percent threshold and for direct mandate votes in a set of target districts.

This plan for an effective campaign was contained in a document submitted by André Brie to the party's leadership in 1993 (Brie, 1993).[7] It began characteristically with the acerbic assertion that "If in an election campaign everyone does whatever he or she wants, and in whatever form desired, that has nothing to do with democracy." Furthermore, although the 1994 elections would have a significance for the PDS that could hardly be overstated, the document stated that no PDS candidate or politician should ever publicly admit that these were crucial elections (*Schicksalswahlen*) for the PDS.

The party's goal was to become a "modern socialist party" as well as a "socially effective opposition force" in Germany. The first step on the long road to this goal was to return to the Bundestag. How realistic was this goal? From the start, the PDS campaign looked both to specific electoral circumstances and general social trends. For example, Brie pointed out that in Berlin, where Gregor Gysi had won a direct seat in 1990, the PDS had gained a plurality of votes in 1992 borough council elections in areas which, after redistricting, represented two additional Bundestag seats. There were thus at least three targets of opportunity in Berlin alone, and there were other tempting districts throughout the new Länder.

The social analysis underlying the PDS' hopes of reaching 5 percent of the national vote rested on the notion that the unification of Germany had transformed but not resolved a variety of social, ecological, and economic problems on both national and global levels. Moreover, strategists argued that the unification of 1990, executed according to "criteria of power politics and the market," had destroyed possibilities for eastern "autonomy, culture, and identity." The inability of the German state to manage these problems would lead to a deepening sociopolitical crisis, whose symptom was the emergence of the first right-wing mass culture since 1945.

What German political forces were there to counter this trend? According to the PDS, the SPD and the Greens were no longer parties working toward general social reform, so that the "[political] space to the left of the SPD and Greens is growing and is in fact unoccupied." The PDS could take advantage of this to campaign for a Germany of "solidarity, cooperation, ecological awareness," as a "leftist, socialist opposition party." The party could also represent eastern German interests, and aim at the ecological and social modernization of Germany – not just the westernization of the former GDR. The political goal of the PDS was to be both Left and East.

What sort of program did the PDS present in order to attract such voters (PDS, 1993; PDS, 1994a; Pfahl-Traughber, 1995)? An examination of the PDS' 1993 program and 1994 campaign program reveals some striking features: the programs were largely atheoretical and contained very limited analysis of the party's (and the GDR's!) past. Rather, these programmatic statements were compendia of reformist and radical demands, combining specific problems of eastern German life with a broad catalog of radical leftist issues. There was little explanation of how these demands might form a coherent whole, or what their theoretical justification might be.

Socialism, the 1993 program declared, while "not an abstract ideal [was not] the realization of a preconceived ideal society either." It was to be attained through lengthy, detailed struggles to overcome the "deficits and contradictions" of present-day society (PDS, 1993). In the election program, this had been watered down to "taking a radical-democratic and anticapitalist" position in current political conflicts while proclaiming: "Our goal remains democratic socialism!"

The party's economic program consisted of a wide variety of measures aimed at creating and maintaining employment and industrial investment (especially in the East), but with due regard for environmental standards. Social policy was to be need-based (*bedarfsorientiert*) and to take special care for social equality for women and other groups. The cost – estimated at DM 3,250 billion – would be met through higher, socially progressive and more efficiently collected taxation.

The international policy of the party stressed engagement with the underdeveloped world, abjuring any military (or, indeed, any leading diplomatic) role for Germany.

Although the PDS expended considerable time and effort on these documents, largely through a *Grundsatzkommission* chaired by André Brie, it is difficult to see these diffuse and internally not quite coherent compilations as serious programmatic documents. They were designed, in part, to satisfy the members who expected a program from their SED days. The all-encompassing catalog of demands for change seemed designed to attract the younger, radical voters. To what extent programmatic appeals accounted for the large percentage (and low numerical) increase in western voting support is unclear.

What constituencies might support such a program? The PDS identified four very heterogeneous elements to be found in social strata outside the working class: 1) former members of the GDR's intelligentsia and party-state apparatus attracted by the PDS's anticapitalist stance; 2) "losers of unification;" 3) those who viewed the GDR in a nostalgic and transfigured light (but who are difficult to recruit for left-wing programs); and 4) left-wing elements in western Germany. To appeal to this mixture of young, partly western radicals, un- or underemployed ex-GDR intellectuals, eastern pensioners, and so forth required a targeted and differentiated election campaign; the PDS would have to stress different appeals in the old and new Länder.

To a surprising extent, the PDS campaign throughout 1994 followed these prescriptions. An energetic, media-clever effort was mounted (partly because the party engaged the services of a competent and expensive campaign and advertising agency). To test the continued validity of its analysis, the party ordered a large-scale survey of public attitudes in the summer of 1994. Finally, the PDS reacted resourcefully to attacks by its opponents.

In the Superwahljahr, German streetscapes in areas where the PDS concentrated its effort were awash in the party's characteristic red and white poster colors, with distinctive and uniform fonts and logo.[8] To draw attention to its campaign and to bolster its claim to be an important alternative force, the PDS' candidates (one fourth of whom were on the PDS' open list although not party members) included a garland of notables: the Bismarck-descendent and member of the wartime Soviet-sponsored National Committee "Free Germany," Count von Einsiedel; the writers Gerhard Zwerenz and Stefan Heym; and even several admitted Stasi informers. Gysi's multi-colored band made for bemused media coverage on both sides of the Atlantic (Kinzer, 1994a; Reiss, 1994).

### Early Returns

From the start of the Superwahljahr, the PDS hoped to establish a track record of good showings at local, state, and European elections. This would both mobilize potential voters and party workers, and attract media attention. The first of these signaling elections, conveniently scheduled on the eve of 1994's many elections, was the local (communal) elections in the state of Brandenburg. The vote totals showed an encouraging upturn in PDS strength. The party increased its share of the vote from 16.5 percent in 1990 to 21.2 percent in 1993 (Crome and Franzke, 1994). Its candidates for mayor in major Brandenburg cities ran strongly. In 14 major rural districts (*Großkreise*) the party won 201 of 934 council seats, although nowhere winning a plurality. In the state capital of Potsdam, the PDS mayoral candidate came in first with 45.3 percent of the vote, compared to the 29.5 percent garnered by the SPD candidate and eventual run-off winner (Crome and Franzke, 1994).

This successful set of elections contained a warning signal for the PDS. The increase in its percentage of the vote had come in the context of a sharply reduced turnout – down to 59.7 percent from 74.6 percent in May 1990. In fact, the actual number of PDS votes was almost the same as three years earlier. This proved to be both a continuing problem for the party, as well as a strategic opportunity. Sometimes the failure of the party to expand its voting base would cost it dearly. And yet, lower turnout levels would benefit a party that had a limited but committed voter base, an effective corps of party workers to get out this committed vote, and many citizens who were fervently hostile to it.

The party's tactical decision was, perhaps not surprisingly, to straddle this issue. It would mobilize its reliable supporters while trawling for the new voter groups described earlier. This ambivalence was possible because the reliable voters were largely in the East, and potential new voters in the West. As an "eastern party" the PDS sought to maximize its vote in the eastern Länder. As a leftist party of socialist opposition, it looked for new votes in the West.

The party's analysis of its good showing in state and European elections of June and September 1994 seemed to validate this dual strategy, and it governed the PDS' approach to the final phase of the national campaign.

## The Emergence of the PDS, Summer 1994

June 1994 saw both state elections in Saxony-Anhalt and elections for the European Parliament. The PDS' showing in these elections marked a turning point in public perception of its chances in the Bundestagswahl and its role in the year's electoral politics more generally. By gaining over 4 percent of the nationwide vote in the European elections, the PDS signaled that its electoral performance in 1994 might well be much better than in 1990 (see Table 1.1). However, low turnout, especially in Brandenburg and in the western Länder, accounted for its narrowly failing to pass the 5 percent threshold. Thus, the PDS just failed to secure representation in Strasbourg with its attendant publicity benefits.

In eastern Germany, the PDS had become the third largest political force in state and local politics – its best showing came where it could point to a record of concrete achievement in local affairs. Where there was no strong PDS presence on the ground, as in the western states, it could not profit from such grassroots approval.

This was demonstrated in the first state elections of 1994, in June in Saxony-Anhalt. The PDS added 7.9 percent to its 1990 totals, winning 19.9 percent to become the third largest party in the state (Table 6.2). Voter turnout was unusually low (54.9 percent). Indeed, the PDS got fewer actual votes in the state than it had received there two weeks earlier in the European elections! Only in Thuringia (the eastern state where it was weakest) was the absolute number of PDS votes in the European election greater than in the 1990 Volkskammer election.

**Table 6.2** PDS Absolute Vote Totals in Eastern Germany

| Land | March 1990 | June 1994 | October 1994 |
|---|---|---|---|
| Thuringia | 217,960 | 230,554 | 246,087 |
| Mecklenberg-W. Pomerania | 305,123 | 230,399 | 231,718 |
| Saxony | 472,037 | 398,150 | 426,378 |
| Saxony-Anhalt | 293,553 | 259,430 | 270,119 |
| Brandenburg | 335,822 | 177,682 | 266,506 |
| East Berlin | 254,771 | 190,729 | – |

*Source*: Brie, 1994a: 6; *Frankfurter Allgemeine Zeitung*, 18 October 1994.

The party used the European Parliament and Saxony-Anhalt results to broadcast its surprising strength, and to critique and adjust its electoral plans (Brie, 1994a; 1994c). In a report to the party, Brie noted that the PDS had not mobilized a majority of its members during the campaign. Too many members, he charged, did not realize that the campaign was not just an event for members but had to be directed at potential voters.

The party's aim to expand its voting base in the West by mobilizing a leftist opposition had not succeeded in the European Parliament election. Its relative strong points were university cities and districts where the peace movement had been strong in the 1980s – not, interestingly enough, in districts where the DKP had done well. Would the PDS be able to mobilize more of this potential in time for the national elections? A good campaign, Brie reminded his party, could realize the potential of previous work, but even the best campaign "cannot change realities . . . volunteer enthusiasm [alone] brings a result of zero point nothing."

In its drive to clear the 5 percent hurdle, the PDS understood that it could generate this vote share only within narrow turnout parameters (Cusack and Eberwein, 1993; INFO, 1994; Forschungsgruppe Wahlen, 1994a). For example, if national turnout was 85 percent, the PDS needed 2.57 million votes to reach 5 percent; if turnout was 65 percent, the party needed only 1.97 million votes (Table 6.3). The election returns in October validated this analysis: the actual PDS vote was 2,067,391 and the turnout 79 percent. In fact, the PDS increased its vote share most in districts with relatively low turnout. In districts where the turnout was below 77.6 percent, the PDS vote averaged 11.2 percent; in districts where the turnout exceeded 80 percent, the

117

PDS' average share of the vote was below 2 percent (Forschungs-gruppe Wahlen, 1994a).

**Table 6.3** Necessary PDS Vote to Surmount 5 Percent by Total Turnout

| National Turnout (in %) | Votes to Reach 5 percent (in millions) |
|---|---|
| 60 | 1.81 |
| 65 | 1.97 |
| 70 | 2.12 |
| 75 | 2.27 |
| 80 | 2.42 |
| 85 | 2.57 |
| 1994 Turnout (79.1) | PDS Actual Vote 2.067 |

*Source*: INFO (1994).

Given these facts, the PDS increased its effort to win at least three direct mandate seats. The party established a priority ranking of districts (all in the East), where it thought it had a reasonable chance for victory. There were three categories of districts: 1) those where the PDS had drawn more votes than CDU and SPD combined, 2) those where it had received a plurality of votes, and 3) those where for various reasons, it expected to do well (Table 6.4).

The most notable of these contests was in the Berlin Center (*Berlin Mitte*) borough. Here the PDS pitted the novelist Stefan Heym (who was a candidate but not a party member) against a leading eastern SPD politician, Wolfgang Thierse. This became the most highly profiled contest for a direct mandate, given its location, and the notoriety of the candidates. Heym displayed a somewhat casual approach to matters of government. For instance, when asked on which committees he might like to serve, he replied that he did not know what committees there were. In addition, Heym would be the new Bundestag's oldest member, if he was elected. This would give him the opportunity to make the traditional opening address of parliament. To counter charges that the PDS was manipulating Heym's candidacy to defeat Thierse, Heym's supporters transformed the contest into one between Heym and the CSU's Alfred Dregger (who was the second oldest candidate), arguing that Thierse would be elected via the state list in any case (PDS, 1994b; Kinzer, 1994c).

**Table 6.4** The "Best Chance" Districts for the PDS [* = won in October]

| Election districts/PDS candidates | 1994 first/second votes |
| --- | --- |
| PDS received more than SPD and CDU combined | |
| 249. Berlin/Heym* | first: 40.6/second 33.2 |
| 258. Berlin/Luft* | first: 44.4/second: 37.7 |
| 260. Berlin/Gysi* | first: 48.9/second 37.7 |
| PDS is the strongest single party | |
| 261. Berlin/Müller* | first 36.8/second: 33.3 |
| 259. Berlin/Hartmann | 35.5 |
| 265. Rostock/Methling | 35.2 |
| PDS has strong chance | |
| 276. Potsdam/Kutzmutz | – |
| 279. Frankfurt/O./Schumann | – |
| 269. Brandenburg/Maleuda | – |
| 267. Rügen/Neumann | – |
| 263. Schwerin | – |

*Source*: Brie (1994a: 31).

**The PDS in the Land Elections**

Although the Bundestag group and party leadership provided the PDS with its national image, the core of its membership, elected representatives, and strategic position remained in the East, especially at the local and regional levels. The strong PDS showing in state elections in Brandenburg and Saxony on 11 September confirmed this. In the Saxony state elections the PDS finished second in twenty-three of sixty electoral districts (including all six in Dresden and five of six in Leipzig); it increased its share of the vote (compared to the 1990 state elections) from 10.2 percent to 16.5 percent and ended up with only one fewer seat in the legislature than the SPD! In Brandenburg, the PDS was placed second in 18 of 44 districts, its vote total rising from 13.4 percent to 18.7 percent; it tied the CDU for second place in the number of seats!

In state elections in Thuringia and Mecklenburg-Western Pomerania (held concurrently with the national elections in October), the PDS increased its Thuringian vote from 9.7 percent to 16.6 percent, running second in 3 of 44 districts; in Mecklenburg-Western Pomerania the PDS vote share increased from 15.7 percent to 22.7 percent; it ran second in 6 of 36 districts. In all the eastern states but Brandenburg the PDS placed second to the SPD; in Brandenburg it was second to the CDU. These strong state-level showings paralleled the PDS' eastern German vote totals in the national elections.

## PDS, CDU, SPD

With the PDS showing some political strength and receiving a great deal more media attention as 1994 progressed, its opponents increased their criticism. Voters' perceptions of the party became an important element in the PDS' campaign strategy. The most strident attacks on the PDS came from the CDU (see Chapter 2). A CDU advertising campaign declared that Germany was ready to march into the future, "but not in red socks." This *rote Socken* campaign was ostensibly designed to warn Germans of the danger from the dictatorial left. It was tied to the formation of an SPD–Greens minority government in early summer that depended on toleration by the PDS in Saxony-Anhalt. In fact, this CDU campaign was not directed at voters in the new Länder – the *rote Socken* posters were not displayed there. As CDU representatives admitted unofficially, it was designed to mobilize an older, Cold War strata of the CDU electorate in the West. The PDS turned the campaign into a fund-raising gimmick, selling red sweat socks at every opportunity.

What effect did these attacks have on the PDS? As early as mid-summer, the PDS had survey data showing that most German voters did not regard voting for the PDS as unacceptable. When voters were asked whether they regarded the PDS as "unelectable," only CDU voters in the West (61.3 percent) showed a majority in favor. All groups in eastern Germany rejected the notion, as did the majority of voters in general (INFO, 1994).

The same survey showed that far higher proportions of voters regarded the Republikaner as unelectable; this was true across party lines and the East–West divide. Indeed, while the PDS faced substantial hostility, especially among older voters, there was no comparison with the disdain shown the Republikaner. Another pre-election survey found that only 41 percent of Westerners thought the PDS was a danger for German democracy, with CDU and FDP voters at 56 percent (Gibowski, 1994). In the new Länder, opinions among these two party groups were 37 percent and 38 percent respectively (overall, 18 percent).

For the national SPD, the PDS was seen as detracting from the total strength of an anti-Kohl coalition. For Social Democrats from eastern Germany, the PDS (or its SED predecessor) had destroyed the social democratic tradition in the East in 1946. Their criticisms of the PDS were marked by angry incomprehension that so many eastern voters could still be fooled by the PDS (Schröder, 1994; Winkler, 1994a; 1994b).[9]

The PDS leadership was concerned that many of its own voters preferred to see the SPD in the government. There was (and is) a strong anti-governmental strain in the PDS. Many PDS supporters preferred opposition to government responsibility (or cooption, as they would see it). They took to heart the ubiquitous PDS slogan, "change begins with opposition." Over 60 percent of PDS voters wanted to see the SPD governing in Bonn. In the national elections, a tenth of those who gave the PDS their first vote (*Erststimme*), voted SPD with their *Zweitstimme*. Almost 17 percent of those voting for the PDS party list gave the SPD their direct mandate votes. While the relative weakness of the SPD in the new Länder accounted for the PDS' strength, it should be noted that the SPD generally finished ahead of the PDS in most eastern German electoral contests (Brie, 1994b; Forschungsgruppe Wahlen, 1994a).

The PDS was clearly confronted by the hostility of the other parties. But did this enmity extend to voters at large? How great was the distance between PDS voters and supporters of other parties? As it entered the final phase of the election campaign, the PDS knew from its opinion polling that it could hope to exploit some striking parallels in the issue preferences of its supporters and those of some other parties (INFO, 1994).

On a variety of issues – ranging from wage guarantees, to German participation in UN Blue Helmet operations, to judging eastern Germans by their present activity, not their GDR past – PDS voters were close to supporters of the Alliance 90/Greens, the SPD, and non-voters. These parallels were more striking if differentiated along East–West lines. The three groups whose views were closest to those of PDS supporters were (in descending order): eastern SPD voters, eastern Alliance 90/

The Political Parties

Green voters, and eastern non-voters. The group most distant from PDS voters were western supporters of the CDU/CSU. Non-voters, a group which the PDS had targeted early in the campaign, were closest to the SPD in the West, but closest to the PDS in the East.

## October 1994: Who voted PDS?

The PDS came out of the national elections of October 1994 with substantial gains. Its share of the national vote total rose from 2.4 percent in 1990 to 4.4 percent (see Table 1.2). By winning four direct mandate seats in Berlin, it gained a total of thirty seats through proportional representation. In the five new Länder, the PDS was especially strong in the northern regions of the ex-GDR, East Berlin, and parts of Saxony-Anhalt. The PDS increased its vote totals as compared to 1990 by between 8 and 9 percent, winning between 16.7 percent in Saxony and 23.6 percent in Mecklenburg-Western Pomerania. The PDS garnered 19.8 percent of the vote in all of the former GDR; in East Berlin it was the leading party with 34.7 percent of the vote. Stefan Heym did become the Bundestag's *Alterspräsident*. The PDS now has over 6,000 representatives in local, regional, and national legislatures.

Despite increasing its share of the vote in each of the eleven Länder of the "old" Federal Republic, the PDS remained an inconsequential force there. Its best showings were in Bremen (2.7 percent) and Hamburg (2.2 percent), where the PDS doubled its vote (Reuter, 1995).[10] Of the thirty PDS Bundestag deputies, five were elected from party lists in the western states, and nine are actually from those states. It is a telling note that in seven of the eleven western states, the PDS actually got fewer votes than the Republikaner.

A profile of PDS voters shows that PDS strategists and outside analysts alike had been correct in anticipating who was likely to vote PDS (Jung and Roth, 1994; Forschungsgruppe Wahlen, 1994a; Chapter 9, this volume). A modal PDS voter was from the former GDR, especially its northern regions and the former main administrative centers (such as the sixteen ex-*Bezirk* capitals). He was a young man in an administrative position, possibly even an independent businessman. Although PDS *members* tend to be over 50 and overwhelmingly former SED members, PDS *voters*

122

The Party of Democratic Socialism

are younger. In the new Länder, 23 percent of PDS voters were under 35, only 17 percent were over 60. The PDS was strongest among voters between 25 and 34; when age and gender were combined, however, it was slightly stronger among women in the age cohort between 18 and 44.

Among occupational groups, the PDS was strongest (5.8 percent) among white-collar salaried employees (*Angestellte*), and weakest among independent farmers (2.7 percent). Workers gave the PDS 4.7 percent; in the eastern states, this reached 14.7 percent.

While most PDS voters, like Easterners generally, were less concerned about their immediate economic situation in October than had been true a year earlier, those who voted PDS believed overwhelmingly that neither major party had a long-term solution for the economic problems of the new Länder and the problems of unification generally. A full 80 percent claimed to be disenchanted with the results of unification. Thus while many PDS voters shared a widespread skepticism as to the reality of the PDS' distance from the old GDR, this mattered less than their need for an authentic voice to represent their grievances (Jung and Roth, 1994).[11]

A view of PDS voters similar to that sketched above is elaborated with rich empirical detail and analytic acuity by Jürgen Falter and Markus Klein (1994). They sketch a PDS voter who is well educated, has a relatively positive view of the GDR, feels socially alienated from western German society and politics, and continues to hold some core values of socialism. They conclude that it is this mixture of "ideology, nostalgia, and protest" that lead some Germans to vote PDS (Falter and Klein, 1994: 34).

Aftermath

After the elections, having saved itself from defeat and obscurity, the PDS has confronted anew some important issues of purpose and identity.

One of these was the ever-present problem of establishing the party in the West (Brie, 1995; Krisch, 1995). Although some local PDS campaign officials eagerly pointed to large percentage increases in the PDS vote, especially in selected election

123

precincts, this was usually on a base so small as to justify the conclusion of party leaders that there had been no breakthrough in the West. Hampering the PDS' western campaign were the party's identification in the popular mind with eastern issues, and the sheer lack of personnel needed to do party work. Insofar as the first problem mirrored a main pillar of PDS strength in the East, it is difficult to see how the party can overcome this without a substantial loss of strength in its present political base.

The lack of personnel, about which campaign leaders complained in 1994, had a practical aspect. The PDS gained support in many eastern communities through constituency and community service at the local level. Such "retail politics" could hardly be undertaken in a city like Mannheim with fewer than a dozen PDS activists, or even in a small state like the Saarland, with fewer than twenty campaign workers.

Since the PDS had identified the loosely organized leftist peace movement and youth in university circles as its recruiting field, rather than acting as a catch basin for the old West German Left, the task of expanding the party's western base will be a lengthy and arduous one. Still, the PDS is bound to try, if it is to become "alternative and nation-wide (*Bundesweit*)," as a banner at the 1995 party congress proclaimed. As noted above, this challenge underlay the decision to hold the next congress in Bremen and channel party resources into the May 1995 Bremen state election.

Now that the immediate – and for months, all-consuming – goal of returning to the Bundestag had been achieved, the PDS faces the strategic issue of its role in German politics. Is it to be a tool for regional interest articulation or a force helping to shape national policy? This question, in turn, is part of a broader issue: does the PDS seek to govern or would it be content to oppose? "Change begins with opposition," the party's slogan proclaimed – but did it end there?

In the wake of its successful electoral effort in 1994 the PDS leadership sought to move the party beyond debates about the past to play an active, participatory role in local, state, and national politics. The struggle over these issues aligns the PDS leadership and many of its (especially younger) voters against those party members for whom the PDS represents a milieu party, sheltering those alienated by unification, as well as a faction of committed ideologues. The latter are centered around the only surviving internal party platform (or faction). Ironically, the formation of these platforms had signaled the PDS' rejection of Soviet-style party unity.

This "Communist Platform" (*Kommunistisches Plattform*, KPF) represents between one and three thousand of the PDS membership (Nawrocki, 1995a), but makes up for its small size by energy, ideological dedication, and a flair for publicity. While the full scope of the ideological and historical discussion within the PDS cannot be considered here, the importance of the KPF is its commitment to the legitimacy of early socialism, that is, the idea of Soviet and GDR history as basically positive phenomena. The overall party leadership would like to remove that stance as political ballast. The KPF sees the cry of Stalinism as an attempt to stigmatize this history and drive adherents of Stalinism out of the PDS or to turn "Marxists into system-conforming leftists" (KPF, 1995).

The leadership's chosen instrument for this struggle was its "Ten Theses" published in advance of the PDS fourth congress (Berlin, January 1995) (Kinzer, 1994b; Nawrocki, 1995a).[12] The Theses declared the PDS to be "not an ideological" party, but a socialist, reform-minded party committed to the democratic institutions and processes of the Basic Law.

Opponents of the PDS leadership attacked this statement as a first step toward a PDS Godesberg. They raised such a storm of opposition within the party in the two months prior to the congress that the leadership tried to mollify the delegates with a "Five-Point Declaration" (PDS, 1995) signed by Gregor Gysi, Lothar Bisky, and Hans Modrow. This trio combined reform figures with Modrow, who could reassure GDR-nostalgic delegates. The declaration portrays possible participation in government coalitions as a form of opposition, but it also declares Stalinist convictions to be incompatible with PDS membership. Despite resignation threats from Bisky and Gysi, the delegates accepted this only with an ambiguous clarification that this did not (necessarily?) mean anticommunist.

Why could the PDS leaders not convince a majority of delegates on the best road to full participation in contemporary German politics? The answer lies in a group of delegates who sought to prevent a showdown within the party. This group reflects the feelings of those for whom the PDS represents a justification of (in the ubiquitous phrase) their biographies. A leader of this group was the innovative SED scholar and (since

1990) Bundestag member Uwe-Jens Heuer, who helped draft and distribute a statement at the party congress (*Declaration of 15 Members*). The group's main point was that the debate about the KPF and Stalinism was an unjustified distraction (Preusker and Baumgartner, 1995).

Forced to retreat on programmatic issues, the PDS leadership did secure removal of KPF leaders from the *Parteivorstand*, although it failed to secure Brie's election as *Bundesgeschäftsführer*. Observers and delegates at the party congress suggested that the election of Angela Marquardt – the young, punk-styled leader of the youth interest group within the PDS – as deputy party chairman was a response to the intense public scrutiny of the KPF's young spokesperson, Sarah Wagenknecht.

The issues at stake within the PDS in early 1995 are largely those that had dominated the party's internal affairs from the start. Is the PDS to be an instrument to defend inherited GDR structures and attitudes or a socialist, leftist national German party? Should its priorities be opposing or governing? Will it be able to be both East and Left, to satisfy both its existing membership base (with a defense of eastern interests and a commitment to economic security) and its potential supporters among younger, socially radical voters?

If it continues to stress regional issues, will it be dependent on the continued existence of an East–West social and political cleavage? While the experience of other countries (Italy and the United States) suggests that such cleavages can sustain political patterns for a long time, it consigns the political organization mobilizing that cleavage to regional stature. If the PDS is to compete with the SPD and the Greens as a national opposition, the direction in which the party leadership is steering, what more must it do to shed suspicions of its ties to the GDR past? How effectively can it compete in the West with the Greens?

That such questions persist indicates how complicated and difficult the road ahead will be for the PDS. That it is worth even asking such questions is a measure of the party's electoral achievements in 1994.

**Notes**

1. I wrote that "the PDS may not survive the 1994 Bundestag election, when there will presumably not be a special 5 percent district. In that event the PDS, now at 8 percent in its Eastern bailiwick, and well below 5 percent nationally, will likely disappear as a parliamentary force." Like other observers, I had – despite the omen of Gysi's victory in an East Berlin electoral district – overlooked the possibility that the PDS would win at least three direct mandate seats, thus voiding the effect of the 5 percent clause.

2. Such countries would include Lithuania, Poland, Hungary, Bulgaria, and Russia.

3. The PDS leadership used this issue for a media crisis, complete with a hunger strike and sit-in by the party's leaders in winter 1994. In June 1995, this issue was settled by a sensible compromise between the PDS and the independent commission overseeing disposition of the old GDR parties' and mass organizations' property.

4. Despite having to relinquish these public party positions, Brie continued as effective head of the party's electoral campaign. The long-term effects of this episode became evident when Brie ran for national party administrator (*Bundesgeschäftsführer*) at the fourth PDS congress in January 1995. The first question directed at him from the floor was a request to explain, once again, what he had done and why. (Author's observation.)

5. Patrick Moreau, generally a very critical observer of the PDS, admits that, apart from the PDS' organizational skills, the poor state of the economy was the main reason for the party's survival in 1992–1993.

6. A particularly vivid expression of this viewpoint appeared in a letter to the editor of the *Frankfurter Allgemeine Zeitung* (19 September, 1994): "Warum man mit 51 Jahren PDS wählt." Gerd Kostrzew wrote that he would vote PDS, "Weil die 'Altparteien' satt sind, weil sie meinen, man hat uneingeschränkt dankbar zu sein und ihnen wie selbstverständlich seine Stimme zu geben." Although "das System [d.h., GDR] ist gescheitert, auch dessen Partei . . . [und ich] weine der DDR keine Träne nach. . . . Heißt das aber, daß sich niemand der Millionen SED-Mitglieder Gedanken machen darf, wir die für

uns neue Gesellschaft gestaltet werden kann? Warum traut mann nicht einigen (nicht allen) einen Wandel zu? Dürfen sich nur die 'Blockflöten' wandeln?"

7. I wish to thank André Brie for letting me use this document as well as another, cited as Brie (1994a), and several surveys commissioned by the PDS, and for the interviews noted in the references.

8. Among the cleverest of PDS posters (reproduced in other formats as well) was one that showed a young couple about to kiss. Under a heading that read „The first time," it enjoined voters that when kissing, to keep eyes closed, when voting, keep them open!

9. Schröder had been a (re-)founder of the East German SPD (originally SDP) in the fall of 1989.

10. For this reason, the PDS decided to hold a party congress there in June 1995; it also made a major effort to win seats in the Bremen state legislature in Land elections in May 1995, where only 15,000 votes would have elected one deputy – but without success. The PDS received only 8,170 votes, or 2.4 percent.

11. What PDS voters have in common, write Jung and Roth (1994), is that "they are unhappy with the consequences of unification, and not only the economic ones; they believe that the PDS is best able to represent their interests; over and above that, almost all of them believe that the PDS has broken with its past . . . [The PDS is for those who wish to] protest current conditions, but for whom the SPD is not a plausible alternative."

12. This PDS fourth congress was important for the further development of the party, but it will be considered here only insofar as relevant to the aftermath of the 1994 elections.

## References

Bortfeldt, Heinrich. 1994. "Die Ostdeutschen und die PDS," *Deutschland Archiv* 27 (12 December): 1283–7.
Brie, André. 1993. "Strategie der PDS zu den Wahlen 1994" (draft).

——. 1994a. "Zur Auswertung der PDS-Ergebnisse bei den Europa- und Kommunalwahlen vom 12.6.1994 und zur Einschätzung des PDS-Wahlkampfes." PDS Vorstand.

——. 1994b. Interview with André Brie.

——. 1994c. "Null-Komma-Partei im Westen, Interessenpartei im Osten," *Frankfurter Rundschau* (6 July).

——. 1995. Interview with André Brie (January).

Crome, Erhard, and Jochen Franzke. 1994. "Toward an East German Party System? The Local Elections in Brandenburg in 1993," *German Politics* 3: 277–83.

Cusack, Thomas R., and Wolf Dieter Eberwein. 1993. "The Endless Election: 1990 in the GDR," in D. Berg-Schlosser and R. Rytlewski, eds. *Political Culture in Germany*. New York: St Martin's Press.

Falter, Jürgen, and Markus Klein. 1994. "Die Wahler der PDS bei der Bundestagswahl 1994," *Aus Politik und Zeitgeschichte*. Beilage zur Wochenzeitung *Das Parlament*, B 51/52–94: 22–34.

Forschungsgruppe Wahlen. 1994a. *Super Election Year 1994*. Reports. Mannheim: Forschungsgruppe Wahlen.

——. 1994b. *Politbarometer*. Mannheim: Forschungsgruppe Wahlen.

Gehrmann, Wolfgang, and Dick Kurbjuweit. 1994. "Rote Socken, schwarze Kassen," *Die Zeit* (9 December).

Gibowski, Wolfgang G. 1994. *Zur politischen Stimmung in Deutschland September/Oktober 1994*. Presse- und Informationsamt der Bundesregierung.

Gohde, Claudia, and Martin Harnach. 1994. *PDS – ein Analysenmaterial*. PDS-Vorstand.

Hartung, Klaus. 1994. "Und der Zukunft zugewandt," *Die Zeit* (23 September).

Hilmer, Richard, and Rita Müller-Hilmer. 1994. "Die Stimmung stimmt für Kohl," *Die Zeit* (7 October).

INFO. 1994. Untersuchung "Wählerverhalten und Meinungsbild in Deutschland-Ergebnisse einer representative Befrgagung in Ost und West in August 1994." Contracted for the PDS.

Jung, Matthias, and Dieter Roth. 1994. "Kohls knappster Sieg," *Aus Parlament und Zeitgeschichte* (B51-52/1994 [23 December]).

Kinzer, Stephen. 1994a. "Germany's Ex-Communists Promise to Behave in Parliament," *New York Times* (19 October).

——. 1994b. "Communists in Germany Seek to Oust Hard Liners," *New York Times* (27 December).

———. 1994c. "Former Communist in Germany Unsure of Political Program," *New York Times* (9 October).

Krisch, Henry. 1993. "From SED to PDS: The Struggle to Revive a Left Party," in R. Dalton, ed. *The New Germany Votes*. Providence and Oxford: Berg.

———. 1995. Questionnaire to PDS Landwahlleiter.

Kuhlwein, Eckart. 1994. "Links sind nur wir," *Die Zeit* (4 November).

KPF. 1995. "Joint Personal Declaration." Author's copy.

Meckel, Markus. 1994. "Bloß keine Nähe," *Die Zeit* (4 November).

Moreau, Patrick. 1994a. "Gefahr von Links? Die PDS auf dem Weg zur Etablierung," *Die Neue Gesellschaft/Frankfurter* 41: 694–705.

———. 1994b. *Was will die PDS?* Frankfurt/Main: Ullstein.

Nawrocki, Joachim. 1995a. "Bisky und die Roten," *Die Zeit* (27 January).

———. 1995b. "Stalinistisches Teufelchen," *Die Zeit* (3 February).

PDS. 1993. "Programm der Partei des Demokratischen Sozialismus," *Disput*.

———. 1994a. *Opposition gegen Sozialabbau und Rechtsruck. Wahlprogramm der PDS 1994*. Berlin: PDS.

———. 1994b. Pressedienst of the PDS. Berlin: PDS.

———. 1995. 4. Parteitag der PDS, 1. Tagung Berlin 27. bis 29. January 1995 Arbeitsmaterial für Delegierte. Berlin

Pfahl-Traughber, Armin. 1995. "Wandlung zur Demokratie? Die programmatische Entwicklung der PDS," *Deutschland Archiv* 28: 359–69.

Phillips, Ann L. 1994. "Socialism with a New Face? The PDS in Search of Reform," *East European Politics and Society* 8: 521.

Preusker, Ingo, and Barbara Baumgartner. 1995. "Das Parteivolk folgt nicht," *Wochenpost* (26 January).

Reiss, Tom. 1994. "Where Marx Meets Perot," *New York Times* (7 October).

Reuter, Christoph. 1995. "Go West," *Wochenpost* 42 (27 April): 12.

Schmitt, Karl. 1994. "Im Osten nichts neues? Das Kernland der deutschen Arbeiterbewegung und die Zukunft der politischen Linken," in W. Bürklin and D. Roth, eds. *Das Superwahljahr*. Cologne: BUND.

Schröder, Richard. 1994. "Die PDS als Verführung für die Unzufriedenen," *Frankfurter Allgemeine Zeitung* (16 September): 8.

Winkler, Heinrich August. 1994a. "Das organisierte Vergessen," *Frankfurter Algemeine Zeitung* (30 July).
——. 1994b. "Von den eigenen Sünden ablenken," *Die Zeit* (11 November).

# 7
# The Republikaner: A Party at Odds With Itself

## *Alexandra Cole*

Since its founding in 1983, the Republikaner party (REP) has experienced successes and failures that have made predictions of its future difficult. A look at other European countries in 1994, such as Italy, France and Austria, shows recent gains in the political power of right-wing parties. The year began with the assumption of government by the Italian right, continued with the maintenance of the National Front in France, and, most surprisingly, saw gains of the right in Austria leading some analysts to speculate of an eventual takeover in Austrian politics by the right.

In contrast, the Republikaner party, the most successful German right-wing party in recent years, did not experience the same electoral success as its European counterparts. In 1994 the Republikaner share of the votes in the 1994 German Bundestag election was lower than in the 1990 Bundestag election (see Table 1.2).

This chapter is primarily interested in how the Republikaner acted through the super-election year of 1994. However, to understand the actions of this newcomer to the German party system, we first describe the evolution of the Republikaner, from its inception as a party to the right of the Bavarian Christian Social Union (CSU), through its successes and failures of the late 1980s and early 1990s, up until its current position. The party's history has been a series of ups and downs. However, the one constant in the history of the Republikaner has been continual party infighting, mostly over the party's policy direction, which may be the best explanation for its poor showing in the 1994 Bundestag election.

## From the Founding of the Republikaner Party to Unification

The Republikaner party was founded in 1983 by two ex-functionaries of the Bavarian Christian Social Union (CSU), Franz Handlos and Ekkehard Voight, and the Bavarian television commentator Franz Schönhuber (Jaschke, 1994). Their goal was to form a political party to the right of the CSU as an alternative for those disenchanted with the policies of the then CSU chair Franz Josef Strauss. Strauss came under wide criticism in Bavaria at the time for his approval of an extension of financial credit to the German Democratic Republic (GDR). Many within the CSU were upset with Strauss' apparent recognition of the GDR – an action at odds with those in the CSU who maintained that the government of the GDR was illegitimate.

The Federal Republic had experienced other right-wing parties, but none had been formed with the explicit intent of challenging a specific established party. Rather, parties such as the National Democratic Party of Germany (NPD) in the 1960s or the Social Reich Party (SRP) in the 1950s were more concerned with the revival of German right-wing extremism of the 1930s and 1940s. The Republikaner were explicitly different from these previous rightist parties because of their initial focus on toppling an established party rather than the regime, and their implicit acceptance of German democracy.

From its beginnings, the REP could name Bavaria as one of its strongholds. In the 1986 state elections it won 3 percent of the vote, and entered into local governments in Oberbayern and Mittelfranken. Although it did not enter the state parliament, the REP did cut into the near monopoly of the CSU in state elections by offering a right-wing alternative to the Union.

The noteworthy aspect of its founding stage lies not in its success in providing a legitimate alternative to the CSU, but rather in the break-up of its founding triumvirate. Within two years of the REP's founding, Handlos and Voight had left the party, leaving Schönhuber to assume the party leadership. This assumption of power would prove pivotal to Republikaner fortunes, for the party would be molded in Schönhuber's likeness.

Schönhuber was well known to Bavarians. Before his entry into politics he was a political commentator on Bavarian television. In 1982, he published a book, *Ich war dabei* (*I was Involved*) that recounted his experiences as a member of the Nazi Waffen SS at the close of the Second World War. Although his experiences were not much different from many of his generation, his portrait of this period in largely positive terms raised some eyebrows, and received commendations from right-wing extremists, such as Gerhard Fry, leader of the German People's Union (DVU) and the largest publisher of right-wing materials in Germany.

As head of the Republikaner party, Schönhuber became the focus of much media attention as his party experienced success in the late 1980s. The Republikaner developed around Schönhuber and his public image. He appeared at numerous rallies and talks, and became the charismatic leader of what seemed to be a growing movement in Germany. Schönhuber gained national recognition although the REPs were primarily a Bavarian phenomenon throughout the mid-1980s. Efforts to form branches in other states were not as successful as in Bavaria, and the REP had to compete with other right-wing parties, such as the DVU, for members and for votes.

Fortune changed for the Republikaner in the Berlin elections of January 1989. The REP fought a campaign heavy with political symbolism. Television commercials showed scenes of Turkish immigrants, intimating how Germany was threatened by immigration and the replacement of a homogeneous German society by more diverse elements. The REP's main campaign theme criticized the high influx of immigrants from countries such as Turkey because of the perception that immigrants took away jobs from 'Germans'. This was underscored by a perceived threat to German culture; Republikaner advertisements highlighted the Islamic culture of the immigrants and implied that Germany would eventually become an Islamic nation given the high number of Turkish immigrants and their high birthrate. With a surprising 7.5 per cent of the vote, the Republikaner gained representation in Berlin's Senat. This success brought the Republikaner the national recognition to which it had previously only aspired.

The Berlin election results showed a diverse voter constituency for the Republikaner. Although most REP voters had previously voted for the Christian Democratic Union (CDU), a significant vote share came from the Social Democratic Party (SPD). REP voters were primarily males, and surprisingly young. A summary of the REP vote concluded "urban areas with inferior housing are characterized by a high REP voter concentration" (Veen, Lepszy and Mnich, 1992: 39).

The success of the Republikaner in Berlin stimulated concerned discussion within the other political parties about how to react to this newcomer.[1] The Christian Democrats eventually studied issues such as immigration in order to claim some of the electoral ground the Republikaner were winning. This discussion intensified in June of 1989, as the Republikaner won entry into the European Parliament with 7.1 percent of the national vote. The Republikaner formed an alliance with other rightists in the European Parliament, such as the French National Front. Many analysts in Germany saw the Republikaner as a serious contender for the next German Bundestag election that was set to take place in 1991.

German unification changed the date of the Bundestag election to December 1990, and more importantly changed the themes of the election campaign. Unification revived debate on the Oder–Neiße line, an issue that could benefit the Republikaner because they had championed this since their inception. Because the REPs had long been associated with this issue, Helmut Kohl's discussion of Germany's border with Poland during the unification debate followed a cautious tone. He did not want to be seen as aligning himself with the right-wing REPs, but he also did not want to give them an opportunity to mobilize support behind a nationalist position. Changes in Eastern Europe, and the influx of immigrants from newly democratizing Eastern European countries, added fire to the immigration issue, because immigrants were perceived as a drain on German coffers. This became especially pertinent as Germans recognized the massive economic and social costs to improve conditions in the new eastern states. While the theme of immigration could have benefitted the REP, it became less salient to the voters who wondered how unification was to be actualized and at what cost.

For the Republikaner, 1990 was an especially bad election year. In state elections held in the Saar, Lower Saxony, North Rhine-Westphalia, and even in their stronghold of Bavaria, their share of the vote was less than the 5 percent needed to gain entry into the state parliaments. Attempts to gain representation in the East were even worse than in the West. In October state elections held in Mecklenburg-Western Pomerania, Brandenburg, Saxony-Anhalt, and Thuringia, the REP could not even garner 1 percent of the vote. In addition, the Republikaner were not allowed to campaign in the new state of Saxony. The East seemed quite a hostile place for the Republikaner.

The Bundestag election in December 1990 brought no better results. The Republikaner share of the national vote was 2.1 percent, substantially lower than forecasters had predicted only one year earlier. Most analysts attributed their loss to the character of the election and its unusual circumstances. The single most important issue of the election for many voters centered on the future of the new Federal Republic. For those in the West, the question was how to pay for unification. While Oskar Lafontaine of the SPD offered a grim assessment of sacrifices needed to finance the venture, Kohl was more optimistic, relying on the prowess of the economic miracle and 40 years of postwar success. Kohl's message attracted voters both from the West and the East who wanted to hear that the situation was not as dire as Lafontaine predicted. Because the election focused on this important economic issue, for the voter it ultimately came down to the question of which party could secure the better future of the Federal Republic. A small party such as the Republikaner could not compete in this atmosphere because of its lack of experience in national governance and lack of ideas on the unification debate.

## Ups and Downs: The Inter-Election Period

After their resounding defeat in the 1990 Bundestag election, the Republikaner future seemed an uncertain one. The following year was full of defeats for the Republikaner. They failed to gain representation in the state parliaments of Hesse and Rhineland-Palatinate, and in the local governments in Hamburg and Bremen. At the end of 1991, the prognosis for the Republikaner was that they were at the end of their life as a political party.

Yet 1992 brought surprises (and further disappointments) that made the 1991 requiem for the Republikaner somewhat premature. In the Baden-Württemberg elections in April, the Republikaner gained 10.9 percent of the vote, and became the third largest party in the state government (Roth, 1993). On the same day in Schleswig-Holstein, the Republikaner received a meager 1.2 percent of the vote in local government elections.

However, the right-wing German People's Union (DVU) won 6.1 percent of the vote (Roth and Schäfer, 1994). Although the REP did not do well in the north, the DVU gains suggested that a significant electorate for an extreme right party still existed.

The successes and failures of the Republikaner in 1993 were so varied that it became hard to predict how they would perform in the next Bundestagswahl. In March, the Republikaner won 8.3 percent of the vote in local government elections in Hesse. In September, the REP won 4.8 percent of the vote in the city of Hamburg, reviving the belief that the Republikaner could attract votes in the north, and perhaps in all of Germany.

Possibly the most intensely debated political issue in this interelection period was the German asylum law. While not considering itself a country of immigration, the Federal Republic had one of the most liberal asylum laws in Western Europe. Individuals were able to come to the Federal Republic, declare political asylum based on fear of return to their former country, and essentially immigrate to the Federal Republic under Article 16 of the Basic Law. While the "asylum seekers," as they were called, made up the smallest percentage of the foreign population in the Federal Republic (guest workers and immigrants of German descent from Eastern Europe were greater in number), they became the target of anti-foreign rhetoric and violence.[2] There was a common impression that the Federal Republic was letting in foreigners too easily. It was widely known that Article 16 was very liberal in comparison with other European countries.

It was not a surprise that the Republikaner favored amending this part of the Basic Law to stem the influx of foreigners, because they had always advocated the concept of "Germany for the Germans." Nor was it a surprise that the CDU took up the issue of asylum reform; it had been losing voters to rightist parties as some of its constituency perceived the party as not focusing on this issue. However, most analysts were surprised that this rhetoric carried over into the broader political spectrum to include parties such as the SPD, and ultimately signaled a rightward shift in the political arena (Young, 1995).

In this same period, violent attacks on asylum seekers and their homes grew in number and intensity. The most infamous incident was an attack in 1991 in Hoyerswerda where a home for asylum seekers was attacked by right-wing extremists. Thirty people were injured in the attack which gained its notoriety from the indifference and tacit support shown by townspeople. The immigration issue included the issue of violence against foreigners, and how to deal with this violence. The Republikaner distanced themselves from this violence because of their desire to be a legitimate part of the German political arena (*Der Spiegel*, 10 May 1992). Schönhuber's comments against more radical right-wing parties were not, however, as virulent as in years past

For Helmut Kohl, violence against foreigners brought little comment at first, despite pressures by the SPD and the Greens to respond to right-wing violence in a manner consistent with how the government dealt with the left-wing Red Army faction violence of the 1970s. Instead, the CDU advocated a change in the asylum law, implying that the violence was due to the permissiveness of the law.

Having always supported changes to the Basic Law on the immigration issue, the Republikaner found themselves in a favorable political position. Their electoral successes in the early 1990s could be linked to the general inactivity of the established parties on the issues of violence and asylum. For the Republikaner, the solution was simple: ending immigration would lessen the violence. In 1993, the established parties reached a similar conclusion: the SPD joined with the CDU to amend Article 16 to make it more difficult for individuals to seek political asylum in the Federal Republic. A mainstay of Republikaner rhetoric was eliminated.

The outlook, then, for the Republikaner in the super-election year of 1994 became mixed. An article in *Der Spiegel* even suggested that the REP could pull 5 percent of the national vote (*Der Spiegel*, 21 June 1993: 58). The super-election year would thus be a pivotal year in the political fortunes of the Republikaner.

## 1994: The Super-Election Year

With nineteen elections on the local and state level occurring before the Bundestagswahl in October, 1994 promised to be a very interesting year. Both politicians and the media often portrayed state elections as test votes for the federal election (Emmert and Stögbauer, 1994: 86). Included in these nineteen elections were elections to the European Parliament in June, previously one of the Republikaner's more successful venues and an indicator to how the party would fare in the Bundestagswahl.

Lower Saxony held the first state election in March 1994. The favorable prognosis for the Republikaner suggested that the party would make it into the state parliament. Although polls had the Republikaner winning 3 to 4 percent of the vote, pollsters felt that potential Republikaner voters were hesitant to express their vote intentions (*Der Spiegel*, 7 March 1994: 25). The pollsters' initial findings held: the Republikaner failed to make it into the Lower Saxony parliament (3.7 percent of the vote). The Republikaner results in the local elections of Schleswig-Holstein later that month were not much better. As in the state elections the year before, the Republikaner did not gain any seats in local governments in Schleswig-Holstein.

As 1994 began with electoral setbacks for the Republikaner, the year also began with controversy surrounding Schönhuber. In responding to inquiries about the inflammatory nature of some of the Republikaner rhetoric, Schönhuber called Ignatz Bubbi, the chairperson of the Central Council of Jews in Germany, the 'worst instigator in Germany' (*Der Spiegel*, 2 May 1994: 41). Schönhuber's pointedly antisemitic remarks were perceived by many in the government, and especially by the Constitutional Commission, as part of a systematic antisemitic campaign by Schönhuber, and by extension, the Republikaner. Coupled with the uproar over Schönhuber's comments were allegations that he took part in an attack on a home for asylum seekers in Bergheim at the end of 1993. While these allegations helped Schönhuber portray the party as being persecuted by the establishment (*Der Spiegel*, 25 April 1994: 18), it also focused the attention of some Länder on having the Republikaner classified as an anti-constitutional party. In the spring, the Constitutional Court's investigators classified the Republikaner as having right-wing extremist elements, but could not concretely classify the Republikaner as anti-constitutional according to Manfred Kanther of the CDU (*Der Spiegel*, 11 April 1994). The Social Democrats claimed these results were politically motivated. They alleged that the Christian Democrats had never completely ruled out working together with the Republikaner (*Der Spiegel*, 18 April 1994: 89).

Feeling the pressure, Schönhuber promised a removal of right-wing extremists and radicals from the party, as well as an "intellectualization of the party," which he hoped would relieve some of the pressure and negative attention. This had been one of Schönhuber's stated goals since 1990 (*Der Spiegel*, 13 April 1992), but seemed especially urgent now that two major national elections were rapidly approaching. Coupled with this pressure were the departures of two functionaries of the party, Udo Boesch and Martina Rosenberger, who alleged the party was doing nothing to intellectualize itself, and that power remained firmly in the grasp of Schönhuber (*Der Spiegel*, 20 June 1994: 32).

The European Parliament election in June was a major test of where the Republikaner stood in the super-election year. In 1989, the REP won 7.1 percent of the vote on its campaign platform of German distance from the European Parliament. The REP had formed a voting bloc in the Parliament with Jean le Pen of the National Front in France, and with Italian neo-fascists. In their campaign platform for the 1994 European Parliament election, the Republikaner used similar themes, opposing the European Union and the Maastricht Treaty. In addition to their opposition to Maastricht, which they felt gave the European Union (EU) too much power over citizens in Union countries, the REP also opposed expanding the membership of the Union to countries, such as Turkey, that did not have the same economic and social characteristics of other EU countries (Republikaner, 1993: 13). They also based their opposition to Turkish membership on the feeling that Turkey is not properly a European country. Although the themes of 1994 were similar to those of 1989, the REP's results were not; they won only 3.9 percent of the German vote, and lost their seats in the European Parliament (see Table 1.1).

Controversy continued to follow the REP's leader after the elections. A meeting in August between Schönhuber and the leader of the German People's Union, Gerhard Fry, refocused attention on whether the party was anti-constitutional, and thus should be banned. Fry was publisher of the biggest nationalistic newspaper in Germany and had ties to the right-wing extremist scene. Schönhuber had previously ruled out the DVU as a working partner because of these links and because of Schönhuber's desire to present the REP as a legitimate right-wing presence in the German political arena. This meeting seemed to end Schönhuber's previous aversion to Fry. The two party leaders promised to work together in upcoming elections by not challenging each other for the right-wing vote, as had happened in Schleswig-Holstein earlier that year.[3]

The uproar raised by this meeting and subsequent announcement of the two leaders was almost predictable. Amid cries from many mainstream politicians and commentators that the REP was continuing its slide into right-wing extremism and should be considered anti-constitutional, there were also cries against this direction from within the party's ranks. The Bavarian party organization issued a statement that the Republikaner would not work more closely with right-wing elements such as Fry; and further, that Schönhuber would not be campaigning in the future as the party's chancellor candidate (*Süddeutsche Zeitung*, 26 August 1994: 2).

In the wake of this controversy, the party continued its downward spiral with a poor showing in the state elections of Bavaria in September. Bavaria, the home base of Schönhuber, and traditionally one of the Republikaner strongholds reflected the national trend for the REP. The party won only 3.9 percent of the vote, not enough to gain entry into the state parliament. This trend was also reflected in the eastern states of Saxony and Brandenburg where the REP was effectively shut out as well.

Defeat for the Republikaner in the eastern states reflected the difficulty the REP had since 1990 in trying to establish eastern party organizations. Although acts of right-wing violence might indicate support potential in the East, the REP could not capitalize on right-wing sentiment. Initially the REP focused its attempts to organize on former SED and National People's Army (NVA) members, which had the effect of alienating most of the mainstream voting public. Compounding their initial attempts was a series of removals and resignation from office of party leaders during 1992 and 1993 which reinforced a perception of the REP as a struggling party in the East (Von Berg, 1994).

On the eve of the Bundestagswahl the situation could not get much worse for the Republikaner; but then a final controversy made the party seem even more fractionalized. On the first weekend in October, only two weeks before the election, the executive committee of the Republikaner announced the removal of Schönhuber as chair of the party because of his meeting with Gerhard Fry (*Süddeutsche Zeitung*, 4 October 1994: 2). The committee termed this meeting as harmful to the interests of the party. This would not be the last of Schönhuber, however.

Schönhuber promised a legal challenge to this decision, and the eastern state committees of the REP vowed to stand by Schönhuber. The fractionalization within the party was not what the party needed as the election drew near. The media and the public were not focusing on the campaign themes of the party as much as the REP's internal political controversies.

## The Federal Election: Slogans and Programs

Posted around most major German cities, in neighborhoods whose demographics reflected a working-class tendency, were the familiar blue and white placards of the Republikaner party. The most distinctive aspects of the placards were not the slogans, nor the basic styling of the placards (white lettering on blue backgrounds), but that most were on lampposts 3 meters off the ground – heights too daunting for anti-Republikaners to remove them. The Republikaner consciously placed their placards where they could not be touched, and most were not. The official party newspaper, *Der Republikaner*, featured advertisements for a contraption that could post the placards in seconds and fit into the trunk of every car (Republikaner, 1994: 11). The placards themselves reflected simplistic slogans that were carried over from previous elections: "Order now" (*Ordnung jetzt*), "Right before Left" (*Rechts vor links*), along with some newer slogans such as "No to Maastricht."

In a discussion I had with a party functionary in Berlin after the election, the functionary stressed that the REP wanted to emphasize two related themes in the election: the Federal Republic faced a threat from parties of the Left, and there must be a renewed emphasis on "German" interests. Both themes reflected a nationalistic element of the Republikaner found in their election program and their campaign literature. The threat from the Left was based on the fear that the SPD would align with the Party of Democratic Socialism (PDS), and thus carry out the century-old specter of a socialist international at the expense of German interests. This imagery was a favorite theme of parties of the extreme right since the start of the movement in Europe. The REP portrayed the PDS as the watered-down remnant of the East German SED. There were no official plans for the SPD and PDS to work together (the issue was a divisive one within the ranks of the SPD, and had threatened the SPD's own election campaign; see Chapter 3). However, there had been some rapprochement within the eastern states between the parties, especially the PDS' tolerance of the SPD-led minority government in Saxony. The Republikaner eagerly seized upon this event as proof that the two parties intended to work together. This theme was not an original one for the Republikaner. The CDU had used the same idea in the 1990 Bundestagswahl and Kohl revived this theme in 1994 (Chapter 2). The Republikaner apparently hoped that this theme would bring success to them as well.

The REP displayed its focus on German interests across a variety of issues that went beyond the threat from the left. Similar to the situation in France, there was a growing anxiety over the introduction of foreign elements into Germany. This threat ranged from the McDonalds in the local *Fußgängerzone* to the influx of immigrants and asylum seekers. The largest component of this perceived threat to German culture came from Turkey, because of the large Turkish guestworker population in Germany. Diversity was not seen as something to be celebrated, but rather feared because of the uncertainties that these new elements brought into society. The REP's idea of German interests implied that all things German in origin (culture, language, and people) should be the predominant focus of policymakers. By having "non-German" elements in society, the Republikaner claimed that German interests did not predominate.

The Republikaner party program presented at the 1993 party congress in Augsburg gave the most comprehensive view of the party's positions on a range of issues. It served as the main election document for both the European Parliament election in June of 1994 and the Bundestag election in October. In it, the Republikaner define themselves as a "society of German patriots. . . . [and] A peaceful and national party with high social and environmental duties." The preamble to the program explicitly stated their democratic nature, belief in a free state, a Europe comprised of sovereign nations, protection from a wave of immigration, a decrease in social differences, and a refusal to criminalize German history (Republikaner, 1993: 3). These themes have been the mainstay of the Republikaner since their inception, albeit with differing emphasis at different times.

A useful way of determining issue priorities is by noting which issues are given the most space within a party's program (Budge et al., 1987). Table 7.1 shows the issues presented by the Republikaner in their 1993 program, along with the amount of space devoted by the Republikaner to these issues. As expected, the platform devoted the most space to the issue of immigration. Because the party expected the election to focus on the costs of unification, the platform also gave substantial space to the issues of economic and financial policy. The program also gave a good deal of space to employment and social policy, although the public gave less attention to the REP's stance on these issues.

Table 7.1 Issues in the 1993 Republikaner Party Program

| Issue | Number of Pages |
| --- | --- |
| Recognition of German Democracy | 2 |
| Foreign and Security Policy | 3.5 |
| European Community Policy | 2 |
| Immigration and Asylum Policy | 9 |
| Family, Women, Youth, Senior Policy | 7.5 |
| Environment and Energy Policy | 4.5 |
| Agricultural, Forestry, and Hunting Policy | 6.5 |
| Economic and Financial Policy | 9 |
| Employment and Social Policy | 6.5 |
| Education Policy | 2.5 |
| Science and Cultural Policy | 1.5 |
| Housing Policy | 2.5 |
| Media Policy | 2.5 |
| Transportation Policy | 3 |
| Health and Sport | 4.5 |
| Church and Religion | 1.5 |
| Animal Protection | 1 |
| Foreign Development | 2 |

*Source*: 1993 Republikaner party platform

The chapter on immigration was titled "Domestic Security, Justice and Foreigner Politics, Right to Asylum and Constitutional Reform." It showed a clear link in Republikaner thinking between domestic security and the presence of immigrants in the Federal Republic. The chapter began by asserting that the Republikaner are the party of law and order, and that it is the duty of a democratic society to provide for the security of all its citizens. To do so, the Republikaner listed a litany of measures to promote security: the strengthening of law enforcement, reforms in anti-crime statutes, and research on the causes of crime (including the ethnic background for various types of crime). The REP implicitly pointed to the relaxing of German border controls as a result of European Union directives as a precursor to crime, especially drug and money smuggling. They demanded a restrengthening of German border controls to stem the flow of crime into the Federal Republic. Interestingly, environmental damage was also viewed as a domestic crime, with the REP calling for harsh penalties against those who pollute the environment.

On immigration policy, the Republikaner stated that Germany is not a country of immigration and should not become a multicultural society. For this reason, the REP called for an immediate end to immigration to the Federal Republic. According to the Republikaner, immigration threatened the FRG because the influx of foreigners threatened the social welfare system, and led to increased crime. To deal with the problems of immigration, the REP proposed sending all guestworkers back to their countries of origin, prohibiting the entry of new guestworkers, strengthening border controls to stop illegal immigration, and preventing the families of guestworkers from immigrating into Germany. The Republikaner allowed for the eventual citizenship of foreigners who had lived in the Federal Republic for a long time, if they were prepared to integrate fully into German culture and society.

The Republikaner pointed to the abuse of asylum laws by foreigners and claimed that the asylum clause in the Basic Law had cost the Federal Republic over DM 40 billion. The REP recommended the elimination of Article 16 (note: the program was made as the change in the asylum law was occurring). While stating that the Federal Republic should have some sort of asylum clause, the REP demanded that asylum seekers must undergo more rigorous verification.

The REP presented its position on economic issues in a chapter titled "Economic, Financial, and Middle-Class Policies." The REP affirmed a desire for financial stability in a democratic state, emphasizing the maintenance of the free market and the importance of private property in benefitting society. However, the REP also named unions as the protectors of the working class and working-class interests. The state, according to the REP, should not interfere in business, but rather offer guidelines for full employment.

Demonstrating their anti-European Union stance, the program called for the German Mark to remain independent of a European currency in order to maintain the integrity of the DM and German-made goods. This was related to their call to build up Middle Germany, that is, the new eastern Länder. The REP called for the development of the new states to western economic and living standards, along with an end to mass unemployment.

In the following chapter, "Employment and Social Policy," the Republikaner pledged a Bismarckian allegiance to social policy as a special duty of the state. To achieve social homogeneity, the Republikaner opposed efforts to diversify society, and believed that all Germans should be free to choose their workplace and their careers. For the REP, unemployment in the Federal Republic could not be separated from the immigration that ultimately hurt the German seeking employment. Thus, they believed that an end to immigration should revitalize the German job market.

Republikaner social policy followed a similar logic. Because of immigration and its associated costs, the Republikaner argued that resources were taken away from needy Germans. The REP stated that immigrants bring other value systems with them, values conflicting with the work ethic of Germans. Thus, social policy also could be restored if immigration was halted.

Although the Republikaner discussed issues of economic and social policy in anticipation of the super-election year, this discussion reverted back to their central nationalistic themes. It should not be surprising, therefore, that Republikaner responses to the major issues of the election were not given much exposure in the election period; they were simply the standard Republikaner themes in new packaging.

## The Federal Election

On the eve of the election, the Allensbach Institute predicted the REP would only get 1.9 percent of the vote (*Der Spiegel*, 15 September 1994: 50). The Republikaner themselves made few references to their chances; little was heard from them excepting intraparty fighting. By winning almost 2 percent of the vote, the Republikaner fulfilled the pollsters' prognoses (see Table 1.2).

What changed over the last year to bring the Republikaner down from their 1993 high?

Voters of the Republikaner are not strong partisans. Studies have shown that the potential Republikaner vote is comprised of people who have voted for parties across the entire party spectrum, including those who had formerly voted for the SPD (Stöss, 1993: 56)! Thus, it is difficult to characterize the typical Republikaner voter. Some analysts posit there are six types of Republikaner voters: the average REP sympathizer; the trade-union worker; the young, authority-oriented worker; the working-class member; the retiree with traditional values; and the highly educated nationalist (Veen, Lepszy and Mnich, 1993; also see Westle and Niedermayer, 1992; Roth, 1993). The Republikaner vote potential includes both adherents of the party and those who are 'protest' voters (Hennig, 1994). These protest voters may ultimately decide the outcome of the Republikaner in any given election because their vote stems from a perceived unwillingness of the major parties to deal with issues that concern these voters.

Another factor contributing to the potential Republikaner electorate has been the increasing number of "floating voters." The German electorate is less partisan than it was twenty to thirty years ago (Dalton and Rohrschneider, 1990). This decrease in partisanship has led to the formation of a type of voter not tied to a single party, who floats from party to party across elections. These floating voters may ultimately decide the fate of an election because political parties may tailor their campaigns to issues the floating voter finds important.

Much of early Republikaner success can be attributed to their attraction to protest voters and floating voters. German voters in the 1980s and early 1990s grew disillusioned with the established political parties, and felt that the parties were not addressing important issues. The Green party capitalized on the perceived inactivity of the established parties on issues such as the environment, and ultimately won a political base within an expanded party system. For the Republikaner, the story is similar. Many Germans were concerned about the immigration issue, for example, and the Republikaner captured votes of those who considered this an important issue. The Republikaner also attracted those protest voters who wanted to send a message of general dissatisfaction to the established parties.

As the Republikaner capitalized on the immigration issue, the established parties took note and addressed this issue. After having lost some of its support to the REP, the CDU began to address this and other Republikaner issues (Young, 1995). This resulted in a change in the German immigration law in 1993, which made immigration to Germany more difficult. At the same time, this action took away some of the impact of the Republikaner message that claimed it was the only party to deal with the immigration issue.

In theoretical terms, Anthony Downs' (1957) model of voter rationality might explain why the Republikaner did not do as well as expected in 1994. In *An Economic Theory of Democracy*, Downs writes that voters will consider the political arena when they make their voting decision. In a multiparty system such as Germany's, a voter "uses his forecast to determine whether the party he most prefers is really a part of the relevant range of choice. If he believes it is not, then rationality commands him to vote for some other party" (Downs, 1957: 48). That is, voters may prefer to vote for a certain party, but if it is unlikely that the party will win, the voter will vote strategically so that the voter's least favorite choice will not win.

Kohl and the CDU had stolen much of the Republikaner steam in 1994: the CDU addressed the foreigner issue with the change in the asylum law in 1993, and advocated a conservative position on related issues. The CDU also attacked the possibility of an SPD/PDS/Green coalition coming into power. The CDU thus blurred the line between itself and the Republikaner on these two key issues. Consistent with Downs's ideas about rational choice in a multiparty system (Downs, 1957: 48), the conservative electorate saw the CDU as the party that had the ability to win the election and govern an effective conservative government. A vote for the Republikaner might be wasted because of the 5 percent hurdle. Thus, within the electoral arena there were two political parties on the right to choose, and many voters opted for the Union parties.

Finally, intraparty squabbling also distracted voters from the Republikaner message in 1994. The REP had always squabbled, and yet had still done relatively well at the polls. By 1994, however, this was taken to a new level. Under Schönhuber's leadership the party had lost two of the three founding leaders, experienced the resignation of key functionaries over the years, and suffered charges that the party was doing nothing to intellectualize itself or distance itself from more extreme right-wing elements. As the number of intraparty conflict have grown, so have doubts in Schönhuber's ability to make the Republikaner into a legitimate right-wing alternative.

As stated previously, the floating voter now plays a large role in election campaigns in Western democracies. In Germany, this floating voter had not shifted just between left and right, but also gravitated to smaller political parties. This occurred because the public did not perceive the establishment parties as adequately dealing with important issues. The floating voter who feared the programs of the Left had a choice to make in the federal election: CDU coalition, or a protest vote for the Republikaner. Because of the intraparty conflict within the Republikaner, a vote for the REP would have been a wasted vote for the floating protest voter. The CDU coalition would thus claim back some of the potential Republikaner electorate.

## Postscript: The Future of the Republikaner

Not long after the Bundestag election, the federal court reinstated Franz Schönhuber to the chair of the Republikaner. The court determined that he was removed unfairly; party law required a vote of the entire membership of the Republikaner. In December of 1994, the removal of Schönhuber became legally valid as he was deposed by a formal vote at the Republikaner party convention. The convention selected Rolf Schlierer in his place. Schlierer is a young (39) party functionary whom Schönhuber had groomed to intellectualize the party and eventually succeed him. Schlierer stated that one of his first goals was to make the party attractive to conservatives (*Der Spiegel*, 26 December 1994: 35). However, he immediately made it difficult to achieve this goal by selecting two known right-wingers to positions on the party's central committee. Furthermore, analysts have downgraded the Republikaner from a potential national force to a regionally based party in Bavaria and Baden-Württemberg.

The REP has been a party that has needed to attract protest voters rather than rely on a stable voter base. Because their voter base contains such heterogeneous elements, the REP faces many difficulties in trying to appeal to each element, as well as appeal to new ones. In a broad sense, they may be more of a catch-all party than the traditional catch-all parties like the CDU. In addition, their emergence indicates a disillusionment with the traditional parties.

The Republikaner's significance for the German party system is twofold: they have emerged as a challenge to a party system that has competed on the same basic political issues for forty years, and they have begun a legitimation of right-wing ideas in the German political arena.

The Republikaner challenge to the established party system is similar to the Greens' challenge to the party system of the late 1970s and early 1980s. As the Greens did, and continue to do, the Republikaner have brought new issues into political discussion that the established parties had not previously discussed. Like the Greens, whose issues have sometimes been coopted by the SPD, the Republikaner have seen some of their issues coopted by the CDU. As the Greens have made clear their disillusionment with establishment politics by attempting to form a political organization differing from the catch-all mold, the Republikaner have formed a different, more hierarchic type of political organization. Both parties have appealed to voters losing faith in the established parties (albeit for different reasons).

Right-wing issues, long taboo in the German political arena, have been openly discussed, if not accepted, since the emergence of the Republikaner. The notion of German interests taking precedence over European interests, and controls on immigration, have their current roots in discussions formulated by right-wing parties such as the Republikaner. The acceptability of voicing opposition to the European Union, and advocating controls on the numbers of immigrants in Germany, was not as widespread in the 1970s as today. Part of this acceptability is because of the success of the Republikaner and cooption of their issues by established parties such as the CDU.

If the Republikaner are to rebound from a disastrous super-election year, then the intraparty fighting needs to be resolved in the West, while in the East more effort must be put into organization. It is too early to know if the new leadership can make any gains in this direction. Whether or not the party does rebound from the events of 1994, there remains a potential for a rightist vote given the successes of the Republikaner in the late

1980s and early 1990s, the lingering of anti-establishment senti-ment in the West, and right-wing sentiment in the East. While there is apparent room in the German party system for a new political party to the right of the CDU, the question is whether the Republikaner are that party.

## Notes

I would like to thank the Friedrich Ebert Stiftung for their support of my research.

1. Republikaner gains in Berlin were quickly followed by advances for the NPD in local elections held in the state of Hesse. These NPD votes were seen as surrogate support for the Republikaner, which had not appeared on the ballot.
2. Kuechler (Chapter 11) notes that the foreign population numbered nearly 7 million at the start of 1993. Roughly 1.5 million were residents of other EU member states; over 3 million were guestworkers and their dependents; and 2 million were refugees or asylum seekers. This last group had grown the most rapidly since 1989.
3. In the Schleswig-Holstein elections the REP had won only 1.2 percent of the vote, and the DVU 6.1 percent (Roth and Schäfer, 1994). This allowed the DVU to win some rep-resentation, but a more even distribution of the right-wing vote could keep both parties below the 5 percent hurdle in subsequent elections.

## References

Budge, Ian, et al. 1987. *Ideology, Strategy and Party Change Spatial Analyses of Post War Election Programmes in 19 Democracies.* Cambridge; Cambridge University Press.

Dalton, Russell, and Robert Rohrschneider. 1990. "Wählerwandel und die Abschwächung der Parteineigungen von 1972 bis 1987," in Max Kaase and Hans Klingemann, ed. *Wahlen und Wähler: Analysen aus Anlaß der Bundestagswahl 1987*. Opladen: Westdeutscher Verlag.

Downs, Anthony. 1957. *An Economic Theory of Democracy*. New York: Harper & Row.

Emmert, Thomas and Andrea Stögbauer. 1994. "Volksparteien in der Krise. Die Wahlen in Baden-Württemberg, Schleswig-Holstein und Hamburg," in Wilhelm Bürklin and Dieter Roth, eds. *Das Superwahl Jahr*. Köln: Bund Verlag.

Hennig, Eike. 1994. "Politische Unzufriedenheit – ein Resonanzboden fur Rechtsextremismus?" in Wolfgang Kowalsky and Wolfgang Schroeder, eds. *Rechtsextremismus*. Opladen: Westdeutecher Verlag.

Jaschke, Hans-Gerd. 1994. *Die Republikaner: Profile einer Rechtsaußen Partei*. Bonn: Verlag J.H.W. Dietz Nachfolger.

Roth, Dieter. 1993. "Volksparteien in Crisis? The Electoral Sucesses of the Extreme Right in Context: The Case of Baden-Württemberg," *German Politics* 2: 1–20.

—— and Hartmut Schäfer. 1994. "Der Erfolg der Rechten. Denkzettel für die etablierten Parteien oder braune Wiedergeburt," in Wilhelm Bürklin and Dieter Roth, eds. *Das Superwahl Jahr*. Köln: Bund Verlag.

Republikaner. 1993. *Wir machen uns Stark ... für deutsche Interessen*. June 26–7, 1993. Augsburg.

——. 1994. *Der Republikaner*. September.

Stöss, Richard. 1993. "Rechtsextremismus und Wahlen in der Bundesrepublik," *Aus Politik und Zeitgeschichte* (12 March): 50–61.

Veen, Hans-Joachim, Norbert Lepszy, and Peter Mnich. 1993. *The Republikaner Party in Germany*. Westport, CT: Praeger.

Von Berg, Heinz Lynen. 1994. "Rechtsextremismus in Ostdeutschland seit der Wende," in Wolfgang Kowalsky and Wolfgang Schroeder, eds. *Rechtsextremismus*. Opladen: Westdeutscher Verlag.

Westle, Bettina and Oskar Niedermayer. 1992. "Contemporary Right Wing Extremism in West Germany," *European Journal of Political Research* 22: 83–100.

Young, Brigitte. 1995. "The German Political Party System and the Contagion from the Right," *German Politics and Society* 13: 62–79.

# III The Election Process

# 8
# The Dynamics of the Campaign

## Hans-Dieter Klingemann and Juergen Lass

Looking at the issue dynamics of the 1994 campaign means distinguishing between two levels. First, there is the supply side of the parties, who are trying to communicate their views of the world to the voters (Klingemann, Hofferbert, and Budge, 1994). Second, there is the demand side of the voters, who are making up their minds about the nation's political course. Therefore, an analysis of campaign dynamics implies a description of the programmatic offerings of the parties and the political agenda as perceived by the voters, which jointly define the nation's most urgent political problems. If we apply models of the rationality of the voters, the voters' attribution of issue competence to the parties is the crucial link between citizen perceptions and party offerings.

The parties fight to promote "their" issues in campaign communications. These issues are associated with each party's program, which constitutes part of the party's identity. The parties have a natural interest in shaping the agenda to be most favorable to themselves – the issues on which they can achieve the highest competency rating – but their capacity to do this is limited by other actors. The definition of the nation's most important problems involves several actors. The media, experts, and interest groups are powerful participants in this play, each guided by its own criteria of rationality. A description of campaign dynamics therefore must consider actors other than the parties.

The success of agenda setting also depends on the attention and the views of the voters. Political events affect the interest and values of the voters in different degrees. As we know since the Bundestag elections of the late 1960s, the parties are associated with special programmatic stereotypes (Klingemann, 1983; 1986;

Klingemann and Wattenberg, 1992; Kaase and Klingemann, 1994). The main job of the parties is to revitalize these stereotypes by political actions and speeches during the campaign. The party stereotypes among the public and their corresponding counterparts within the party define the long-term component of electoral dynamics, which changes only gradually between elections. The parties adapt their offerings to the political circumstances of an election, emphasizing some things while de-emphasizing others. Thus, the question in each election is: How successful were the parties in revitalizing their stereotypes? To answer this question, we have to examine the process of mobilization. This process lies within the middle- or short-term component of campaign dynamics, which depends on the impact of events, the input of interest groups, the input of the media and other experts, and the skillful actions of the parties.

Looking at the dynamics of the campaign, therefore, requires attention to the special features of a campaign. These dynamics are partially contingent on exogenous events that are out of the parties' control, but which shift attention to the parties and demand their reaction. In addition, in 1994 there was the extra-ordinary circumstance of having nineteen elections on the local, state, federal, and European level during this Superwahljahr, as well as the election of the federal president. The horse race between the parties was thus measured by public opinion and by this series of elections. This election series earns special attention for two reasons. First, election results give useful information to the voters who use short cuts to make their political decisions (Popkin, 1991). Elections are valuable opportunities for the voters to observe themselves. One's own vote preference can be examined in the light of the preferences of the entire electorate. Why should a rational voter ignore the voice of others in a political world of ambiguities and insecurities? One's own voting preference might be adjusted based on this information about the entire electorate's preferences. Thus, a sequence of elections can create an underlying voting trend. The second reason lies on the side of the parties. Election cycles are characterized by the parties' campaign spending, an increased polarization of political communication, and increased media coverage of politics. In 1994 the series of elections built a framework within which the parties were constrained. Mobilizing voters requires doing and saying the right thing at the right moment before an election.

After an election, the winners see a confirmation of their past actions and strategies, and have to prevent a demobilizing euphoria among their followers. The losing parties have to issue a warning of premature generalization, and intensify their efforts to win the next election.

Because of the character of the Superwahljahr, we first examine how the campaign generally mobilized partisan support during the election cycle. Then, we specifically examine how the parties and the public jointly converged on the issues of the 1994 campaign. We are fortunate to have an unparalleled data source as the basis of our analysis. During 1994 the German Research Foundation (DFG) supported an extensive series of public opinion surveys to monitor public opinion during this series of elections: "Wahlstudie 1994."[1] These data allow us to track German attitudes and interests in a way that was previously not possible.

## The Superwahljahr: The Mobilization of the Voters

It is a truism in voting research that the voters remember their prior preferences during a campaign that structures their attitudes in terms of enduring partisan stereotypes. This is the long-term component of campaign dynamics: the revitalization of party stereotypes and generalized competence attributions. If partisans have deviated from these preferences, they may be drawn back into the party fold. This pattern of mobilization depends on how the political agenda is construed and how the mobilization occurs. This also held true for 1994.

During 1994 the voters closely followed the media coverage about the elections. When asked what were the most interesting topics of the media coverage, the proportions in the Wahlstudie 1994 surveys answering "elections" ranged from 40 percent to almost 80 percent immediately before the election. This media coverage stimulated the public to become more involved in politics. Thus we can expect that the proportion of the undecided should drop as media coverage grew as the election approached. The proportion of people who cannot articulate a clear party preference is thus a measure of political mobilization.

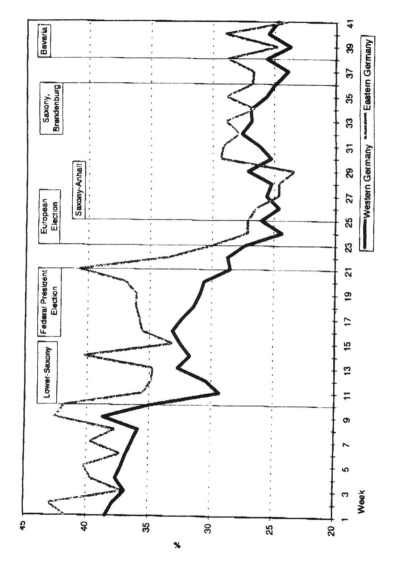

**Figure 8.1** Mobilization of the Electorate in 1994: Percentage of Undecided Voters and Non-Voters

Figure 8.1 shows that there are three clear waves of election-related mobilization. In the beginning of the year, we find the traces of *Parteienverdrossenheit*. Almost 40 percent of the electorate said that they did not have a party preference or that they would refuse to participate in the elections. This hesitancy endured until the 13 March election in Lower Saxony, when non-partisanship weakened. Some weeks after the Lower-Saxony election mobilization levels ebbed slightly. The second wave of mobilization coincided with the election of the Federal President in May. From the week of his election until the week of the European election (18 June), the proportion of non-partisans decreased more in eastern Germany than in the West. This indicates that this symbolic event, in which the public was only indirectly involved, had some impact on the electorate. From this point on, the vast majority of the western and eastern publics expressed some voting preference. We also find that mobilization again ebbed slightly a few weeks after this mobilization wave. In western Germany a third mobilization wave paralleled the state elections in Brandenburg and Saxony in September. By the last weeks of the campaign, less than a quarter of Westerners did not express a voting preference.

The development of voting preferences tells us nothing about the content of these preferences: Which party profited from the mobilization process? How did the party preferences develop in 1994? Figures 8.2 and 8.3 display strong differences across the parties. Most remarkable is the extreme increase in support for the main government party, the CDU/CSU, during 1994. If we compare the curve of the non-partisans (Figure 8.1) to the curve of CDU/CSU-supporters (Figure 8.2), it appears that people who had been dissatisfied with the government's policy were CDU partisans who returned to the CDU/CSU in the course of 1994. Such a mechanism is not implausible, because there are high psychological barriers against changing party preferences. That is, people dissatisfied with the performance of the CDU/CSU first changed to an ambivalent state of non-partisanship, then they were mobilized back into CDU/CSU partisanship during the 1994 campaign.[2]

There are a few ripples in this general pattern. For example, the little jump in the eighth week is a consequence of the CDU party convention in Hamburg. However, the main impression is that the development of party preferences followed a trend.

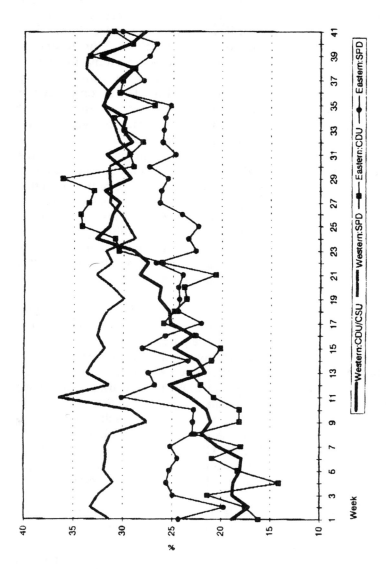

Figure 8.2 1994 Voting Intentions for CDU/CSU and SPD

Beginning in the third week of 1994, support for the CDU/CSU rose steadily. After the election of the federal president the rate of increase speeded up. After the European election the mobilization process of CDU/CSU voters flattened temporarily, and a last downtick occurred shortly before the federal election. In the last two weeks of the Bundestagswahl campaign, the CDU/CSU lost voters.

This picture differs sharply for SPD preferences (Figure 8.2). SPD voters had been highly mobilized at the beginning of the year. The serious economic difficulties and the resulting social problems offered sufficient stimuli to mobilize the SPD's potential followers. The SPD peak in the eleventh week may be a euphoria or so-called bandwagon effect triggered by the party's victory in Lower Saxony. Around the twenty-third week the election of the federal president produced a visible drop in support for the Social Democrats. The picture changed in the hot phase in the campaign, when the SPD succeeded in (re)mobilizing its constituency with its emphasis on classic social democratic issues and a competence-cuing "troika" of Scharping, Schröder, and Lafontaine.

The impact of election events is also visible in the preferences for the other parties, if one is willing to interpret slight changes (see Figure 8.3). The preferences for the Greens corresponded to the pattern of election results. The good results in Lower Saxony and in the European election mobilized the Green supporters in western Germany. The situation in eastern Germany looked somewhat different. The Green trend in the East was negative, and the Green party's losses in the Brandenburg and Saxony elections in September discouraged potential supporters.

The impact of the election for the European Parliament is observable in the PDS' level of support. Although the PDS failed to meet the 5 percent threshold, they received an impressive 4.7 percent. After that, the inclination of PDS support increased slightly.

The strongest mobilization effect before the election helped the FDP: from the thirty-ninth week until the forty-first week, the FDP garnered an additional 4 percent in western Germany. Rational and tactical voters of the government coalition, activated by the news about the possible failure of the FDP to surmount the 5 percent hurdle, supported the FDP even though they preferred the CDU/CSU in a narrow sense (*Leihstimmen*). In

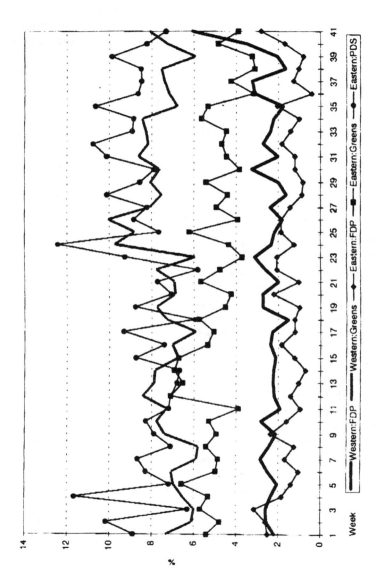

**Figure 8.3** 1994 Voting Intentions for Alliance 90/Greens, FDP, and PDS

the end, this mobilization of support enabled the Liberals to win reentry into the parliament. This behavior by the voters had been observed in prior elections (Brettschneider, 1992).

## The Input of the Parties

After examining the shifting patterns of party support, we should look for the driving forces behind these patterns. According to our model, these changes are caused by the import-ance attached to specific political problems and perceptions of which party is most competent in handling these problems.

A key element of this process is the behavior of the parties. The political parties act both as political organizations and (potentially) as an actor in government. The parties use govern-mental resources, if possible, to pursue their goals. Governments normally have more prestige than the opposition parties among the public. However, the parties also try to show a com-plementary position between their governing actions and partisan actions. Thus, the CDU/CSU exercised two roles to cultivate the voters in 1994, as a party and as a member of the federal government. In this way it could combine the programmatic function of a party at a symbolic level and the function of a government on the operative level. The SPD tried to use its position in the state governments in a similar way.

In January the CDU presented its economic program, which advocated supply-orientated, neo-liberal policies. According to the program, the main aim of economic policy should be to strengthen the attractiveness of Germany as a production place (*Wirtschaftsstandort Deutschland*). The instruments of this policy were a reduction of business taxes and the conversion of research knowledge into new products. In February the party adopted this program at the party convention in Hamburg. The main innovation of this program was to supplement the concept of a social market economy with ecological ideas.

In its governmental role, the CDU/CSU (and the FDP) pub-lished the annual economy report in January, which expressed optimism about several economic indicators. The government said that economic growth would be positive for the year and that inflation would decline. The government conceded that the high rate of unemployment would remain stable in 1994. In the beginning of March the government supported development of a new high-speed train (*Magnetschwebebahn Transrapid*) as an example of the type of technological innovation it had promised as an economic stimulus. The decision illustrated the concrete promises of the CDU's economic program.

The CDU/CSU thus set the relevant cues early in the election year. Later it repeated these economic messages. In this early period the first positive economic news appeared, but many analysts initially doubted these reports. Because the CDU/CSU's optimistic expectations were later confirmed, this gave it additionally competence in the eyes of many voters. These shared expectations of prosperity gave the CDU/CSU another clever campaign argument: the economic recovery should not be disturbed by a change in government.

In the economic area the SPD concentrated on the issue of the public debt. On the one hand, this was not an easy job because a considerable part of the electorate associated the Social Democrats with the stereotype that the party could not work with money. On the other hand, the extremely high public debt constituted an enormous danger for the economy and a source of public concern. At the end of September the last Bundestag session debated the federal budget plan for 1995. The SPD launched massive attacks that were registered by the population. The SPD promised to reduce new public debt and to cut expenditures and subsidies. The SPD has published a tax plan earlier in the year after the election in Lower Saxony. The SPD favored replacing the CDU's tax surcharge for all citizens (*Solidaritätszuschlag*) by taxes paid only by the "better earners" (*Ergänzungsabgabe*). When the SPD published its tax plan, it created a great confusion because the definition of the "better earners" was not clearly stated (see Chapter 3). The CDU/CSU argued that such a plan would destroy economic recovery.

All the parties offered answers to how unemployment could be reduced. There was a common feeling that shortening the working week and increasing part-time jobs would help. The main difference involved the parties' ideological positions and timeframes for solving the unemployment problem. The CDU/CSU and the FDP said that unemployment could not be solved in the short term; instead, basic economic conditions should be improved. For example, employers should be stimulated to make investments that would spur economic growth. The SPD and

Alliance 90/Greens wanted to use the instruments of social policy, such as support of employment agencies and expenditure to reduce long-term unemployment.

On the governmental level, the CDU/CSU and the FDP also took action. In January the government initiated a short-term program to reduce unemployment by having private brokers help the unemployed to find jobs. In May the government installed new measures for the unemployed in eastern Germany. Additionally the government increased the budget to provide more publicly financed jobs for the unemployed (*Arbeitsbeschaf-fungsmaßnahmen*). In eastern Germany the government pressed down the unemployment rate by 0.8 percent. The Bundesanstalt für Arbeit, in its role as the expert on labor, explicitly related this reduction to the government's measures.

Economic-based discussions also occurred for social policy. The state tried to find a solid financial basis for the growing number of elderly, who are sick and need help (*Pflegever-sicherung*). The governing parties wanted to compensate employers for their payments to the program; the CDU/CSU and FDP proposed abolishing two paid holidays. The SPD proposed a one-day reduction. Shortly before the election in Lower Saxony, the governing parties and the SPD came to an agreement. Both sides saved face: the governing parties established an employer-friendly compensation scheme and the SPD reduced the burden for working people.

In summary, these policy actions led to reactions by the public. Additionally, the dynamic of the agenda was dependent on trends in objective conditions that the parties and experts interpreted.

## The Dynamic of the Agenda

Our aim is to describe the development of the public's issue interests during the Superwahljahr that emerged from the party actions and objective conditions described in this chapter. The weekly Wahlstudie 1994 surveys asked respondents to list the most important problems facing the nation.[3] We found that the development of issue concerns over the election year falls into three periods. The first period is labeled by the dominance of socioeconomic perceptions; the second by the emergence of

167

The Election Process

libertarian/authoritarian issues; and the third by the hot phase of
the campaign.

*First Period: Programming of the Base Line*

In the period from the first to the twelfth week, the basic
conditions for issue perceptions were set for the rest of the year.
In addition to unemployment, several other issues competed for
the top of the agenda: the general economy and social policy
(Figures 8.4 and 8.5). The vast majority of the western public
(averaging around 70 percent) and eastern public (averaging
over 80 percent) saw unemployment as an important problem
facing the nation. Record unemployment statistics troubled the
German public; the peaks in these perceptions are caused by
reports from the Bundesanstalt für Arbeit (weeks 6, 10, 14, 18,
and 23). There is a visible reaction to the report in the sixth week
that unemployment had passed the 4 million level. In both West
and East, concern for unemployment increases by about 5
percent within one week. After the tenth week the news was a bit
more positive. Unemployment sank slightly from 4 to 3.7 million.
Throughout the rest of 1994, Germans in both West and East
ranked unemployment as the most important problem facing the
nation.

In early 1994 the general health of the economy was also hotly
debated. In the second week of the year the Federal Central
Bureau of Statistics said that some economic indicators were
signaling a recovery. The optimistic news began to cumulate. The
proportion of people who expected a better economy for the
future began to increase slowly but steadily (see also Chapter 10).
For a time, the ritualized wage conflicts between employers and
employed reinforced the public's economic concerns. The
negotiations were concluded by the tenth week, and media
coverage turned positive along with the public's mood.
However, concerns about the contemporary state of the national
economy remained unchanged during this first period.

Undoubtedly the governing parties benefitted over the course
of the year as the public forgot the petrol tax that had been
introduced at the start of 1994. The public reduced its attention
to this issue over the first ten weeks of the year. With the
publication of his tax plan shortly after the election in Lower
Saxony, Scharping and the SPD diverted attention from the petrol

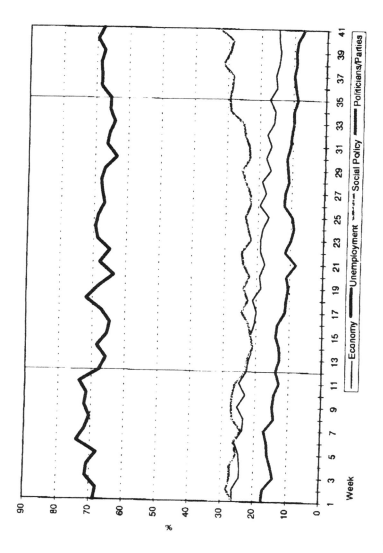

**Figure 8.4** 1994 Political Agenda in Western Germany: Socioeconomic issues and Politicians/Parties

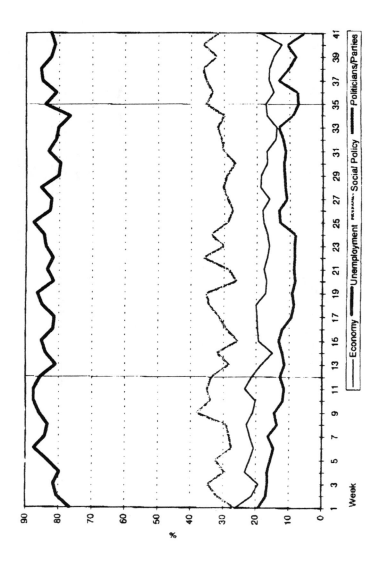

**Figure 8.5** 1994 Political Agenda in Eastern Germany: Socioeconomic Issues and Politicians/Parties

tax. This attention shift relieved the governing parties.

Social policy was also a significant concern during this first period, especially among Easterners. About a third of the western and eastern publics mentioned social policy as a national concern. For many Germans, the issue of *Pflegeversicherung* was the most visible controversy in social policy. The parties and political elites skillfully stimulated the public's wish to find an acceptable solution and to end the political battle. The parties compromised shortly before the Lower Saxony election in March (week 10). After this breakthrough, concerns about social policy decreased for at least a short while in both West and East. Political elites did not offer a picture of fruitless rhetorical battle to the voters, but produced a policy compromise.

In return for economic and social performance, trust in political actors was changing. In the first period insecurity, political scandals (especially in Bavaria), and the public discourse about *Parteienverdrossenheit* led almost a fifth of western and eastern Germans to list problems with politicians/parties as a major concern. The public criticized political actors on a professional and moral level. However, this inclination declined toward the end of the first period. This trend was strengthened by the opportunity for the electorate to observe themselves. In Lower Saxony the "Party of the Non-voters" and the protest parties were weaker than expected. Political leaders and the media interpreted these facts positively. Individual citizens felt that their more positive evaluation of politicians and parties, caused by economic and social performance, was not an isolated phenomenon.

The "deproblematization" of economic issues and politicians/ parties after this first period created a vacuum, especially in the West, which demanded to be filled. The question of which issue would profit from the appearing vacuum was open. The parties could influence the issue interests of the electorate only in a limited manner. The public's attention depended on the stimuli of events.

*The Second Period: The Strengthening of New Issues*

The second period, lasting from the thirteenth to thirty-fifth week of the year, was characterized by a structural change of the issue agenda. During this period the media coverage of the economy turned steadily more positive. Experts communicated positive economic news to the public, and politicians' interpretations of these statistics created an increasing optimism in the population. In its governmental role, the CDU/CSU explained the recovery as a result of its policies. Although concern about unemployment remained high, other economic concerns trended steadily downward in the West and at a slower rate in the East (Figures 8.4 and 8.5). During the second period the ranking of the issues was clear: concern about unemployment was followed by worries about right-wing extremism, the problems of foreigners, and social policy. This pattern was particularly evident in western Germany.

In general, issues corresponding to libertarian/authoritarian values gained attention during this second period (Figures 8.6 and 8.7). On the one hand, actions by right-wing extremists mobilized a call by other political actors for improved minority protection and the ostracism of the extremists. The fire in the synagogue in Lübeck in the thirteenth week, the anti-foreigner riots in Magdeburg in the twenty-first week, and later events produced intensive media coverage. In the first half of the year the public in both regions reacted with increased sensitivity. After the riots in Magdeburg the law committee of the Bundestag declared that the laws dealing with right extremism would be strengthened. The corresponding bill passed the Bundestag in September. Following these actions, attention to these issues declined after the twenty-first week. After these political actions, the public's attention to this issue declined.

On the other hand, a part of the western electorate felt a threat of violence by protesting Kurds, which appears as the "foreigner" trend in Figures 8.6 and 8.7.[4] In the eleventh week, Kurds started dramatic protest actions against the government's prohibition of the Kurdish communist worker party and against the suppression of the ethnic Kurdish minority in Turkey. They protested with blockades of autobahns and with self-immolations. These events led to an intense debate about whether the Kurds who broke German law should be deported. The Federal Minister of the Interior, Kanther, announced that Kurds should be deported to Turkey rapidly. However, the debate moved in another direction. There was a bloody civil war between Kurds and Turks in Turkey. Opponents of deportation described the danger of torture for Kurds who would be sent

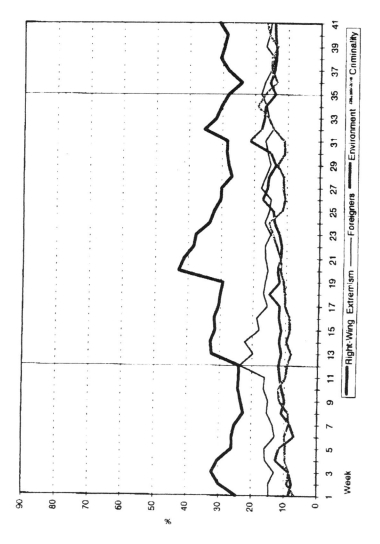

Figure 8.6 1994 Political Agenda in Western Germany: Libertarian and Authoritarian Issues

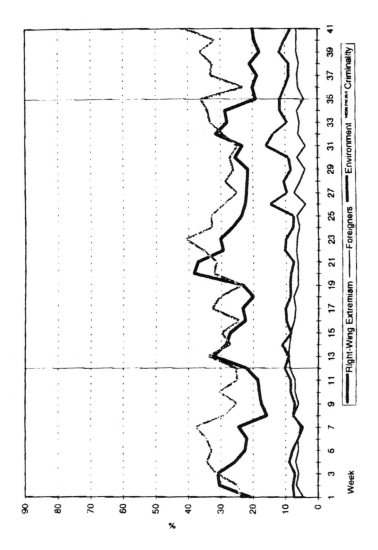

**Figure 8.7** 1994 Political Agenda in Eastern Germany: Libertarian and Authoritarian Issues

back to Turkey. Churches gave asylum to Kurds threatened with deportation. The courts intervened and strengthened a libertarian position. The SPD and Alliance 90/Greens supported a libertarian position that called for an interruption of deportation. The SPD used its leadership position in the state governments to interrupt the deportation in SPD-governed states; the CDU/CSU continued the deportation in CDU/CSU-governed states.

The public registered these different pieces of information: the violent demonstrations, the civil war between Kurds and Turks, and the political debate. The issue of how to deal with foreigners continued to attract the attention of a significant minority of Westerners up until the Bundestagswahl.

During this second period two other issues profited from the vacuum left by the decline in economic worries: the environment and criminality (Figures 8.6 and 8.7). Again, events stimulated the salience of these issues. Already in the first period, an ecological disaster – a ship in the stormy North Sea losing a cargo of poison that threatened the German coast – showed the population that ecological risks still existed. After some minor ripples in environmental concerns, the major debate focused on how to reduce summer smog. After the twenty-fifth week, some SPD-governed states implemented speed limits to reduce traffic on the highways. The government parties in Bonn opposed this policy; they argued that speed limits would not help to reduce summer smog. This debate stimulated a growing western attention to environmental issues during the second period, although interest in these issues remained limited in the East.

The issue of criminality also became more important during this second period. The publications of federal crime statistics had an impact because Germany was experiencing a very high growth in crime rates during the 1990s. The residents of eastern Germany were especially troubled by the high crime rates in their states. The question of how to deal with criminality was hotly debated between the government parties and the SPD. It is no coincidence that this issue reached a peak around the time of the European parliament election in the twenty-fourth week. In September, the parties agreed to formulate a law against criminality, and attention dropped off toward the end of this period.

In summary, during the second period the development of the campaign agenda was directed by exogenous events. The parties then translated these events into the political debate. In this way the parties shaped the public agenda.

## Third Period: The Hot Campaign

Between the thirty-sixth and forty-first weeks the parties strengthened their efforts to communicate their views to the voters as interest in the campaign increased. As we noted earlier, the public's interest in the campaign and elections grew as a topic of media coverage through the course of 1994.

The issue agenda changed slightly during the third period. Social policy grew in importance in both the West and East so that it ranked above the issues of hostility to foreigners and right-wing extremism. This was caused by the political cues sent by the parties and other actors. After the CDU/CSU had caught up with the SPD in voter preferences, the SPD sought to mobilize support via its classic issue bases; social pressure groups reinforced this message by publishing statistics on national poverty levels. In response, lobbyists of the market economy called for cuts in social programs. The CDU/CSU announced its intention to cut social programs for the next legislative period; the SPD and the trade unions responded by sharply criticizing the government. In addition, social policy issues that touched middle-class interests were part of the party debate. For example, the parties differed on family policy: the CDU/CSU favored a preferential tax treatment of families while the SPD promised to increase expenditures for families.

Finally, the SPD succeeded in keeping the issue of unemployment in the minds of western and eastern voters. The increase in attention to this issue in both regions between the thirty-fourth week and election week was a mobilization effect of the Social Democrats.

## Issues and the Vote

If the voters define the nation's problems in a special way, they should also prefer the party that is most competent in dealing with these problems. The voters' views of the good and bad points of the parties over seven federal elections (1969 to 1990) shows a consistent result: the CDU/CSU is perceived as the party that can deal best with economic problems (Klingemann, 1990).

To test these ideas in 1994, we asked the following questions: How did voters perceive the political agenda the week immediately before the Bundestagswahl, and how did these perceptions influence voting preferences? To answer these questions we measured issue salience with a question about the nation's most important problems. To gather information about voting decisions and the reasoning behind them, we asked "which issue did or will most influence your vote decision?"

The first two columns of Table 8.1 present the salience of various issues during the last week of the campaign, and the proportion of the electorate who said an issue would influence their voting decision. The table highlights the importance of socioeconomic conflicts: unemployment (73.1 percent), the economy (16.8 percent), social policy (39.1) are all highly salient. In addition, over a fifth of those surveyed list each of these issues as an influence on their voting decision. These issues represent the long-term components of party programs and voter stereotypes. The importance of these socioeconomic conflicts are not surprising because of the economic recession in the early 1990s and the feeling of deep crisis at the beginning of 1994 that we have described in this chapter.

The rightmost column in Table 8.1 displays the partisan preferences of individuals interested in each of these specific issue interests. In 1994 the CDU/CSU benefitted from its perceived competence in economic matters (see also Chapter 10). For example, among those who listed the economy as an important problem, voters favored the CDU/CSU (44.0 percent) over the SPD (29.8 percent). The SPD reaped the fruits of its perceived competence in social policy and of unemployment.[5] The FDP's policy problems are also clearly visible. The FDP did not possess any distinctive area of competence.

A second, less salient package of issues involve postmaterialist (or libertarian/authoritarian) values of improving life quality (environment protection), along with opposition to threats against minorities (fight against right-wing radicalism). The anti-pode is support for law and order and feelings of being threatened by foreigners. The issues grouped around postmaterialist values are not negligible. For example, the

**Table 8.1** Issues and Vote Reasons Before the Federal Election

| Type of Issue | Saliency of Issue Decision | Major Reason for Vote | Party Elected for that reason |
|---|---|---|---|
| Economy | 16.8 | 21.4 | CDU/CSU 44.0 SPD 29.8 |
| Unemployment | 73.1 | 29.1 | SPD 51.0 CDU/CSU 33.9 |
| Social policy | 39.1 | 21.3 | SPD 64.0 CDU/CSU 17.8 |
| Environment | 13.3 | 7.5 | A90/Grüne 60.0 SPD 26.0 |
| Hostility against foreigners/ rightextremism | 29.9 | 4.4 | SPD 36.7 A90/Grüne 33.3 |
| Crime | 23.4 | 3.1 | (SPD 47.8) (CDU/CSU 43.5) |
| Foreigners | 13.8 | 2.6 | (CDU/CSU 44.4) (SPD 27.8) |
| (N) | (2423) | (876) | |

*Source*: Wahlstudie 1994; respondents interviewed the week before the election.
*Note*: Multiple responses were possible for the listing of salient issues and issues that were a reason for the respondent's vote. Brackets indicate that the basis of a calculation is smaller than 30 respondents.

environment – the prototypical issue of the postmaterialists – is seen as an issue of Green party competence. The table shows that people who wanted environment protection in 1994 supported the Alliance 90/Greens to a disproportionate degree (60 percent).

## Conclusion

At the beginning of this chapter we claimed that an understanding of the dynamics of the campaign in 1994 requires an examination of the supply side of the parties, who provide programmatic solutions to the nation's problems, and the demand side of the voters, who determine what are the important problems. Voters following rational calculations support the party that is perceived as the most competent in the most important issue areas. Such perceptions are not invariable over time. Of course, there are also rather stable programmatic profiles of the parties. The electorate has stereotypic ideas about which party can handle which issue best: the CDU/CSU is perceived as the party that can deal with economic problems; the SPD "owns" the issues of social policy; and the Alliance 90/ Greens "own" the environmental issues.

In an election year there are strong time-dependent elements in issue perceptions, which form the dynamics of the campaign. This was the case in 1994 too. First, perceptions of the important problems changed with events and media coverage, and with the problems discussed by the politicians and the experts. After the first three months the public expected the economic situation to improve. Similarly, the parties and the government solved a major social problem (*Pflegeversicherung*). Consequently, the public's readiness to criticize the old parties declined. These changes gave other issues the possibility to attract more attention. Libertarian issues such as environmental protection, as well as the counterpart issue of law and order, gained in importance. Second, the parties succeeded to different degrees in revitalizing their traditional images. The electorate was mainly interested in economic and social bread-and-butter-issues. The CDU/CSU succeeded in convincing an increasing part of the electorate that it possessed the ability to push the economic recovery. The CDU/ CSU communicated successfully in its role both as a party with programmatic messages and as the main government actor. In the last weeks of the campaign the SPD influenced the political views of the electorate by promoting its traditional social democratic issues. The decision of the SPD chancellor candidate, Scharping, to install a new "troika" was fruitful, but it compensated only for prior losses in the party's image. At the end of the campaign, the SPD stood where it stood at the beginning of the election year.

The Alliance 90/Greens profited from the media coverage of environmental issues and its mobilizing effect on the electorate. This issue motivated many voters to support the Greens. The FDP, however, did not possess a distinct issue area of its own. It survived at the federal level because CDU/CSU adherents "rationally" calculated that support of the FDP would be necessary in order to perpetuate the governing coalition.

Third, twenty elections took place in 1994. This was a special characteristic of the Superwahljahr. These elections heightened the public's attention to politics and they offered the voters multiple opportunities to observe themselves, as well as the political actors. Two elections played a special role during this year. The results of the Lower Saxony election in March were interpreted as indicating that the delegitimization of the old parties had been stopped. The symbolically important election of the federal president in May let the CDU/CSU appear as a strong, powerful party, and the SPD as a bad loser. Both elections were accompanied by a wave of mobilization. In those weeks the proportions of people who knew which party they would support substantially increased.

Finally, we concentrated our analyses mainly on the whole of Germany, neglecting some important peculiarities in eastern Germany. For instance, party affiliations were (and are) much lower in eastern Germany than in the West. This was illustrated in the higher proportion of Easterners who could not say which party they would support (Figure 8.1). In addition, the postcommunist PDS emerged as a relatively strong, regional party in eastern Germany. The PDS recruited its voters mainly from the former SED-supporters (see Chapter 6). This recruitment was made easier through the radical economic and social changes in eastern Germany – and the public concerns that followed from these changes.[6]

On the whole, however, we have downplayed regional differences because eastern and western Germans generally reacted to political events and to the inputs of the political actors in a similar way. Despite sharply contrasting socialization experiences, political differences between East and West are beginning to disappear.

**Notes**

1. The survey conducted weekly samples from the first week of 1994 up until the election. The average weekly sample was 2,500 respondents, and a total of more than 100,000 respondents were surveyed. The fieldwork was conducted by FORSA, Berlin and Dortmund.

   This survey is a central element of the "Wahlstudie 1994: Massenmedien und Wähler" which was conducted by the Institut für Kommunikationssoziologie und -psychologie of the Free University Berlin, the Zentralinstitut für sozialwissenschaftliche Forschung of the Free University Berlin, and the Wissenschaftszentrum Berlin für Sozialforschung. The project has been funded by the Deutsche Forschungsgemeinschaft (DFG) and was supported by FORSA and Radio-Television Luxembourg (RTL).

2. This hypothesis is also confirmed by an examination of the party recall question. The CDU/CSU recruited the "new" voters in 1994 from the potential of the CDU/CSU voter from 1990.

3. The wording of the question was "Was sind Ihrer Meinung nach in Deutschland zur Zeit die drei größten Probleme?"

4. The foreigner issue was largely a western concern, and attention to these issues was consistently lower in the East.

5. Norpoth and Roth (Chapter 10) note that the 1994 election presents a puzzle in that the most salient problem, unemployment, was a natural issue for the SPD. Yet, these perceptions of competence did not benefit the SPD to a substantial degree.

6. We did not discuss whether the CDU/CSU campaign against the "left front" helped the PDS to mobilize its supporters. There is some evidence in our data that this took place. In the first weeks of the "left front" campaign the proportion of Easterners who said that they felt something of a "wall in the mind" between East and West increased very slightly.

## References

Brettschneider, Frank. 1992. "Der taktische und rationale Wähler," *Politische Vierteljahresschrift* 33: 55–72.

Kaase, Max, and Hans-Dieter Klingemann. 1994. "The Cumbersome Way to Partisan Orientations in a New Democracy," in M. Kent Jennigns and Thomas Mann, eds. *Elections at Home and Abroad*. Ann Arbor: University of Michigan Press.

Klingemann, Hans-Dieter. 1983. "Die Einstellung zur SPD und CDU/CSU 1969–80," in Max Kaase and Hans-Dieter Klingemann, eds. *Wahlen und politisches System*. Opladen: Westdeutscher Verlag.

———. 1986. "Der vorsichtig abwägende Wähler: Einstellungen zu den politischen Parteien und Wahlabsicht: Eine Analyse anläßlich der Bundestagswahl 1983," in Hans-Dieter Klingemann and Max Kaase, eds. *Wahlen und politischer Prozeß: Analysen aus Anlaß der Bundestagswahl 1983*. Opladen: Westdeutscher Verlag.

———, Richard Hofferbert, and Ian Budge. 1994. *Parties, Policy and Democracy*. Boulder: Westview Press.

——— and Franz Urban Pappi. 1970. "Die Wählerbewegungen bei der Bundestagswahl 1969," *Politische Vierteljahresschrift* 11: 111–38.

——— and Martin Wattenberg. 1992. "Decaying Versus Developing Party Systems: A Comparison of Party Images in the United States and West Germany," *British Journal of Political Science* 22: 131–49.

Popkin, Samuel. 1991. *The Reasoning Voter*. Chicago: University of Chicago Press.

# 9

# The Two German Electorates

## *Russell J. Dalton* and *Wilhelm Bürklin*

We are interested in probing beneath the vote counts and party actions described in other chapters to determine how political alignments are forming in the East and possibly reforming in the West as a consequence of unification. In 1990 the party system and democratic politics itself was new to eastern voters. Voters in the new Länder were only superficially familiar with the FRG parties that had expanded eastward. The pattern of interest group competition that underlies the western electoral process was still forming in the East. The 1990 elections were a tentative test of what partisan politics would look like in the new Länder.

What emerged in 1990 were several anomalies in eastern voting behavior when compared to the West (Dalton and Bürklin, 1993). Electoral research in western democracies almost uniformly finds that parties of the left gather most of their support from the working class, and parties of the right draw their support from the middle class. The emerging class structure in eastern Germany displayed a *reversal* of this partisan alignment in 1990. In addition, the lack of religious attachments by most Easterners changed the nature of the religious cleavage in the FRG's party system.

In this chapter we determine if the anomalies we originally noted in the 1990 election had resolved themselves by 1994. The peculiarities of voting choice in 1990 may have been a transitory phenomenon of this first election. After four years the capitalist infrastructure has developed, interest groups have formed, and the aura of unification has been overtaken by a closer approximation of normal politics. To what extent have eastern voters been integrated into the party system of Federal Republic, or to what extent have the distinctive experiences of Easterners created new or different bases of partisan cleavage within the same party system? Our analyses focus on several social groupings that reflect the existing cleavage alignments of the West, or which have the potential to structure the voting behavior of Easterners: social status, religion, rural/urban residence, age, and gender.[1] Each of the following sections examines the relationship between a social characteristic and vote choice in the 1994 Bundestagswahl. These findings lead to a discussion of the contrasting political alignments that have developed in East and West, and their implications for the German party system.

### Social Status and the Vote

The Federal Republic's party system is partially built upon the traditional class conflict between bourgeoisie and proletariat, and more broadly the problems of providing economic well-being and security to all members of society. These economic conflicts were important in defining the initial structure of the party system. Moreover, the CDU and SPD are embedded in their own network of support groups (business associations and labor unions) and offer voters distinct political programs catering to these group interests. Although the class cleavage has gradually weakened as an influence on voter choice in the West, it remains an important element in structuring partisan competition (Dalton, 1992b).

At the first democratic elections of 1990, Easterners understandably may have had a difficult time using the social class cues that guide electoral choices in the West. It is hard to apply western notions of social class to the occupational structure inherited from the communist GDR. The economy was overwhelmingly comprised of state-owned enterprises; the GDR was ostensibly a state *of* and *for* the working class. Similarly, in place of the new middle class in the West, the East had party functionaries, governmental appointees, and managers of state enterprises. Furthermore, the GDR did not allow the formation of interest groups that could challenge the SED-controlled mass organizations and thus could serve as a basis for political cleavage. Thus, the traditional contrast between the bourgeoisie and proletariat in a free market economy was largely irrelevant in East Germany. Market-based class distinctions are developing in the new Länder, but in 1990 they were still weakly defined.

Electoral researchers found that class voting patterns in the 1990 Bundestagswahl were relatively unchanged for Westerners when compared to prior elections (Roth, 1990; Dalton and Bürklin, 1993). Although the SPD lost considerable overall support in the election, the party still polled a plurality of working-class voters in the West. Conversely, most middle-class voters supported the CDU/CSU, especially among members of the self-employed and professionals. If one simply calculated the difference in the percentage supporting leftist parties (SPD and Greens) between working-class and middle-class voters, the 12 percent gap in party support in 1990 barely differed from the two prior elections.

To the extent that researchers could apply capitalist class distinctions to the eastern electorate in 1990,[2] public opinion surveys found striking evidence of a *reversal* of class voting patterns among Easterners. The eastern CDU won most of the working-class vote, but fared less well among the middle class. Conversely, the socialist-oriented parties – SPD and PDS – garnered more votes among the middle class than among their "normal" constituency in the working class. The Alliance 90/Greens also gained greater support from the middle class. The few self-employed professionals in the East supported the CDU, but white-collar salaried employees in the East disproportionately endorsed leftist parties. Eastern voters thus began their experience with the FRG party system in 1990 with the opposite of the class voting pattern in the old Länder and most Western democratic party systems.

It is possible that this reversal of the class cleavage in the new Länder was a temporary occurrence. The 1990 campaign was an exceptional election. The unification issue dominated the Bundestag campaign, temporarily eclipsing other political concerns. Debates on the course of unification overshadowed ongoing public interests in the structure of social welfare programs, social benefits, issues of environmental quality, and many other topics (Kuechler, 1993). In addition, the intermediary institutions that could link the parties to class groups, such as the unions and business associations, were themselves still developing in late 1990 (Löbler et al., 1991).

The 1994 Bundestagswahl is the important second election that can measure whether the class voting anomaly of Easterners in 1990 has converged with voting alignments in the West, or maintains its own course. Indeed, following the 1990 election a series of events provided a stimulus for Easterners (and Westerners) to revise their partisan preferences. Tax increases in the West and a struggling economy in the East led to a marked decrease in support for the CDU in public opinion polls and state elections. Thomas Emmert suggested that these trends produced a realignment in class voting after the 1990 election (Emmert, 1994). Indeed, since 1989 many political analysts pointed out the Social Democrats' traditionally strong working-class base in the East, evidenced by the elections of Weimar and the first postwar elections (Schmitt, 1993; 1994).

Alternatively, the upswing in the economy in 1994 and Kohl's remarkable comeback in the months before the election may have signaled a different realignment among Easterners. The promised prosperity of unification was finally becoming apparent, and the CDU was benefitting from these sentiments (Chapter 2). As the CDU surged in late 1994, it could have been gathering the support of middle-class voters who were benefitting from the upswing.

To examine these questions, Table 9.1 displays the class alignment in 1994 for both western and eastern voters. The class divide in the West mirrors recent elections. The working class gives the bulk of its support (55.9 percent) to the Social Democrats. Indeed, one of the SPD's successes in 1994 was to recapture its electoral strongpoints (*Hochburgen*) in the West; the party's greatest gains were in traditional industrial districts. Middle-class voters, especially members of the traditional middle class of self-employed and professionals, give the largest share of their vote to the Christian Democrats. If one were to compare the leftist (SPD and Greens) share of the vote between working-class and middle-class strata, the 14 percent difference is very close to the gap in prior elections.

More striking are the results from eastern voters. In 1994 a majority of eastern workers (and the lesser-educated) give their vote to the CDU – exactly the opposite of the relationship in the West. The bulk of the eastern middle-class vote goes to parties of the Left. More than a fifth of the middle class in the East voted PDS, and another two-fifths vote SPD or Alliance 90/Greens. The worker–middle class gap in class voting in 1994 is a *negative 15 points*, even greater than in 1990.

The anomaly of eastern class voting patterns in 1990 and 1994

**Table 9.1** Class Voting Patterns in 1994

| Party | Worker | Self-Employed | Salaried Employees | Combined Middle Class |
|---|---|---|---|---|
| Western Germany | | | | |
| CDU/CSU | 37.2 | 59.7 | 38.6 | 42.9 |
| FDP | 1.1 | 17.1 | 8.0 | 9.9 |
| SPD | 55.9 | 14.6 | 39.4 | 34.5 |
| Alliance 90/Greens | 3.6 | 5.9 | 12.7 | 11.5 |
| Other (REP/PDS) | 2.2 | 2.6 | 1.4 | 1.1 |
| Total | 100% | 100% | 100% | 100% |
| (N) | (264) | (98) | (391) | (489) |
| Percent | 35.1 | 13.0 | 51.9 | |
| Eastern Germany | | | | |
| CDU | 51.5 | 39.1 | 33.5 | 34.3 |
| FDP | 2.5 | 9.4 | 3.9 | 4.6 |
| SPD | 34.1 | 26.6 | 32.5 | 31.6 |
| Alliance 90/Greens | 1.8 | 7.8 | 8.0 | 8.0 |
| PDS | 9.8 | 17.2 | 21.6 | 21.0 |
| Other (REP) | 0.3 | 0.0 | 0.5 | 0.4 |
| Total | 100% | 100% | 100% | 100% |
| (N) | (396) | (64) | (388) | (452) |
| Percent | 46.7 | 7.5 | 45.8 | |

*Source*: September 1994 Politbarometer Study, conducted by Forschungsgruppe Wahlen for the Zweites Deutsche Fernsehen (ZDF). The salaried employee category in the West includes civil servants.

could reflect continuity between these elections, or the ebbs and flows of counterbalancing events between the elections. Therefore, we tracked the class bases of CDU voter support in the East between 1990 and the third quarter in 1994 (Figure 9.1). The first two timepoints redisplay the 1990 results for Westerners and Easterners (Dalton and Bürklin, 1993). The subsequent timepoints are from monthly Politbarometer surveys of the East, cumulated by quarter.[3] To simplify the presentation, we track only support for the CDU. Because of the CDU's role in government and its position as the major conservative party, this methodology generally provided a good representation of Left/Right party preferences in the East.

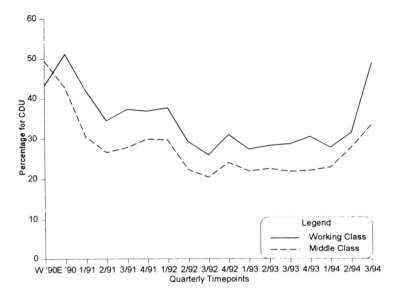

*Source*: December 1990 Politbarometer (East and West); 1991–1994, Politbarometer-Ost surveys conducted by the Forschungsgruppe Wahlen. Monthly surveys in 1991–1994 were cumulated by quarter.

**Figure 9.1** Class Voting Patterns in Eastern Germany, 1990–1994

The crossing of the two lines at the start of the figure illustrates the reversed class cleavage among Westerners and Easterners in 1990. In this election the eastern working class preferred the CDU by 8 percent over the party's support from the middle class. Over the next three years the CDU lost support among both class groups, but the working-class bias toward the party persisted or even increased. Even while the Treuhand was creating a free market economy in the new Länder, and the framework of the FRG's interest group and partisan structure was becoming more firmly established in the East, the anomaly in class voting continued. Probably the most dramatic shift in Figure 9.1 is the increase in CDU support in 1994. Yet, this is a broad-based gain across all social strata, and the reversed class alignment actually widens.

Occupation remains a somewhat uncertain measure of social status because of the fluidity in the eastern economy; thus we also examined educational level as a more stable measure of social position. Educational differences in the West are fairly muted, averaging a few percentage points difference. In contrast, we find very sharp social status differences for educational groups in the East. In December 1990 the lesser-educated Easterners gave disproportionate support to the CDU by a margin of 29 percent. In September 1994 this gap remains at 30 percent.

Because of the centrality of class to German politics and the political identity of the parties, these contrasting East–West patterns of class support are a striking finding. Moreover, they have now endured across two national elections, and many more state elections.[4] The continuity from 1990 to 1994 suggests that this is not a transient phenomenon. A new class cleavage has developed in the East, and it is grounded in citizen identifications with the parties. Voters entering their next election will have partisan predispositions based on these class patterns.

How did this class reversal develop? In part, it reflects the different historical experience of the East. Most analysts attribute this class reversal in 1990 to a backlash against the policies of the GDR. Despite the rhetoric of being a state for farmers and workers, the GDR disproportionately benefitted the party elite and intelligentsia. Especially in the last decade, the GDR showed all the characteristics of a consolidating class society (Solga, 1994). The ideological heirs of the GDR – the parties of the Left – represent some of the same principles as espoused by the SED, albeit in more moderate and democratic forms. Because of this, the elite class of the old regime continued its leftist orientation by disproportionately supporting the SPD and PDS.[5] Similarly, the PDS' support is concentrated in the quarters of East Berlin formerly identified with GDR employment and SED membership.

At the other end of the social spectrum, the workers struggled under the old regime, and looked toward the West and unification as a way to improve their situation. Eastern workers were hesitant to support leftist parties that could be identified with the socialist past of the GDR, even when the link was modest, as with the newly formed eastern SPD.[6] The political system of the GDR did not allow these class conflicts to surface, but they have manifested themselves in the open democratic system of the Federal Republic.

This different historical experience also gives a different meaning to a working-class identity in the East. Faced with the failure of the GDR, workers in the new Länder turned their attention and support to the party group that promised a change and improvement in their situation. In early 1990 the leading figures in the SPD were hesitant to offer a dramatically new vision of the future, thinking of a partial stabilization of the socialist model via a federal solution (*Staatenbund*). Thus eastern workers were suspicious, fearing that a vote for the SPD would not bring about real change. In contrast, Kohl and the CDU leadership promised a radical and immediate change in the economic and political conditions in the East. The CDU (or the Alliance for Germany) thus gained the support of many Easterners in the elections of 1990, and the CDU still benefits from this image today.

To sum up, two different class alignments exist in East and West. These contrasts are caused by the differences of the class structure of East and West, as well as the different political experiences of class groups under the GDR. Normally, parties with conservative economic and political programs should reach middle-class voters. Because of their different ideological value systems, neither the CDU nor the FDP is attractive to middle-class voters in the new Länder.[7] These differences will persist as long as the eastern middle class contains the remnants of the former leadership class of the GDR.


### Religion and the Vote

Historically, the religious cleavage provided a second basis for electoral division in the German party system. This conflict goes back to the Kulturkampf of the 1870s, when Protestant Prussia attacked the position of the Catholic Church and its adherents. Originally this line of conflict divided Catholics and Protestants. With the foundation of the CDU after the Second World War, religious differences in the Federal Republic shifted toward a cleavage between secular and religious voters within each confessional group (Schmitt, 1988). The gap in SPD voting support between Catholics and Protestants, and the gap between secular and religious voters, has remained considerable for most of the past three decades. Furthermore, perceptions of the partisan leanings of the Catholic Church suggest that religious cues also remain distinct (Dalton, 1992a: ch. 8).

The impact of the religious cleavage on eastern voters initially was uncertain because of the GDR's history. The government forced the replacement of religious rites (such as *Taufe* or *Konfir-mation*) with secular rites (e.g. *Jugendweihe*). The existence of the churches was not questioned, but their loyal adherents who rejected the secular rites would be deprived of life-chances for themselves and their children. Still, the churches were one of the few institutions that could act independent of the SED-state. Especially in larger cities like East Berlin, the churches played a significant role in fostering political dissidence that eventually led to the 1989 revolution.[8]

Table 9.2 describes the pattern of religious voting in the West and East in 1994. Among Westerners in 1994, a 16 percent gap continues to separate Protestants and Catholics in their support for leftist parties (SPD and Greens). The voting gap between religious and non-religious Westerners displays a similar divide. Both patterns are similar to the results for 1990 and other recent Bundestagswahlen (Dalton, 1992b).

**Table 9.2** Religious Voting Patterns in 1994

| Party | Catholic | Protestant | No Religion |
|---|---|---|---|
| Western Germany | | | |
| CDU/CSU | 49.5 | 37.4 | 30.7 |
| FDP | 7.8 | 4.2 | 5.7 |
| SPD | 31.9 | 49.2 | 42.0 |
| Alliance 90/Greens | 9.0 | 7.9 | 17.0 |
| Other party | 1.7 | 1.4 | 4.5 |
| Total | 100% | 100% | 100% |
| (N) | (372) | (356) | (88) |
| Percent | 45.6 | 43.6 | 10.8 |
| Eastern Germany | | | |
| CDU | 72.7 | 56.5 | 32.1 |
| FDP | 4.5 | 2.5 | 3.9 |
| SPD | 18.2 | 29.1 | 34.5 |
| Alliance 90/Greens | 2.3 | 6.1 | 5.1 |
| PDS | 2.3 | 5.7 | 20.7 |
| Other party | 0.0 | 0.0 | 3.6 |
| Total | 100% | 100% | 100% |
| (N) | (44) | (244) | (588) |
| Percent | 5.0 | 27.9 | 67.1 |

*Source*: September 1994 Politbarometer Study; conducted by Forschungs-sgruppe Wahlen.

In the East, Catholics and Protestants disproportionately support the CDU. The voting gap between denominations is 18 percent in leftist voting preferences. This is almost exactly the same voting gap as for the western electorate, although one should remember that eastern Catholics are a distinct and relatively homogeneous minority, compared to the large and diverse nature of the Catholic constituency in the West. The more relevant dimension for Easterners involves the secular/religious divide or religious attachments such as church attendance. Secular voters favor parties of the Left by a large margin; the size of this gap is similar to the West. Eastern voters thus mirror the religious voting patterns found in West German elections. Furthermore, the religious gap at the end of 1994 remains as wide as it was during the 1990 Bundestagswahl.

Religious voting apparently follows a similar pattern in West and East, yet this commonality overlooks a basic difference in the composition of the two electorates. One area of cultural change where the GDR government had been successful was in promoting the secularization of society. For instance, a 1991 opinion poll found that 59 percent of Westerners never doubted the existence of God, compared to only 27 percent of Easterners (Times Mirror Center, 1991). The vastly different composition of the two electorates also can be seen in Table 9.2. Only a tenth of the western public say they are non-religious, compared to 67.1 percent of Easterners! With respect to its religious values, the GDR was a much more modernized society than western Germany, but in a totalitarian form (Zapf, 1994).

These compositional differences between East and West will change the political makeup of the parties and thus possibly their policy positions. More generally, the addition of non-religious eastern voters to the electorate will accelerate the general secularization process in German society and attenuate the importance of the religious cleavage. As with the class cleavage, the impact of religion will further weaken in a unified German party system.

## Generation/Age and the Vote

Another possible influence on party preferences, and an indicator of the potential for electoral change in the future, is the distribution of party support across age groups. Age groups display both the differentials of party support for individuals at various points in the life cycle, as well as the legacy of historical experiences.

Survey research in western Germany has routinely found a tendency for younger Germans to support parties of the Left, especially since the Greens offered a distinct counterculture option to German youth (Bürklin and Dalton, 1994). The data in Table 9.3 display this same general pattern for Westerners. Support for the CDU/CSU, for instance, increases from about a third among the youngest cohorts to over half of elderly Westerners. There is a corresponding decrease in support for the Greens (and to a more irregular extent the SPD) among older cohorts.

Again, our expectations for Easterners are more ambiguous. The demonstrations that brought down the GDR were filled with

Table 9.3 Age Group Voting Patterns in 1994

| Party | Under 30 | 30–39 | 40–49 | 50–59 | 60 and over |
|---|---|---|---|---|---|
| **Western Germany** | | | | | |
| CDU/CSU | 38.8 | 26.7 | 33.9 | 55.2 | 51.7 |
| FDP | 4.4 | 5.4 | 6.4 | 7.4 | 8.1 |
| SPD | 38.1 | 49.2 | 46.5 | 31.8 | 37.5 |
| Alliance 90/Greens | 16.1 | 16.2 | 9.9 | 4.4 | 1.9 |
| Other party | 2.6 | 2.5 | 3.3 | 1.2 | 0.7 |
| Total | 100% | 100% | 100% | 100% | 100% |
| (N) | (152) | (162) | (136) | (145) | (229) |
| Percent | 18.4 | 19.7 | 16.5 | 17.6 | 27.8 |
| **Eastern Germany** | | | | | |
| CDU | 35.4 | 39.7 | 45.6 | 38.4 | 49.0 |
| FDP | 7.6 | 3.0 | 3.8 | 2.4 | 2.3 |
| SPD | 33.3 | 31.7 | 26.1 | 38.6 | 33.1 |
| Alliance 90/Greens | 10.5 | 8.4 | 4.4 | 3.3 | 1.7 |
| PDS | 13.1 | 16.5 | 20.1 | 17.3 | 13.8 |
| Other party | 0.1 | 0.6 | 0.0 | 0.0 | 0.0 |
| Total | 100% | 100% | 100% | 100% | 100% |
| (N) | (172) | (138) | (143) | (181) | (232) |
| Percent | 19.9 | 15.9 | 16.5 | 20.9 | 26.8 |

*Source*: September 1994 Politbarometer Study; conducted by Forschungsgruppe Wahlen.

youthful faces. Even before the collapse of the Berlin Wall, there were signs of growing liberalism among eastern youth. Yet, the young also were socialized under the closed system of the GDR. Compared to their elders who had lived in the West or travelled there before 1961, the young only knew life under the communist regime. Moreover, the GDR had intensified its indoctrination programs over time, especially its emphasis on the political socialization of the young.

The data in the lower half of Table 9.3 display a muted Left/ Right difference in the party preferences of generations. Older Easterners generally express a greater preference for the CDU, though differences are narrower than in the West. The Leftist preferences of young Easterners are not displayed in support for the SPD or the PDS, but in a leaning toward the Alliance 90/Greens. In fact, a comparison between 1990 and 1994 suggests that the PDS' voter base became more diversified in its age composition between these elections. In 1990, 17 percent of young Easterners (under 30) expressed a preference for the PDS, compared to only 5 percent among the oldest age group (over 60). In 1994 there is very little age gradient in PDS support.

These findings, both from 1990 and 1994, suggest that the generational shift toward the Left is continuing in the West. The Greens are the major benefactor of this trend. The FDP are potentially the greatest losers, since their support among the young falls below the critical 5 percent threshold. Because age differences are more muted in the East, and still more fluid across elections, it is more difficult to speak of generational demographics as a driving force in electoral change there.

## Gender and the Vote

The last cleavage we examine is gender. Our interest in gender stems more from the situation of Easterners than from the traditional importance of this cleavage in the western Länder (see Chapter 12). Gender-based voting differences were pronounced in the early Federal Republic, with women leaning toward the more conservative CDU/CSU. The gender gap steadily narrowed during the 1970s and 1980s as social differences between the sexes converged and the women's movement transformed social norms linking gender and politics. Voting preferences in

1994 reflect this gender convergence (Table 9.4). Women in the West still favor the CDU/CSU, but by less than a 2 percent margin.

**Table 9.4** Gender Voting Patterns in 1994

| Party | Men | Women |
|---|---|---|
| **Western Germany** | | |
| CDU | 41.1 | 42.6 |
| FDP | 6.0 | 6.9 |
| SPD | 39.8 | 41.4 |
| Alliance 90/Greens | 10.0 | 8.2 |
| Other party | 3.2 | 0.8 |
| Total | 100% | 100% |
| (N) | (390) | (437) |
| Percent | 47.2 | 52.8 |
| **Eastern Germany** | | |
| CDU/CSU | 41.9 | 42.1 |
| FDP | 3.8 | 3.5 |
| SPD | 32.8 | 32.8 |
| Alliance 90/Greens | 3.7 | 6.8 |
| PDS | 17.0 | 14.7 |
| Other party | 0.6 | 0.0 |
| Total | 100% | 100% |
| (N) | (412) | (452) |
| Percent | 47.7 | 52.3 |

*Source*: September 1994 Politbarometer Study; conducted by Forschungsgruppe Wahlen.

While the women's movement faced a protracted struggle in the West, the GDR proclaimed itself to be an emancipated state. There were the much-advertised statistics on the high participation of women in the labor force, and the provision of childcare services by the state. While abortion rights were limited in the West, these rights were guaranteed in the GDR. Reality often fell short of the regime's rhetoric, but the rhetoric of the GDR strongly promoted gender equality. Furthermore, these gender differences were often worsened by the political decisions that accompanied German unification. The debate on abortion reform polarized opinions on this issue, and women were often the main losers in the policy choices that followed unification

(Schlegel, 1995; Hahn, 1995).

Despite the different legacy of the East, the lower panel of Table 9.4 shows that gender had little impact on the party preferences of Easterners during the 1994 Bundestagswahl. The CDU garnered a bit more support from eastern women, but all of the differences in the table fall below conventional levels of statistical significance. Furthermore, this voting pattern is little changed from the 1990 Bundestagswahl. The overall lesson, therefore, is that gender plays little role in structuring the partisan preferences of Easterners (or Westerners).

## The Combined Impact of Social Characteristics

Until this point we have looked at specific social characteristics as discrete influences on voting choice. Yet, the total impact of social cleavages comes from the combination of these elements. Moreover, social characteristics are often interrelated; the young, for instance, also tend to have higher levels of education and lower levels of religious involvement.

Therefore, we combined the various social traits discussed in this chapter into a multivariate model of partisan choice. Instead of explaining vote choice, we predict public sympathy toward political parties as measured by an 11-point scalometer.[9] This allows us to measure reliably public sentiments toward a set of parties, even when the parties may garner only a small percentage of the vote. We focused our analyses on the two major parties that structure the broad framework of the party system, as well as two smaller parties that highlight the distinct counter tendencies of West and East (the Alliance 90/Greens for the West and the PDS for the East).

Table 9.5 presents the results of these multiple regression analyses. If we start with the western models, the pattern of partisan support follows our previous analyses of political cleavages in the German party system. The CDU draws disproportionate support from those who attend church regularly, older voters, and rural residents; each of these effects is strong and statistically significant. The SPD voter base presents an almost mirror image. The Social Democratic base is located among the less-educated, the less-religious, and younger voters. The Alliance 90/Green clientele reflects the parties' distinctive postmaterial appeal, drawing support from the young, the better-educated, and the secular sectors of German society.

**Table 9.5** A Multivariate Analysis of Party Sympathy in 1994

|  | West | | | East | | |
|---|---|---|---|---|---|---|
|  | CDU/CSU | SPD | A90/G | CDU | SPD | PDS |
| Middle-class occupation | −0.01 | 0.04 | 0.01 | −0.03 | −0.02 | 0.06 |
| Better education | 0.02 | −0.10* | 0.11* | −0.10* | −0.04 | 0.14* |
| Catholic | 0.01 | −0.07 | 0.03 | 0.05 | −0.04 | −0.06 |
| No church attended | −0.23* | 0.10* | 0.08* | −0.16* | 0.06 | 0.18* |
| Age | 0.18* | −0.13* | −0.19* | 0.06 | 0.05 | 0.00 |
| Female | 0.01 | 0.07 | 0.18* | −0.05 | 0.00 | 0.04 |
| Urban residence | −0.07* | 0.00 | 0.02 | −0.05 | 0.09* | 0.06 |
| Multiple R | 0.32 | 0.21 | 0.31 | 0.27 | 0.13 | 0.30 |

*Source*: September 1994 Politbarometer Study; conducted by Forschungsgruppe Wahlen. Table entries are standardized regression coefficients predicting the separate scalometer ratings for each party.

More noteworthy, however, are our results for the eastern public. Even controlling for the other variables in the model, the eastern CDU supporter is significantly less likely to be drawn from the better-educated; there is also a weak working-class leaning among CDU sympathizers. This is a direct reversal of the CDU class base in the West. In addition, the Christian Democrats also lose significantly among non-religious voters. The primary contrast is not with SPD adherents, who are a fairly diffuse group in social terms (the Multiple R is the lowest of any model). Instead, the PDS represents the core leftist constituency in the East – and the PDS draws upon almost the opposite clientele from the eastern CDU. Better-educated Easterners (and to some extent those with middle-class occupations) are overrepresented in this party of socialist reform. The PDS also garners significantly more support from the non-religious Easterners.

## Two Electorates

The most significant aspects of our findings are the contrasts in the social bases of party support in western and eastern

Germany. Our analyses suggest that there are two distinct elect-orates within the one German nation. One source of these differ-ences is the *different composition* of western and eastern Germany. The sharply different religious preferences of Easterners and Westerners is the most distinctive evidence that two separate electorates now exist in Germany. The western electorate is fairly religious, as well as conservative on economic and social welfare issues; the eastern electorate is more secular and liberal on social issues (Mayer, 1994; Glatzer and Noll, 1995; Schmitt, 1995).

The difference in the religious composition of the two electorates creates two distinct constituencies within the political parties. This can be graphically seen in Tables 9.6 and 9.7, which describe the social composition of the parties in West and East. In the West (Table 9.6), 53 percent of CDU voters are Catholics, 39 percent are Protestants, and only 9 percent are non-religious. In the East (Table 9.7), 53 percent of the CDU's voters describe themselves as having no religious attachment. Among Western democracies, this is probably the only party explicitly espousing religious values that has such a secular base.

Other studies have shown similar results in comparing attitudes toward the social welfare state between West and East; Easterners are much more likely to favor an expanded social role for government and favor government protections of individual well-being (Bauer-Kaase, 1994; Wegener and Liebig, 1993).

A second source of the distinctiveness between electorates is the *different relationship* between social characteristics and party choice. The reversal of the normal class alignment among eastern voters creates distinctly different constituencies within the same parties in the West and East. Taking the Christian Democrats as an illustration, the CDU's electorate in the West is largely made up of middle-class voters, especially members of the new middle class (Table 9.6). This provides a political base for the Christian Democrats' conservative economic policy and their preference for modest social spending. In the East, however, the bulk of the CDU's support in 1994 (46 percent) comes from working-class voters (Table 9.7).

The opposite pattern exists for parties of the Left. The PDS offers the most graphic example. This leftist party garners more than two-thirds of its eastern voters from among the middle class (Table 9.7). The SPD electorate proportionately overrepresents working-class voters in the West (Table 9.6), and slightly

**Table 9.6** Electoral Coalitions of the Parties Among Western Voters in 1994

|  | CDU/CSU | SPD | FDP | Greens | Total public |
|---|---|---|---|---|---|
| **Occupation** | | | | | |
| Worker | 28 | 43 | 6 | 13 | 34 |
| Self-employed | 17 | 5 | 32 | 8 | 12 |
| White collar/ | | | | | |
| government | 44 | 46 | 58 | 66 | 46 |
| Other | 11 | 6 | 3 | 13 | 9 |
| **Union member in house** | | | | | |
| Yes | 21 | 45 | 9 | 32 | 31 |
| No | 79 | 55 | 91 | 68 | 69 |
| **Education** | | | | | |
| Primary | 54 | 51 | 32 | 18 | 49 |
| Secondary | 25 | 30 | 20 | 27 | 27 |
| Advanced | 21 | 19 | 48 | 55 | 23 |
| **Religion** | | | | | |
| Catholic | 53 | 35 | 54 | 44 | 44 |
| Protestant | 39 | 52 | 29 | 37 | 42 |
| Other, none | 9 | 13 | 17 | 19 | 14 |
| **Age** | | | | | |
| Under 40 | 30 | 42 | 29 | 68 | 40 |
| 40–59 | 36 | 32 | 36 | 26 | 33 |
| 60 and over | 34 | 26 | 35 | 6 | 27 |
| **Gender** | | | | | |
| Male | 46 | 46 | 44 | 52 | 47 |
| Female | 54 | 54 | 56 | 48 | 53 |
| **Size of town** | | | | | |
| Less than 5,000 | 34 | 28 | 27 | 16 | 29 |
| 5,000–20,000 | 25 | 22 | 25 | 26 | 24 |
| 20,000–100,000 | 22 | 23 | 23 | 29 | 22 |
| More than 100,000 | 19 | 27 | 25 | 28 | 24 |
| (Maximum N) | (346) | (336) | (53) | (75) | |

*Source*: September 1994 Politbarometer Study, conducted by the Forschungsgruppe Wahlen (Weighted N = 1013).

underrepresents them in the East (Table 9.7).

Another example of this regional polarization is the overall level of support for specific parties in the two regions. The PDS is

**Table 9.7** Electoral Coalitions of the Parties Among Eastern Voters in 1994

|  | CDU/CSU | SPD | FDP | Greens | PDS | Total public |
|---|---|---|---|---|---|---|
| **Occupation** | | | | | | |
| Worker | 46 | 47 | 32 | 16 | 29 | 49 |
| Self-employed | 7 | 6 | 21 | 10 | 8 | 6 |
| White collar/ | | | | | | |
|   government | 36 | 44 | 48 | 66 | 61 | 43 |
| Other | 11 | 2 | 0 | 8 | 2 | 3 |
| **Union member in house** | | | | | | |
| Yes | 25 | 32 | 13 | 15 | 32 | 27 |
| No | 75 | 68 | 87 | 85 | 68 | 73 |
| **Education** | | | | | | |
| Primary | 44 | 43 | 37 | 7 | 25 | 39 |
| Secondary | 42 | 37 | 33 | 26 | 40 | 40 |
| Advanced | 14 | 21 | 30 | 67 | 36 | 21 |
| **Religion** | | | | | | |
| Catholic | 9 | 3 | 4 | 1 | 1 | 5 |
| Protestant | 38 | 25 | 21 | 35 | 10 | 28 |
| Other, none | 53 | 71 | 75 | 64 | 89 | 67 |
| **Age** | | | | | | |
| Under 40 | 32 | 36 | 52 | 47 | 33 | 39 |
| 40–59 | 37 | 37 | 31 | 26 | 44 | 36 |
| 60 and over | 31 | 27 | 17 | 9 | 23 | 25 |
| **Gender** | | | | | | |
| Male | 48 | 48 | 50 | 33 | 52 | 46 |
| Female | 52 | 52 | 50 | 67 | 48 | 54 |
| **Size of town** | | | | | | |
| Less than 5,000 | 35 | 35 | 31 | 38 | 28 | 35 |
| 5,000–20,000 | 13 | 13 | 24 | 7 | 16 | 13 |
| 20,000–100,000 | 30 | 25 | 7 | 10 | 30 | 27 |
| More than 100,000 | 17 | 27 | 38 | 45 | 26 | 26 |
| (Maximum N) | (364) | (285) | (32) | (46) | (137) | |

*Source*: September 1994 Politbarometer Study, conducted by the For-schungsgruppe Wahlen (Weighted N = 1068).

now almost exclusively based in the East, in terms of both its voter base and rank-and-file membership (see Chapter 6). Conversely, the Alliance 90/Greens and the FDP are disproportionately western parties in their voting base and political appeals.

When we first observed sharp regional contrast in the 1990 election, we speculated that this might be a passing phenomenon because of the unusual circumstances of unification and the undeveloped nature of democratic politics in the East. Now, four years later, we are more inclined to see these patterns as enduring features of the two electorates unless there is a major political intervention. Repetitive voting experience tends to strengthen party ties and lead to the formation of partisan identifications that endure across elections. Moreover, even with the anomalous partisan alignments of the East, once partisan networks and support groups start to develop, they create a framework for perpetuating these alignments. Local politicians and party activists realize who their voters are, and build ties to these individuals; these linkages strengthen with each new election. State party leaders similarly recognize where the party's base is located, further strengthening these orientations.

These regional differences can create sharp intraparty tensions. Because CDU voters in the new Länder are significantly less religious and less Catholic than their western counterparts, their attitudes toward abortion and other social issues conflict with the policy program of the western CDU. An eastern wing of the CDU that is oriented toward the ideal of christian socialism would strengthen the labor-oriented wing of the party (*Sozialausschüsse*) and could create new policy strains within the Union (Bürklin, 1995). If CDU politicians from the East represent these views, this places them in conflict with the party's official policies. If eastern CDU deputies do not reflect these views, then this produces a representation deficit for Easterners. Thus, the complex relationship between horizontal integrations with the national party elite, and vertical integration between party elites and their social bases, has been unbalanced by German unification.

The SPD faces a similar question of establishing its identity among Easterners. A middle-class-oriented SPD in the East might fit into the modernizing image of the current party leadership. However, this eastern constituency could handicap the SPD's efforts to renew its working-class constituency in the East and

West. Similarly, there are growing signs of tension between the eastern and western wings of the Alliance 90/Greens, partially because of the divergent constituencies in the two regions (Chapter 5).

Such sharp regional contrasts are unusual phenomena in disciplined, unified party systems. One possible model for understanding the implications of this contrast is the historic North–South divide in the United States. Sharp compositional differences in social and political attitudes separated American Northerners and Southerners. Furthermore, the Civil War led to an anomalous party alignment in the South; Democrats in the South found themselves representing an electorate that was distinctly more conservative than Democrats with constituencies north of the Mason–Dixon line. Republicans in the South often were more liberal than their northern counterparts (until recently). Despite the inconsistencies that this created in the American political process, and the tensions generated within the political parties, this situation persisted for over a century.

Clearly there are basic differences between the American South and the German East, but the comparison suggests some potential implications for German politics. One implication is the potential for intraparty conflict along regional lines. Because the eastern wings of the major parties reflect a different electoral base, this pressures eastern politicians and especially Bundestag deputies to reflect these alternative views within the national party. At the same time, the requirements of a disciplined party system make it difficult to tolerate such divergence. This tension is clear in many of the votes involving the economic and social aspects of German union. Eastern CDU voters endorsed reforms in the Treuhand's privatization policies and a review of the implementation of the unification treaty (Ferchland et al., 1993); yet eastern CDU deputies accepted party discipline on these issues and voted with their western colleagues in the Bundestag. In other instances, such as the Bundestag vote on abortion reform, eastern CDU deputies voted with their constituents and against the majority of western CDU deputies. These conflicts are atypical for a system of responsible party government.

These partisan and political contrasts between West and East also can reinforce a regional identity in the new Länder. Regardless of their party attachment, eastern CDU and SPD voters can feel that their views are not well represented in the present democratic party system. Like American Southerners, these experiences can strengthen feelings of regional solidarity. This representation deficit within the major parties undoubtedly contributed to the PDS' success in 1994 as spokesperson for the disenfranchised East (Moreau and Neu, 1994).

If eastern politicians within the major parties respond to these feelings of alienation, this may further reinforce regional divisions. As in the United States, the federal system of German government creates an opportunity for such regional variation that is not commonly found in unitary political systems. Indeed, the SPD leadership in Brandenburg and the CDU leadership in Saxony have both charted courses that distinguish them from their national parties and put them in closer touch with their own electorates; they have benefitted electorally from this strategy. This may be a common result of having two separate German electorates.

Regional variations in voter support and party positions have existed in the Federal Republic before unification, such as differences between the SPD in Bavaria and North Rhine-Westphalia. However, the present gap between West and East is a different phenomenon. Party differences in the past did not involve conflicts over central ideological positions, but in the intensity of these positions. The two different electorates in East and West create the basis for two different party systems, much as existed in American politics for the century after the Civil War. These regional differences created real political tensions in the American party system. Because of the centralization and more ideologically focused nature of German political parties, the potential for intraparty conflicts is even greater.

The existence of these intraparty tensions makes it difficult for the German parties to represent these two electorates within a single system of disciplined party government. Which voters will lose when party discipline enforces a common party position? How will party government function with less party discipline? It will be difficult for the present government to function effectively, especially with its small majority in the Bundestag, when it represents such distinct constituencies. These challenges for the party system are an enduring legacy of German union.

**Notes**

We presented a portion of these findings at the conference on the
1994 Bundestagswahl organized by the Center for Western European Studies at the University of Washington; another portion
was published in a special issue of *German Politics and Society*
(April 1995). We want to thank Alexandra Cole, Roberto
Heinrich, and Falk Reckling for their assistance on this project.

1. The data analyzed here were collected by the Forschungsgruppe Wahlen for the Zweites Deutsches Fernsehen (ZDF).
   The data were made available through the Zentralarchiv für
   empirische Sozialforschung, University of Cologne. The
   authors are solely responsible for the analyses and interpretation presented here.
2. See Kitschelt's (1992) provocative discussion about the
   potential class basis of politics in postcommunist systems. We
   use a traditional western definition of class because the
   western economic system was quickly extended to eastern
   Germany and the fine class distinctions in Kitschelt's model
   are difficult to examine with the Politbarometer surveys.
3. The Forschungsgruppe Wahlen conducts two or three
   monthly surveys each quarter, for a base sample size of two to
   three thousand respondents per quarter. We measure party
   preferences with the question of vote intention if the election
   were held on the next Sunday.
4. We extended our analyses to consider whether there was a
   generational aspect to these patterns, which might suggest
   future trends. Class polarization is slightly weaker among
   those between 25 and 44 years old (-11 Alford index) than
   among those 45 years and older (-17 Alford index). The con-
   sistency of this negative class voting among both age groups
   strengthens the evidence that this will be an enduring pattern.
5. Because of the ambiguous meaning of social class for eastern
   voters in 1990, we also compared educational differences
   between the two regions. In the December 1990 Politbarometer survey, Left/Right party preferences differed very
   little between the better and lesser educated groups in the
   West (by only 4 percent), though there was a slight leftward
   tilt among the better educated because of the Greens' appeal
   among younger, university-trained Westerners. In the East,

the education gap is much wider (21 percentage points), with a distinct leftward bias among the better educated.

6. At the same time, Easterners continue to express belief in the idea of socialism. A recent public opinion poll found that 79 percent of Easterners believed the idea of socialism was good, but the politicians were incompetent (*Der Spiegel*, 3 July 1995: 46).

7. The competition between the PDS and CDU is not a class conflict in Lipset and Rokkan's (1967) sense, but a cleavage based on nation-building issues.

8. Unification also upset the religious balance of politics in the Federal Republic; Catholics and Protestants are roughly at parity in the West, but the East is heavily Protestant. Thus, unification significantly shifted the religious composition of the new Germany.

9. Respondents were presented with a scale that ran from -5 (very negative opinion) to +5 (very positive opinion).

**References**

Bauer-Kaase, Petra. 1994. "German Unification: The Challenge of Coping with Unification," in W. Donald Hancock and Helga Walsh, ed. *German Unification: Process and Outcomes*. Boulder: Westview Press.

Bürklin, Wilhelm. 1995. "Perspektiven des Parteiensystem," in Heinrich Oberreuter, ed. *Das Wahljahr 1994: Eine Bilanz*. Munich: Olzog.

—— and Russell Dalton. 1994. "Das Ergrauen der Grünen," in Hans-Dieter Klingemann and Max Kaase, eds. *Wahler und Wähler*. Opladen: Westdeutscher Verlag.

Dalton, Russell. 1992a. *Politics in Germany*, 2d ed. New York: HarperCollins.

——. 1992b. "Two German Electorates," in Gordon Smith et al., *Developments in German Politics*. London: Macmillan.

—— and Wilhelm Bürklin. 1993. "The German Party System and the Future," in Russell Dalton, ed. *The New Germany Votes*. Oxford: Berg.

Emmert, Thomas. 1994. "Politische Ausgangslage vor der Bundestagswahl 1994," in Wilhelm Bürklin and Dieter Roth, eds. *Das Superwahljahr*. Köln: Bund Verlag.

Ferchland, Rainer et al. 1993. *Ost–West-Wahlanalyse 1/1993*. Berlin: Institut für Sozialdatenanalyse.

Glatzer, Wolfgang, and Heinz-Herber Noll, eds. 1995. *Getrennt vereint: Lebensverhältnisse in Deutschland seit der Wiedervereinigung*. Frankfurt: Campus.

Hahn, Toni. 1995. "Frauen und Arbeitslosigkeit," in Hubert Sydow, Uta Schlegel, and Andreas Helmke, ed. *Chancen und Risken im Lebenslauf: Wandel in Ostdeutschland*. Berlin: Akademie Verlag.

Kitschelt, Herbert. 1992. "The Formation of Party Systems in East Central Europe," *Politics and Society* 20: 7–50.

Kuechler, Manfred. 1993. "Framing Unification: Issue Salience and Mass Sentiment 1989–91," in Russell Dalton, ed. *The New Germany Votes*. Oxford: Berg.

Lipset, Seymour Martin, and Stein Rokkan, eds. 1967. *Party Systems and Voter Alignments*. New York: Free Press.

Löbler, Frank, Josef Schmid, and Heinrich Tiemann, eds. 1991. *Wiedervereinigung als Organisationsproblem: Gesamtdeutsche Zusammenschlüsse von Parteien und Verbänden*. Bochum: Universitätsverlag Dr. Brockmeyer.

Mayer, Karl-Ulrich. 1994. "Vereinigung soziologisch: Die soziale Ordnung der DDR und ihre Folgen," in Hansgert Peisert und Wolfgang Zapf, eds. *Gesellschaft, Demokratie und Lebenschancen*. Stuttgart: Deutsche Verlaganstalt.

Moreau, Patrick, and Viola Neu. 1994. "Die PDS zwischen Linksextremismus und Linkspopulismus." Internal study nr. 74. St Augustin: Konrad Adenauer Stiftung.

Niedermayer, Oskar. 1991. "Parteimitglieder im Leipzig." Unpublished research report. Mannheim: University of Mannheim.

Roth, Dieter. 1990. "Die Wahlen zur Volkskammer in der DDR," *Politische Vierteljahresschrift* 31: 369–93.

Schlegel, Uta. 1995. "Ostdeutsche Frauen in neuen gesellschaftlichen Strukturen," in Hubert Sydow, Uta Schlegel and Andreas Helmke, ed. *Chancen und Risken im Lebenslauf: Wandel in Ostdeutschland*. Berlin: Akademie Verlag.

Schmitt, Karl. 1988. *Konfession und politisches Verhalten in der Bundesrepublik* Berlin: de Gruyter.

——. 1993. "Politische Landschaften im Umbruch: Das Gebiet der ehemaligen DDR, 1928–1990," in Oscar Gabriel and Klaus Troitzsch, eds. *Wahlen in Zeiten des Umbruchs*. Frankfurt: Lang.

——. 1994. "Im Osten nichts Neues? Das Kernland der deutschen Arbeiterbewegung und die Zukunft der politischen Linken," in Wilhelm Bürklin and Dieter Roth, eds. *Das Superwahljahr*. Köln: Bund Verlag.

——. 1995. "Die Landtagswahlen 1994 im Osten Deutschlands," *Zeitschrift für Parlamentsfragen* 26: 261–95

Solga, Heike. 1994. "Auf dem Weg in eine klassenlose Gesellschaft? Klassenlagen und Mobilität zwischen Generationen in der DDR." PhD dissertation. Berlin: Free University Berlin.

Statistisches Bundesamt, eds. 1994. *Datenreport 1994: Zahlen und Fakten über die Bundesrepublik Deutschland*. Bonn: Bundeszentrale für politische Bildung.

Times Mirror Center. 1991. *The Pulse of Europe*. Washington, D.C.: Times Mirror Center for People & the Press.

Wegener, Bernd, and Stefan Liebig. 1993. "Eine Grid-Group-Analyse sozialer Gerechtigkeit: Die neuen und die alten Bundesländer im Vergleich," *Kölner Zeitschrift für Soziologie und Sozialpsychologie* 45 :668–90.

Zapf, Wolfgang. 1994. "Einige Materialien zu Gesellschaft und Demokratie im vereinten Deutschland," in Hansgert Peisert und Wolfgang Zapf, eds. *Gesellschaft, Demokratie und Lebenschancen*. Stuttgart: Deutsche Verlagsanstalt.

# 10
# Timid or Prudent? The German Electorate in 1994

## Helmut Norpoth and Dieter Roth[1]

The opposition never wins, as the saying goes about elections, it is only the government that loses. That holds for the opposition in federal elections in Germany; but to make matters worse, German governments refuse to lose. The parties out of power in the Federal Republic once again learned that lesson to their chagrin in 1994, as Chancellor Helmut Kohl led his party coalition to reelection. That was his fourth consecutive victory, giving him a triumph unsurpassed in German national elections during this century. Only Konrad Adenauer was victorious as many times, although his fourth win in 1961 was marred by the refusal of his coalition partner to back him for another full term. No such demands overshadowed Kohl's prospects on election night 1994, notwithstanding his own hint that this might be his last term.

The completion of that term, however, may be highly taxing in light of the razor-thin margin of victory. Election night 1994 was one of the most suspenseful ever, as the governing coalition of CDU/CSU and Free Democrats struggled to edge the combined opposition ranks of Social Democrats, Greens, and PDS by barely 0.3 percent of the popular tally (second vote). The headline of *Bild*, Germany's notorious tabloid, screamed *Zitterwahl* (thriller election). Taken by itself, the vote margin was good enough for a minimal majority of two seats in the next Bundestag. Thanks to the "overhang" rule, it expanded to ten seats, but that still equaled the smallest initial seat margin of any federal government.[2]

As the suspense lifted, the outcome of the 1994 election revealed a glaring paradox: all the winners lost and all the losers gained. As compared with the previous election, there were losses for both the CDU/CSU (-2.3 percent) and FDP (-4.1

percent), and gains for the SPD (2.9), Greens (3.7), and PDS (2.0) (see Table 1.2). Unfortunately for the parties out of power, the drop of voter confidence in the governing parties halted just before the point where it would have shifted the political balance. The German voter, so it looked, stepped to the edge of the cliff, peered over it, teetered for a moment, but then refused to take the plunge. Was the drop too steep? Was the water below too murky? Too turbulent? Or was the diver just too timid?

This chapter probes the tug-of-war inside the German electorate in 1994. We begin with an examination of the policy issues pulling voters in opposite directions. Much of our analysis focuses on the perennial issue of the economy, which blossomed with special vigor as a result of the mounting costs of unification. If there was one issue that had initially promised the SPD a return to government, it was the economy. Among issues of more recent vintage was a highly explosive one, the foreigner problem. The influx of asylum seekers and violence against non-Germans had inflamed passions. This is the kind of issue that typically stirs up electoral support for parties at the fringes of the spectrum. Beyond this, the environment continued to command public attention, especially among the western electorate where these issues kept alive the Greens' prospects.

Aside from issues, we examine the appeal of the key contenders for the chancellorship. What did the German electorate see in Helmut Kohl that it did not see in Rudolf Scharping, the Social Democratic leader? To what extent was this a question of idiosyncratic personal qualities? And how much of it had to do with incumbency, namely the value that accrues from being chancellor (*Kanzlerbonus*)? Did issue concerns intersect with candidate evaluations in a way that gave the chancellor an edge over the challenger? Beyond policy issues and the personnel of leadership, the political parties merit our attention as more long-term forces of electoral politics. The 1994 election took place amidst symptoms of deepening disaffection with party politics (*Parteienverdrossenheit*). Our chapter probes the extent of partisan dealignment in the German electorate by 1994 and its consequences for political participation.

With the new Germany barely four years old in 1994, it is also imperative to examine how the eastern voters adapted to the electoral game. The spectacular showing of former communists (under the PDS banner) in eastern Germany points to a persisting, even deepening, division within unified Germany. What were the sources of electoral strength on which the PDS drew? What was the balance between ideology and resentment? How deep did the party's roots extend in the soil of the eastern electorate? Our analysis of all those questions relies on a survey of more than 2,000 eligible voters conducted by the Forschungsgruppe Wahlen a few days before the election of 16 October 1994.[3]

## The Imprint of Issues

At the beginning of the Superwahljahr of 1994, most observers expected that the SPD – led by a Clintonesque chancellor candidate unburdened by the party's recent failures, and in concert with a more pragmatic Green party – would defeat the Christian–liberal coalition of Helmut Kohl. Many signs pointed to an end of the twelve-year reign of conservative government, just as they had in the United States two years earlier. Like its American counterpart, the German electorate entered the election year with a "throw-out-the-rascals" mood.

### The Economy

The most compelling reason for that sour mood was the economy. That was the issue, after all, that helped Helmut Kohl capture the chancellorship twelve years earlier from Helmut Schmidt (SPD), ending thirteen years of social–liberal rule (Goergen and Norpoth, 1992). The 1994 election shaped up as a contest focused to an unusual extent on economic issues. For one thing, there were Kohl's promises in the campaign four year earlier: an economic miracle in the East, and painless financing by the West. The collapse of the East German economy had unleashed a flood of bankruptcies and job losses, forcing the West to consider substantial tax hikes and/or spending cuts. The government reneged on its pledge not to raise taxes. To contemplate what happened to political leaders who broke their tax vows, Kohl only had to look at George Bush in the US presidential election of 1992.

Then, to add injury to insult, the economy in western Germany fell into a recession that lasted through most of 1992 and 1993.

The SPD hammered home the message that the government's economic policy had failed. Unemployment dwarfed any other issue on the public's list of concerns (see Chapter 8). On the eve of the Bundestag election, according to our survey, that issue ranked as the nation's most important problem among 63 percent of Westerners, and 75 percent of Easterners. The salience of unemployment ought to have guaranteed victory for the SPD. This is the party that normally "owns" this issue. Even better, as an opposition party, the SPD could deny any responsibility for the rise of unemployment during the past four years. Had the SPD triumphed on election day in 1994, everyone would have pointed to the high voter concern with unemployment as the reason.

In the end, maddening as it was for the SPD and perplexing as it may be to students of voting, the unemployment issue failed to cut much electoral cloth in 1994; just as it had not prohibited Margaret Thatcher's victories in Britain during the 1980s (Norpoth, 1992). Does high unemployment no longer pose a mortal threat to the electoral survival of parties in power? As for Germany, one reason might have been that this was an issue only for SPD-partisans, who were planning to vote for the party anyway. Concern with unemployment was high among SPD supporters (68 percent in the West, and 79 percent in the East), but hardly any higher than it was among CDU/CSU voters (64 percent in the West, 70 percent in the East). How could those citizens rate unemployment as so important and still vote for the governing parties?[4]

As our survey shows, few Germans personally feared unemployment: less than one in six in the West, though understandably more in the East, expressed worry about the security of their own jobs. To overstate the case, perhaps, unemployment was like a natural disaster that struck far from home. What is more, the SPD failed to inspire much public confidence in its ability to deal with this problem any better than the CDU/CSU.[5] It is a myth to believe that unemployment automatically helps the SPD and hurts the CDU/CSU. Whether that did not happen in 1994 because the SPD offered few convincing proposals to create more jobs, or because the CDU/CSU offered good enough policies, is a question we cannot resolve here.

Most important perhaps, unemployment was only one part of

the economic picture. No matter how strongly Germans felt about the problem, the public also embraced the opinion during 1994 – first in the West, and then in the East – that the economy was moving into recovery (Figure 10.1). The general public saw few signs of recovery at the beginning of the election year. The sudden rise of optimism remains one of the more intriguing subplots of the 1994 election. While it is debatable how keenly the general public monitored the course of the economy, the shift of public perceptions did not come totally out of thin air. The turnaround in economic perceptions mirrored movement in offic-ial data.[6] An upbeat report by Germany's leading economic institutes in the spring of 1994 received much publicity.

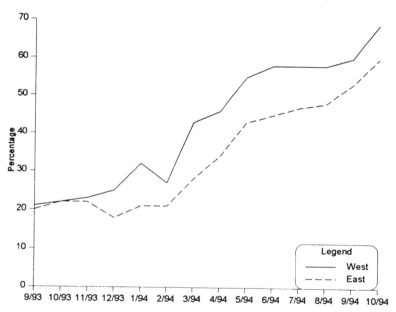

Source: Forschungsgruppe Wahlen

**Figure 10.1** Opinion that Economy is Getting Better

Chancellor Kohl seized on that news with glee, first in the campaign for the European Parliament election, and then for the Bundestag. For the SPD, of course, good economic news made bad electoral news. Rudolf Scharping must have felt the sting of truth of a remark about a British prime minister some 200 years ago: "A Government is not supported a hundredth part so much by the constant, uniform, quiet prosperity of the country as by those damned spurts which Pitt used to have just in the nick of time" (as quoted by Butler and Stokes, 1969: 389). Whatever the "damned spurt" of the German economy in 1994, the CDU/CSU made sure that the voters noticed it by touting Kohl as the *Kanzler des Aufschwungs* (chancellor of economic recovery). That was one of the campaign roles Kohl was happy to play in 1994.

Whatever the process of persuasion, the public gave the state of the German economy a favorable rating by the time of the Bundestag election. The same was even more true for appraisals of personal finances (Forschungsgruppe Wahlen, 1994). The prospects for the future, be it the overall economy or voters' own pocketbooks, were downright ecstatic by the fall of 1994. Such good economic news paid electoral dividends, as can be seen in Table 10.1. The question that aligned partisan choices especially closely was the one about economic recovery. A majority of Westerners who sensed an economic recovery was underway voted CDU/CSU or FDP (together 56 percent), whereas a majority of those not seeing signs of recovery voted SPD (57 percent). By October, the electoral balance tilted in favor of the governing parties because those who felt good about the economy outnumbered those who felt bad by a 3–1 margin in the West.

**Table 10.1** Economic Opinion and Partisan Choice

| Partisan Choice[a] | Westerners Opinion Economic Recovery is Underway? | | Easterners Opinion Economic Recovery is Underway? | |
|---|---|---|---|---|
| | Yes | No | Yes | No |
| CDU/CSU | 48 | 24 | 51 | 26 |
| SPD | 36 | 57 | 31 | 38 |
| FDP | 8 | 5 | 2 | 1 |
| Alliance 90/Greens | 8 | 14 | 6 | 7 |
| PDS | 0 | 0 | 10 | 28 |
| Total | 100% | 100% | 100% | 100% |
| (Number of Cases) | (620) | (215) | (536) | (325) |

*Source*: Forschungsgruppe Wahlen pre-election survey, October 1994.
[a]Partisan vote intention prior to election.

Compared to the West, the economic picture was more complicated in the East. On one hand, few Easterners had kind words for the present state of the economy; even CDU-partisans did not. On the other hand, much of the economic blame fell on the pre-1990 rulers, and thus would not greatly affect current voter choices. Moreover, Germans in the new states were not unhappy with their personal financial situations, and they felt optimistic about the future of the economy. That did not mean, however, that the CDU had an easy time capturing their votes. In the end, the CDU in the East rallied electoral support and edged the SPD by appealing to the same sense of economic recovery as it did in the West. The CDU beat the SPD by 51 to 31 percent among Easterners positive on recovery, while the SPD beat the CDU by 38 to 26 percent among the naysayers, with a staggering 28 percent of naysayers going to the PDS (Table 10.1). In the East, as in the West, believers in an economic turnaround far outnumbered doubters. For the governing parties, those sentiments could not have come at a better time.

*Foreigners*

However much the parties' electoral standing depended on the economy, that was not the only pressing concern of the German electorate. Issues related to foreigners in Germany preoccupied the general public for most of the previous four years (see Chapter 11). The rapid surge in the number of foreigners seeking political asylum in Germany coupled with a series of violent, and in some cases deadly, assaults on foreigners in Germany had generated this interest. In western Germany the asylum/foreigners issue ranked above all others in public concern from late 1991 to the summer of 1993 (Jung and Roth, 1994). Granted, much of the German public, in West and East, reacted with revulsion to the violence against foreigners. But at the same time, voter patience with the accelerating influx of asylum seekers was running out. Public opinion polls made it clear that Germans overwhelmingly demanded a halt of that flow (Wiegand, 1992).

The drastic change in Article 16 and the asylum law, enacted with the support of the SPD, deflated the salience of the issue. It may also have diminished the partisan tilt of public opinion, as can be gathered from Table 10.2. In both East and West, respondents expressed nearly as much faith in the ability of an SPD-led government to deal with the foreigner issue as they did with a CDU/CSU-led government. Best of all for the democratic forces, the proportion trusting neither major party was not particularly high, indicating perhaps that not many Germans were looking for extremist alternatives. For all its early bark, the foreigner issue had little electoral bite in 1994.

**Table 10.2** Preferred Party Coalition to Deal with Foreigners, the Environment, and Foreign Threats

| | Foreigners | | Environment | | Foreign Threat | |
|---|---|---|---|---|---|---|
| Preferred Party Coalition | West | East | West | East | West | East |
| CDU/CSU-led Government | 33 | 28 | 13 | 13 | 35 | 28 |
| SPD-led Government | 30 | 31 | 41 | 37 | 10 | 12 |
| Both equal | 24 | 23 | 33 | 34 | 42 | 47 |
| Neither of them | 13 | 17 | 14 | 16 | 13 | 12 |
| Total | 100% | 100% | 100% | 100% | 100% | 100% |
| CDU/CSU Lead | +3 | –3 | –28 | –24 | +25 | +16 |

*Source*: Forschungsgruppe Wahlen, pre-election survey, October 1994. The number of total cases is 1,117 for the West, and 1,056 for the East.

*Environment*

While it may be surprising, it is no great news to learn which side the environmental issue benefitted. The general public preferred an SPD-led government over a CDU/CSU-led one by a huge margin on environmental matters (Table 10.2). This had less do with the SPD by itself, than with the presence of the Greens in such a government. Without the distraction of unification that harmed them in 1990, the Greens were able in 1994 to draw on their strength as the party of the environment. Among Westerners who rated the environment as the most important problem, one of every five voted for the Greens. Although this issue failed to give the red–green combination an electoral majority, its continued salience helped the Greens mount a successful electoral comeback in 1994.

*Foreign Policy*

By most survey measures, foreign policy concerns did not arouse much public concern in 1994. The Cold War was history. For the first time in decades, Germans had lived four years without a palpable threat from abroad. Europe remained a bureaucratic abstraction, and the horrors of the Bosnian war were distant cries. To the extent that voters were divided in their assessments of the parties' abilities to deal with a foreign threat to Germany, opinion sharply favored the governing coalition over the opposition (Table 10.2). As we shall see below in examining the qualities of the chancellor candidates, those sentiments packed more electoral punch than it might seem.

### The Pull of Leaders

It is a staple of electioneering in Germany that chancellors decide elections ("Auf den Kanzler kommt es an"), even though voters cannot mark their chancellor preferences on the ballot. The campaigns of the major parties typically key on their top leaders, featuring them in larger-than-life posters, rallies of the party faithful, and television advertisements. Only the Greens have tenaciously resisted this personality cult. If anything, changes in the mass media have increased the leverage of top political leaders to reach mass audiences and personify political issues. The expansion of private television, in particular, has invited as well as compelled politicians to confront the electorate in hitherto unfamiliar settings.

Most observers would agree that the 1994 campaign concentrated heavily on the personalities of the contenders for the chancellorship. The SPD made headlines by trying out a new, more democratic means of selecting its leader, who then became the party's chancellor candidate. In the manner of an American primary, rank-and-file members of the SPD could vote directly for one of the nominees, with Rudolf Scharping the winner (see Chapter 3). In the CDU/CSU Kohl was undisputed for reelection. Campaign advertisements depicted Kohl as statesman, but also as a man of the people, and as already noted, engineer of economic recovery. If that was overkill, it was justifiable in view of Scharping's early lead over Kohl in the trial heats (Figure 10.2).

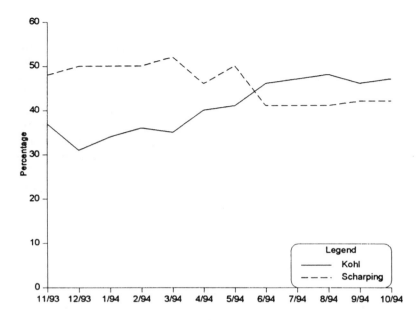

Source: Forschungsgruppe Wahlen

**Figure 10.2** The Race for Chancellor in the Opinion Polls

As the fresh challenger of a faltering incumbent, the SPD-candidate for chancellor seemed to hold the winning hand at the beginning of 1994. But then, in the spring of 1994, Kohl's standing in the eyes of the German public brightened as Scharping's star fell. "It's the economy, stupid," the attentive reader of this chapter will be quick to shout, joining many other observers. Indeed Kohl's recovery in his popular standing coincided with the economic recovery in the minds of Germans (see Figure 10.1). As they became convinced that the economy was on the mend, there was no more reason, so it would seem, to dismiss Kohl and look for another chancellor.

On the other hand, as even pundits without a friendly bone for Kohl pointed out, the challenger was not blameless for this reversal of fortune. Theo Sommer of *Die Zeit*, Germany's leading opinion weekly, listed a series of Scharping's miscues and missteps (Sommer, 1994). There was his failure to prevent a CDU/CSU victory in the presidential election; the confused discussion

**Table 10.3** The Perceived Qualities of the Chancellor Candidates

| Who is more likely to | Westerners Kohl | Scharping | Kohl Lead | Easterners Kohl | Scharping | Kohl Lead |
|---|---|---|---|---|---|---|
| Stand up for German interests | 57 | 11 | +46 | 57 | 11 | +46 |
| Lead government | 45 | 21 | +24 | 45 | 22 | +23 |
| Be forceful | 40 | 22 | +18 | 43 | 22 | +21 |
| Be responsible | 33 | 17 | +16 | 31 | 28 | + 3 |
| Be trustworthy | 30 | 21 | + 9 | 30 | 29 | + 1 |
| Be honest | 19 | 22 | − 3 | 15 | 26 | −11 |
| Advance social justice | 13 | 54 | −41 | 13 | 65 | −52 |

*Source*: Forschungsgruppe Wahlen, pre-election survey, October 1994. The total number of cases is 1,117 for the West, and 1,056 for the East.

of taxes and incomes; and the brush of the SPD with the PDS in Saxony-Anhalt, tarring the party red (once again). Moreover, the creation of an SPD leadership troika (Scharping, Oskar Lafontaine, the SPD's standard bearer in 1990, and Gerhard Schröder) only increased doubts that Scharping could take on Kohl by himself. Ironically, many Germans believed, as documented by our October survey, that the SPD would have done better in the 1994 election with Gerhard Schröder, than it did with Scharping.

Whatever Scharping's shortcomings, the electorate's verdict in 1994 must also recognize an "iron law" of German electoral politics. Scharping was by no means the first challenger to suffer from the comparison with the incumbent chancellor. In the history of federal elections, no challenger has ever outshone the incumbent chancellor in the public estimate. On election day, German voters revere the incumbent and doubt the challenger. It is nothing personal. Some political leaders, including Kohl himself, have found that their standing with the public miraculously brightened once they moved from the position of chancellor candidate into the office. Hence, Scharping can console himself with the fact that all challengers have faced an almost insurmountable block in the public's mind.

If there is one domain where the challenger, almost by definition, suffers discrimination, it is foreign policy. Asked who was more capable of safeguarding German interests *vis-à-vis* other nations, respondents overwhelmingly picked Kohl over

Scharping (Table 10.3). Even SPD voters conceded that Kohl was better in this domain than was the candidate of their own party. The CDU/CSU missed no opportunity to remind voters of Kohl's standing on the world stage as a leader equal to Bill Clinton, François Mitterrand, and Russian leaders Gorbachev and Yeltsin. The departure of Allied forces from Berlin during the election year provided a picture-perfect backdrop for Kohl to act the statesman-role. Such displays of chancellorship simply left Scharping at a loss, inevitably creating an unfavorable comparison for him. On the surface, specific issues of foreign policy may not have aroused much concern in 1994, but the credentials of government leaders in that domain remained salient to German voters.

Table 10.3 indicates that there were several other areas where Kohl's qualifications surpassed Scharping in the eyes of the German public. By varying margins, Kohl enjoyed the higher rating with respect to leading the government, being forceful, responsible, and trustworthy. There was only one item where Scharping was rated decidedly better than Kohl: the question of who was the better champion of social justice. But that seemed to be the party's reputation rubbing off on the nominee. While the challenger's personal assets derived from his party, the chancellor's personal assets derived from his office. Only by holding the chancellorship could Kohl demonstrate his abilities, in particular, the ability to safeguard German interests in foreign policy. In the end, challengers for the chancellorship face a catch-22 dilemma: the electorate measures them by criteria that they can only meet if they were chancellor. It is unlikely that Kohl has forgotten the frustration of coming up short as a challenger, as he did in 1976.[7]

The unwillingness of German voters to give the challenger the benefit of the doubt seems closely intertwined with their reluctance to throw the governing parties out of office on election day. In German elections one cannot find the likes of Jimmy Carter and George Bush, that is, incumbents whom the voters rejected at the polls in 1980 and 1992, respectively. The first election in Germany to produce such a turnover most likely will be the one in which the public finally rejects the incumbent chancellor in favor of the challenger.

## The Hold of Parties

Our detailed attention to the issues and candidates in the 1994 election should not obscure the fact that these opinions were often derived from voters' general sense of partisanship – what American researchers would recognize as party identification. An enduring attachment to a particular party makes many voters give their party the nod on handling an issue like the economy, or prefering its chancellor candidate. Viewed from that perspective, the continued success of the CDU/CSU in defeating the SPD in Bundestag elections may be attributed to its superior partisan firepower rather than to specific circumstances of the 1994 election.

Many analysts, however, do not find this a compelling interpretation of electoral choices in western Germany, let alone in the East. In the age of partisan dealignment the established political parties have been losing their grip on the electorate (Bürklin and Roth, 1994; Dalton, 1992). There is no dispute that the traditional bastions of party support, namely church-going Catholics for the CDU/CSU and unionized workers for the SPD, have shrunk. Moreover, the parties themselves have lost members, and voter turnout has fallen. In the years leading up to the 1994 Bundestag election, the talk of partisan decline reached a shrill pitch with claims of *Politikverdrossenheit* (disgust with politics) in Germany (e.g., Scheuch and Scheuch, 1992). To be sure, several state elections between 1990 and 1994 produced the unusual results of both CDU and SPD suffering simultaneous losses. The normal interchange between government and opposition seemed disrupted. As the stocks of those parties tumbled, a newly formed party with the curious oxymoron, *Statt-Partei* (Instead Party), captured more than 5 percent of the vote in the 1994 Hamburg election. Were Germans clamoring for their version of a Ross Perot? Or for an Italian-style party upheaval? Or worse, was it true that "the German people cannot love politics."[8]

One could not see signs of partisan upheaval in the vote outcome of the 1994 election. The major party in government, the CDU/CSU, slipped barely two percentage points, which roughly equaled the gain of the SPD. Neither the *Statt-Partei* nor any other newcomer made any electoral headway. To be sure, the western Greens nearly doubled their vote share, but that simply reinstated them in the Bundestag. And yes, the PDS grew to a pesky size, defying all the premature obituaries (see Chapter 6). Apart from this rather special case, to be dealt with below in more detail, the raw numbers of the 1994 returns speak more of partisan stability than of volatility. So was all the talk about party decay much ado about nothing?

To gain some perspective on this question, we charted a critical indicator of partisanship for the western public. Figure 10.3 documents the change in the strength of party identification between 1976 and 1994. There can be no dispute that the share of strong identifiers has dropped sharply, from close to 50 percent in 1976 to less than 30 percent by 1994. At the same time, the proportion of people without any party identification rose from a tiny minority in 1976 to over 30 percent in 1994. Like Caesar's Gaul, the electorate in western Germany is now divided in three parts (of equal size): strong, weak, and no partisans. In all fairness, it should be noted that 1976 represents a postwar peak of partisan intensity. Partisanship in the Federal Republic grew steadily until the mid-1970s even while other countries such as the United States were already experiencing partisan dealignment (Norpoth, 1983). It was only in the 1980s, it seems, that Germany caught up with the trend.

But as always, latecomers and converts catch up with a vengeance. The 1990–1994 period unravelled voter ties to political parties most brutally, lending some credence to the current alarm about disgust with parties, if not disgust with politics altogether. The 1994 election reversed the sharp drop somewhat, but that kind of rally is typical for election years and has yet to produce a lasting benefit for partisanship. Most disturbing perhaps was that both major parties lost devoted partisans at about the same rate between 1980 and 1994. If the CDU/CSU suffered from exhaustion in government, the SPD failed to re-charge its electoral energy in opposition. Partisan dealignment is a perverse form of a non-zero-sum game. All partisan players lose.

For some parties this loss in partisans can turn into a life-or-death question. By one clinical test of electoral science, the FDP died in 1994: the incidence of identification with the FDP was barely one in a hundred in the old Federal Republic. What kept the party alive at the polls was a large vote transfusion from CDU/CSU identifiers. Without it, the FDP would have fallen short of the 5 percent requirement. True, the FDP has benefitted

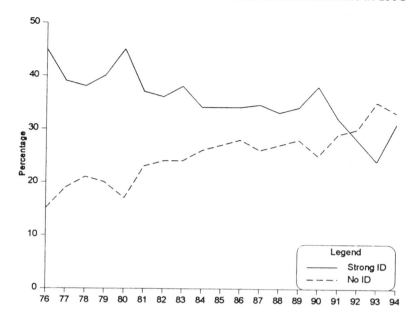

Source: Forschungsgruppe Wahlen. Note that partisanship tends to strengthen in election years (1976, 1980, 1983, 1987, 1990 and 1994).

**Figure 10.3** Percentage of Western Germans with Strong or no Party Identification

from such transfusions before, but it could always count on a critical mass of loyalists. That no longer existed in 1994. The typical FDP voter in the old Federal Republic in 1994 had CDU/CSU loyalties. It was purely through the kindness of its partner in government that the FDP survived in the West. Not being able to count on such generosity among the newer voters in the East, the FDP fell below 5 percent (4.0 percent). By May of 1995, after state elections in North Rhine-Westphalia and Bremen, the FDP was no longer represented in eleven of the sixteen state parliaments.

The cooling of partisan ardor in the electorate spells trouble beyond the fate of specific parties. It saps the energy of democratic politics. Nobody should be surprised, for example, to see voting turnout drop sharply, just as the share of strong partisans falls. Whereas in 1976, 91 percent of eligible voters participated in the Bundestag election, only 81 percent did so in the old Federal Republic in 1994. The strength of party identification is a proven determinant of electoral turnout, in Germany as in the United States (Abramson and Aldrich 1982; Rattinger, 1994: 95–6). Falling participation cannot wholely be explained by declining partisanship, but it is one of the more powerful forces, and for good reasons.

As in sports, it is difficult for a citizen to get involved in the game of politics without a team to support. Who follows football or basketball just for the intrinsic beauty (or savagery) of the game? If anything, this would seem even more difficult to do in politics than in sports. Independents (non-partisans) are notoriously low in voting turnout. What is at stake for them in electoral contests? Analysts have debunked the myth that non-partisans size up parties and candidates on their merits; instead, compared to partisans, most non-partisans lack the motivation to follow politics and go to the polls. It is simple arithmetic that, as this group grows, the percentage of citizens showing up at the polls declines, barring other changes that would feed voter desire to participate.

Oddly enough, this points to a self-adjusting tendency of the body politic. If partisan dealignment increases the ranks of non-partisans and thus the ranks of non-voters, the consequences for electoral outcomes may be mitigated. In other words, a growing mass of floating voters may not materialize if they simply drift to non-participation. If that is so, the fraying of partisanship need not spell greater electoral turbulence.

### The Roots of PDS Support

There were many instances in the 1994 election where the voters in the East felt, thought, and acted just like the voters in the West. Even where opinions changed, whether it be on economic recovery or chancellor candidates, they did so in close tandem on both sides of the former border. Still, four years after unification, there is also evidence of a deepening estrangement between eastern and western voters. In the electoral arena, the most palpable difference between East and West is the PDS. Practically invisible as a partisan force in the West with barely 1 percent of the vote in 1994, this party of former Communists captured one of every five votes in the East. Its strength in the East was twenty times that in the West, marking it as a truly eastern regional party; all other parties in the Bundestag, by varying margins, did better in the West than in the East. For the once-disgraced party of the old regime, living well electorally in the age of democracy must be the best revenge.

The PDS' survival should not be all that surprising for a party that monopolized the attention of its citizenry for almost half a century, however unpleasant that was for many of them. From the point of view of political socialization, the party of socialism (SED then, PDS now) was in a perfect position to foster partisan identifications. The leading party of the old regime missed few opportunities to instill the correct party spirit in its captive audience. The western concept of party identification is not inapplicable in the East (Rattinger, 1994; Schmitt, 1994). In our October 1994 pre-election survey, one in ten Easterners expressed an attachment to the PDS. Anyone unimpressed with that proportion should note that almost half of the Easterners lacked any party tie whatsoever, and that neither CDU nor SPD commanded the allegiance of more than one in five each. Even more important, the devotion to their party ran much deeper among PDS-partisans: almost half of them expressed a strong attachment, whereas that was true for just over one quarter of CDU and SPD partisans. As for sheer devotion, the PDS can hold its own with the two major parties in the East. In addition, there are probably good reasons to be skeptical of the true attachments of Easterners to the CDU or SPD, many of whom probably fit the image of a *Wendehals*, that proverbial creature of opportunity.

The PDS drew its voters in 1994 heavily from the ranks of identifiers (66 percent), compared to the votes for the CDU and SPD (55 percent each). PDS-voters also surpassed voters for all the other parties in their political interest. Only one in four eastern CDU-voters expressed a strong interest in politics – the lowest for any party – compared to one in two for the PDS. The PDS is not a "flash party," scraping the bottom of the electoral barrel, but a firmly entrenched party with a cadre of devoted and involved loyalists.

Another distinctive feature of PDS voters was their ideological profile. Asked what they thought of the idea of socialism, eight in ten PDS supporters expressed a high or very high regard for socialism (Table 10.4). For some respondents, this may have been

*The Election Process*

**Table 10.4** Opinions about Socialism and Unification by Partisan Choice (Easterners only)

| | Voting Preference | | | |
| | CDU | SPD | A 90/G | PDS |
| --- | --- | --- | --- | --- |
| Opinion of Socialism | | | | |
| High, Very High | 10 | 27 | 48 | 80 |
| Medium | 39 | 51 | 39 | 15 |
| Low, Very Low | <u>51</u> | <u>22</u> | <u>12</u> | <u>5</u> |
| Total | 100% | 100% | 100% | 100% |
| Feeling about Unification | | | | |
| Joy | 72 | 38 | 51 | 20 |
| Worry | <u>28</u> | <u>62</u> | <u>49</u> | <u>80</u> |
| Total | 100% | 100% | 100% | 100% |
| (Number of Cases) | (358) | (288) | (56) | (145) |

*Source*: Forschungsgruppe Wahlen, pre-election survey, October 1994.

just another way of professing a partisan identification, but for many this response squared with their broad ideological positions (Falter and Klein, 1994). The question of socialism sharply segregated the vote of Easterners, with CDU-voters on one side and PDS-voters on the other. On this dimension, SPD-voters resembled CDU-voters far more than they did PDS-voters. It augurs well for an avowedly socialist party that one in three Easterners holds the idea of socialism in high or very high regard.

PDS-voters in the East were also the partisan group deploring unification the most. By a 4–1 margin, they expressed worry over the problems unification had wrought rather than joy that the division of the country was over (Table 10.4). To be sure, a narrow majority of Easterners shared this point of view, but what distinguished PDS-voters was that they combined a negative assessment of unification with a positive view of socialism. That is the gestalt of the PDS-voter. This is the kind of voter who is a died-in-the-wool socialist and hence objects to unification because it tossed socialism in the trash compactor of western capitalism. Such reasoning applies to the hard core of PDS-voters, but it does not account for the surge of the party's vote in the East in 1994. The principled opponents of unification were already in its fold in 1990. For the PDS to enlarge its electoral support in 1994, it had to make strides elsewhere.

In appealing to discontent over unification, the PDS had stiff competition from other parties such as the SPD and Alliance 90/Greens. Yet, by 1994 the two latter parties were largely, or appeared to be, extensions of their western origins. This left the PDS as the only partisan voice speaking with an eastern accent. At the same time, as the Wall and the Stasi began to fade into the darkness of history, the PDS could conjure up an endearing image of a socialist wonderland. Already in state elections before 1994, the PDS succeeded in converting disappointments and resentments arising from unification into a growing fondness for socialism. Any voter troubled more by the shortcomings of today than by the deprivations of yesterday became a natural target of the PDS appeal.

For all the ideological commitment, partisan zeal, and anti-Western resentment of its supporters, the PDS needed extra help in getting into the Bundestag with a sizable presence. By the rules of the German electoral system, a party has to win more than 5 percent of the second vote nationally, or else at least three districts, to secure a proportional share of Bundestag seats. With the 5 percent goal out of reach, the PDS banked on the district route (see Chapter 6).[9] In two districts the PDS candidates won handily: Gregor Gysi and Christa Luft, with 48.9 and 44.4 percent, respectively. But in the other two, the winning margins were quite close. Some data suggest that the PDS candidates benefitted from the generosity of SPD voters. According to a special exit poll conducted by the Forschungsgruppe Wahlen in East Berlin, 17 percent of SPD voters (second vote) chose the respective PDS candidate in their district with their first vote (Forschungsgruppe Wahlen, 1994: 16–17). That amounted to roughly 6 percent of the total vote volume, enough to make the difference in the two close contests. It remains puzzling, however, that this vote-splitting denied the district to the SPD, whose candidates had the next best chance of winning. Whatever the explanation, in three of the four districts that the PDS captured it surpassed the SPD in the second-vote count as well. PDS support may have been deep enough to pull off victories in three districts without the kindness of strangers.

## Conclusion

What lessons can we draw from our analysis of German voters in 1994? The most obvious conclusion would be that economics decides elections. The classic ingredients of official statistics, public perceptions, and partisan evaluations came together in a perfect mix for the incumbent parties in 1994. The German economy experienced "one of those damned spurts in the nick of time," the public noticed, and decided to give Kohl's government electoral credit for it. A corollary lesson might be a vindication of the political business cycle (Tufte, 1978). The government pursued an economic policy that, while creating hardship in the first part of its term, was designed to ignite an upturn close to the election. In so doing, the policymakers banked on the short-sightedness of an electorate that would not remember distant pain or broken promises. Others might note the special sensitivity to economic performance that has long been considered a trademark of German political culture (Almond and Verba, 1963). Of all people, Germans need no reminder of the political consequences of the economy. The twin calamities of hyperinflation and depression in the 1920s did much to snuff out the Weimar Republic, while the "economic miracle" of the 1950s solidified the fledgling Federal Republic.

The economic interpretation of the German vote in 1994 nonetheless has limitations. Consider the US presidential election two years earlier. That election was largely fought over the economy as well. But in the US election the incumbent, George Bush, lost. In light of the economy, Chancellor Kohl should have fared no better in 1994 than President Bush did in 1992. The US economy recovered from a recession at roughly the same time before the 1992 election and grew at about the same pace during the election year as did the German economy relative to the 1994 election.[10] Under those same conditions, one incumbent of a twelve-year old administration won his bid for reelection, while the other one lost. How come the German voters saw an economic recovery, whereas their American counterparts failed to see one? If anything, the much higher unemployment rate should have made the German public less inclined to see good times.

To resolve this puzzle, we may draw on another lesson from our analysis: the *Kanzlerbonus* (chancellor effect). As in previous elections, the German electorate preferred the incumbent for the job of chancellor. Helmut Kohl may very well have been the better man for the job in 1994 by some expert judgment. Yet it is revealing that the public gave Kohl his best ratings over Scharping in domains where Scharping, as the challenger, had almost no chance to prove himself, such as in foreign policy. The public's criteria for judging prospective chancellors seem biased in favor the incumbent, hinting at a strong aversion to risk. In the Federal Republic, it is not the challenger, but the incumbent who gets the benefit of the doubt from the general public. The flaws of the challenger always loom larger than the disappointments with the incumbent. It would take us far beyond our electoral evidence to fathom the depth of that risk aversion. Is it the old reverence of the powers-that-be? Or is it the lesson of taking an ill-fated electoral gamble some sixty years ago with disastrous consequences? If that made German voters demand proof beyond reasonable doubt from challengers for the highest office, being timid may be the prudent thing to do.

## Notes

1. Dieter Roth wishes to acknowledge his collaboration with Matthias Jung, also of the Forschungsgruppe Wahlen. See the analysis by Jung and Roth (1994).
2. A party obtains "overhang" seats by winning more single-member districts in a given state than it is entitled to based on its percentage of second votes (those cast for party lists) in that state. This typically happens when a party sweeps all district races in a given state, yet garners fewer than 50 percent of the second votes in that same state. For the specific details of the 1994 results see Chapter 1.
3. In western Germany, 1,117 respondents were interviewed by telephone (10–14 October); in the East, 1,056 respondents were interviewed in person (4–14 October). The method of selection in both cases was by multi-stage probability sampling. Respondents were weighted to reflect household size as well as the age and gender distribution of the voting-age populations

in East and West. With a sample of 1,000, chances are 19 in 20 that results close to 50 percent differ by no more than 3 percentage points in either direction from what would have been obtained if all eligible Germans had been interviewed.

4. Strictly speaking, the reference to "voters" should be qualified since the data come from a pre-election survey. Our measure elicits the party a respondent planned to vote for on election day, not the one that was actually chosen. In 1994, however, those vote intentions proved to be highly accurate predictors of actual vote decisions.

5. Asked who was better able to deal with unemployment, western respondents in our October survey favored an SPD-led government over a CDU/CSU-led government by only 31 to 24 percent, with 42 percent seeing no difference. The gap, however, was somewhat wider among eastern respondents: 39.5 percent favoring the SPD side, compared to 23 percent for the CDU side.

6. After four consecutive quarters of decline, the real gross domestic product in the West rebounded in the second quarter of 1993, and proceeded to grow at the rate of more than 2 percent in the first half of the election year (*Week in Germany*, September 10, 1993; September 23, 1994; October 14, 1994). In the East, the economy rose from depression-type devastation, posting a 9 percent growth rate in the first half of 1994. Even the unemployment rolls began to descend from their record-breaking 4 million level, further diminishing the electoral sting of this issue.

7. In the 1976 election, the incumbent Helmut Schmidt (SPD) led the chancellor trial heat over challenger Helmut Kohl by 53 to 40 percent, and the governing SPD–FDP coalition defeated the CDU/CSU in the Bundestag election. In that year Chancellor Helmut Schmidt (SPD) enjoyed all the advantages in personal qualities that Kohl did in 1994.

8. Thomas Mann said this in a book of political essays written during the First World War and entitled, with characteristic irony, *Betrachtungen eines Unpolitischen* (*Reflections of an Apolitical Man*). See Mann (1922: xxxiv).

9. It was the first time since 1957 that a party successfully used that strategy, and probably the only time without an agreement involving other parties. In 1957, the German Party (DP) won enough districts, but only because the CDU did not field

candidates of its own in several districts and encouraged its voters to vote for the DP candidates.

10. The US recession that began in July 1990 officially ended in March 1991, compared to the second quarter of 1993 for the (West) German economy. Real GDP in the United States grew at an average of 2.5 percent during the first three quarters of 1992, practically the same as the rate for western Germany in the first half of 1994. For the US data, see Hershey (1992), for the western German data, see note 6.

## References

Abramson, Paul R., and John H. Aldrich. 1982. "The Decline of Electoral Participation in America," *American Political Science Review* 76: 502–21.

Almond, Gabriel, and Sidney Verba. 1963. *The Civic Culture.* Princeton: Princeton University Press.

Bürklin, Wilhelm and Dieter Roth, eds. 1994. *Das Superwahljahr.* Köln: Bund-Verlag.

Butler, David, and Donald Stokes. 1969. *Political Change in Britain.* New York: St Martin's Press.

Dalton, Russell. 1992. "Two German Electorates?" in Gordon Smith et al., eds. *Developments in German Politics.* London: Macmillan.

Falter, Jürgen W., and Markus Klein. 1994. "Die Wähler der PDS bei der Bundestagswahl 1994," *Aus Politik und Zeitgeschichte* (23 December): 35–46.

Forschungsgruppe Wahlen. 1994. *Bundestagswahl 1994.* Eine Analyse der Wahl zum 13. Bundestag am 16. Oktober 1994. Bericht Nr. 76. Mannheim: Forschungsgruppe Wahlen.

Goergen, Christian and Helmut Norpoth. 1992. "Government Turnover and Economic Accountability." *Electoral Studies* 10: 191–207.

Hershey, Robert D. 1992. "This Just In: Recession Ended 21 Months Ago," *The New York Times* (23 December): D1.

Jung, Matthias and Dieter Roth. 1994. "Kohls knappster Sieg," *Aus Politik und Zeitgeschichte* (23 December): 3–15.

Mann, Thomas. 1922. *Betrachtungen eines Unpolitischen*. Berlin: S. Fischer.

Norpoth, Helmut. 1983. "The Making of a More Partisan Electorate in West Germany," *British Journal of Political Science* 14: 53–71.

——. 1992. *Confidence Regained: Economics, Mrs Thatcher, and the British Voter*. Ann Arbor: University of Michigan Press.

Rattinger, Hans. 1994. "Parteiidentifikationen in Ost- und Westdeutschland nach der Vereinigung," in Oskar Niedermayer and Klaus von Beyme, eds. *Politische Kultur in Ost- und Westdeutschland*. Berlin: Akademie Verlag.

Scheuch, Erwin K. and Ute Scheuch. 1992. *Cliquen, Klüngel und Karrieren*. Reinbeck: Rowohlt Taschenbuch Verlag.

Schmitt, Karl. 1994. "Im Osten nichts Neues? Das Kernland der Arbeiterbewegung und die Zukunft der politischen Linken," in Wilhelm Bürklin and Dieter Roth, eds. *Das Superwahljahr*. Köln: Bund-Verlag.

Sommer, Theo. 1994. "So wenig Aufbruch war noch nie." *Die Zeit*, Oct. 14.

Tufte, Edward R. 1978. *Political Control of the Economy*. Princeton: Princeton University Press.

Wiegand, Erich. 1992. "Zunahme der Ausländerfeindlichkeit? Einstellungen zu Fremden in Deutschland und Europe," *ZUMA Nachrichten* 31: 7–28.

# IV Social and Political Developments

# 11
# Deutschland den Deutschen? Migration and Naturalization in the 1994 Campaign and Beyond

## *Manfred Kuechler*

The shameful riots in the eastern German city of Rostock in the summer of 1992 provided a particularly poignant reminder that Germany had become home – at least, residence – to a large segment of foreigners, and that the relationship between native Germans and foreigners had become precarious. More generally, 1992 produced a steep increase in criminal acts against foreigners (*fremdenfeindliche Straftaten* in the terminology of Germany's official statistics) from 2,426 in the previous year to 6,336, including 32 cases of (attempted) murder and homicide (Beauftragte der Bundesregierung für die Belange der Ausländer, 1994: 59). The increased level of violent hostility continued in 1993 with 6,721 criminal acts officially recorded before a marked decline in 1994 to 3,100.

Drawing on a variety of public opinion data, Kuechler (1994) showed that the spectacular rise of xenophobic expression in 1992 was embedded in a much longer period of strained relations between western Germans and foreigners. While German attitudes towards the *Gastarbeiter* had gradually turned more positive, a new wave of migrants in the form of asylum seekers and (to some extent) resettlers had triggered new hostility.[1] This analysis indicated that the driving force behind xenophobic attitudes were economic and social fears and a perception of relative deprivation. Despite vast differences in their actual exposure to the foreign population – 97 percent of all foreigners live in the former West Germany – Germans in East and West displayed strikingly similar patterns of hostility towards foreigners. Moreover, a comparison of attitudes towards foreigners across the publics of the European Union revealed the same pattern of social envy and fear.

Xenophobia, then, is not a uniquely German problem; it is widespread in Western Europe including France and Great Britain (see also Wrench and Solomos, 1993). Xenophobia is not restricted to small groups of marginal extremists, neo-Nazis, skinheads, and similar groups, although a majority of manifest violent acts against foreigners can probably be attributed to members of those groups, especially among youths (see Otto and Merten, 1993). Rather, xenophobia is a latent trait found in a much broader segment of the population. It is nourished by a mindset receptive to right-wing populism. Ideas and policy preferences stemming from right-wing populism are not restricted to openly right-extremist or fascist parties. The electoral success of such parties, though, is the most visible indication of an emergence of xenophobia (see e.g., Betz, 1994).

In Germany, right-wing parties enjoyed spectacular success in several Landtagswahlen during the 1990–1994 legislative period (see Chapter 7). The Republikaner reached a record 10.9 percent of the vote in Baden-Württemberg in April 1992, the DVU gained parliamentary seats in Bremen (September 1991) and Schleswig-Holstein (April 1992) with over 6 percent of the vote. Though both parties failed the 5 percent threshold in Hamburg (September 1993), their combined total of 7.6 percent in a city-state that was long seen as a bastion of liberalism and civic liberties was shocking. Across the border, in France, the National Front and its leader Jean-Marie Le Pen have exploited xenophobic sentiment for a long period, although the party was severely handicapped in winning parliamentary seats by the French electoral system. As a candidate in the presidential elections of 1988 and 1995, however, Le Pen received 14.3 and 15.0 percent of the popular vote running on a blatantly anti-immigrant platform. In addition, a second openly xenophobic candidate, Philippe de Villiers, won another 5 percent of the popular vote in 1995. Similarly, the National Front and the group headed by de Villiers fared extremely well in the 1994 elections to the European Parliament, which used a proportional electoral system. Together they garnered about 20 percent of the vote.

In Germany, then, the emergence of overtly xenophobic behavior, the rise of criminal acts against foreigners, the early success of right-wing parties in state elections, and the concern abroad seemed to indicate that migration and naturalization issues would play in major role in the 1994 Bundestagswahl. However, this was not the case. Unlike the 1995 French presidential elections, where the extreme Right forced the immigration issue on the political agenda putting the mainstream contenders on the defensive, a discussion of migration and naturalization was strangely absent from the German campaign in 1994 – despite stark differences in party programs and election platforms. True, the change in asylum rights in mid-1993 alleviated the sense of urgency to deal with these issues. However, the larger problems of immigration, integration, and naturalization remained un-solved (see Hoskin, 1991). The 1994 campaign was an exercise in collective denial. From the point of view of each political party, this was a rational – meaning: vote maximizing – decision, as we will show below. Yet, sooner or later, both the public and the political actors will have to face these issues.

In this chapter I briefly summarize the objective situation of foreigners to outline the quantitative scope of the problem. Second, I present trend data on mass sentiment towards for-eigners updating and expanding earlier work (Kuechler, 1994). Then I discuss policy and legal changes effected during the legislative period 1990–1994. This leads to a comparative assess-ment of party platforms and programs and, subsequently, an explanation of why no party talked about the foreigner issue during the campaign. I conclude with an outlook on what pro-gress may be made in the new Bundestag.

### Foreigners in Germany: Facts and Figures[2]

As of 31 December 1993, the foreign population in Germany was 6.8 million or 8.5 percent of the total population. After a period of relative stability between 1980 and 1988 at a level of roughly 4.5 million, the foreign population has grown steadily by about 400,000 each year since then. By 1994, the share of non-citizens in Germany clearly exceeded the levels in France (6.3 percent) and Great Britain (4.3 percent). The proportion of foreigners in Germany is second only to Belgium (9.1 percent) among the countries in the European Union.[3] Even without new immigration, the share of foreigners in Germany will rise as a consequence of generational replacement and a marked and growing difference in the fertility rate between Germans and foreigners. In 1993, 12.9 percent of all children born in Germany were foreigners, a level well above the share of 8.5 percent foreigners in the total population.[4] The spatial distribution of foreigners is highly uneven. Just over 200,000 foreigners or a mere 3 percent live in eastern Germany. Almost 75 percent of all foreigners live in just four states: North Rhine-Westphalia, Baden-Württemberg, Bavaria, and Hesse. Furthermore, foreigners are heavily concentrated in the urban areas with shares exceeding 20 percent in the cities of Frankfurt, Stuttgart, and Munich.

Non-citizens fall into three major groups with significant differences in their legal status and in the policy problems they constitute. First, roughly 3 million are workers and their dependents from countries outside the European Union, commonly referred to as *Gastarbeiter* (guest workers). The term *Gastarbeiter* dates back to the 1950s when the German economy experienced a labor shortage and the Federal Republic recruited foreign labor from several countries including Italy, Spain, Portugal, Turkey, Greece, and Yugoslavia. The foreign labor force increased from less than 100,000 in 1955 to 2.6 million in 1973. These workers were considered temporary residents and were expected to eventually return to their home countries. However, many of these workers decided to stay and to bring their families to Germany as well. As a result of the economic crisis in the early 1970s, the German government reversed itself and issue a ban in November 1973 on further recruitment (*Anwerbestopp*). It is still in effect today. Over the years, various attempts were made to reduce the number of guest workers, with very limited success (see Edye, 1987). However, the legal status of many of these workers and their families has changed significantly, not due to a change in German laws but rather as a by-product of European integration.

The second group of foreigners arises from the free movement of goods *and people* as laid down in the Treaty of Rome. As of January 1993, citizens of member countries of the European Union have a legal right to take residence in other member countries and pursue gainful employment as they wish. Consequently, workers and their dependents from Greece, Spain, or Portugal are no longer subject to the restrictive regulations of other guest workers. Likewise, Germany could experience a significant immigration from within the European Union despite its continuing claim not to be an "immigration country." In practice, however, this has not happened. The number of foreigners that are EU citizens increased by just 2 percent from 1992 to 1993 while its share among all non-citizens even decreased from 23.2 to 22.3 percent in the same time period.

The third group of 2 million refugees in Germany is rather heterogeneous. It is comprised of people who were granted political asylum in accordance with Articles 16 and 16a of the German constitution (11.9 percent in 1993), people whose application for asylum is under review (27.5 percent), *de facto* refugees (37.8 percent), and refugees from countries affected by war or civil war (20 percent). The last category consists of people from the former Yugoslavia. A modification of the foreigner law that took effect on 1 July 1993 introduced a simplified admittance procedure for this group. Their stay, however, is considered as only temporary since they waived their right to apply for political asylum. The truly problematic subgroups are asylum applicants and *de facto* refugees which together account for about two-thirds of all refugees. Given the extremely low rates of success for asylum applications (the rate was well below 10 percent of all cases decided in any given year since 1986 and reached a low of 2.3 percent in the first half of 1993), a large segment of asylum applicants eventually ends up in the category of *de facto* refugee. In theory, persons whose application is rejected will be deported. Yet, for a variety of political, legal, and humanitarian reasons, deportation is often stayed.

Across all three categories of foreigners, the largest national group is the Turks with 1.9 million or 27.9 percent of all foreigners in 1993, followed by the Yugoslavs with 930,000 or 13.5 percent (not counting people from the now independent territories of Croatia, Bosnia, Slovenia, and Macedonia which together make up about another 300,000). Other major groups include Italians (563,000), Greeks (351,000), and Poles (260,000). To put things in perspective, there are under 100,000 French residing in Germany, and there are 108,000 Americans.[5] The number of Turks has increased from 1.6 million in 1989 to 1.9 million in 1993 (roughly 20 percent); however, their share among all foreigners decreased from 33 percent to 28 percent. In this period, about 90,000 Turks came to Germany seeking political asylum, but most of the growth of the Turkish population in

Germany is due to fertility. In contrast to workers from countries that are (now) members of the European Union, e.g., Italians, Greeks, or Spaniards, there are few legal avenues for Turks to take up residence in Germany or to shift their residence freely back and forth between their home country and Germany.

Overall, more than half of all foreigners have been living in Germany for more than ten years, and about one quarter have stayed for more than twenty years. There are marked variations by national origin. As of December 1992, 85 percent of the Spanish, 73 percent of the Italian, and two-thirds of the Turkish population had been in Germany for at least ten years. Unfortunately, these figures do not correct for minors. The share of foreigners that have spent a significant part of their life in Germany, then, is even higher. In elementary schools, Turkish students account for over 40 percent of all foreign students, an indication of the roots the Turkish population has developed in Germany, notwithstanding their unsatisfactory legal status and the lack of integration.

German naturalization procedures are another distinctive aspect of this issue. Traditionally, Germany has not encouraged foreigners to become German citizens. Apart from fairly recent attempts at liberalizing the German naturalization law – to be discussed below – Germany has maintained its position as a non-immigration country. In each year from 1972 to 1991, the percentage of naturalizations did not exceed one half of a percent of all foreigners.[6] In 1992, after some modest reforms, the naturalization rate rose to 0.6 percent. In absolute numbers, naturalizations rose from about 20,000 in 1990 and 27,000 in 1991 to 37,000 in 1992. Among Turks, the naturalization rate is even lower: below 0.2 percent in 1990 and 1991 and just 0.4 percent in 1992.

The process of European integration has opened new avenues for legal migration that seem irreversible. Since 1993, citizens of countries belonging to the European Union can freely take residence and seek employment in Germany. This has not (yet) spurred a new wave of immigration, but it has improved the legal status of many who originally came as guest workers. Non-EU citizens need to apply for residence, which is granted in various forms ranging from an *Aufenthaltsbefugnis* (the least desirable form) to an *Aufenthaltsberechtigung* (the most desirable form – roughly equivalent to a "green card" in the United States).

After certain periods of stay and contingent upon other requirements, the residence status can be upgraded. Until very recently,
however, much was left to the discretion of the local authorities.

Despite an often long residence in Germany, many foreigners
enjoy only limited civil rights. As in the United States, non-
citizens are not eligible to vote or to seek political office. As part
of the Maastricht Treaty, however, citizens of EU countries will
be able to vote in municipal elections and in elections for the
European Parliament. To accommodate this provision of the
Maastricht Treaty, Article 28 of the Basic Law was changed
accordingly (by an amending act passed in December 1992).[7]

In summary, the vast majority of the foreign population in
Germany is permanent, an important part of the labor force, and
growing due to age structure and fertility behavior. Foreigners
are a constitutive part of German society, though they are by no
means universally accepted or fully integrated. The legal status
of foreigners in Germany differs vastly and these legal differences need to be taken into account when policy options are
discussed. Yet the seemingly sharp distinctions between recent
asylum seekers and guest workers with long residences in
Germany get blurred when the underlying social and economic
process is considered. As one of the most affluent nations and
geographically situated in the middle of Europe, Germany has
attracted migrants living in less fortunate conditions and will
continue to do so. The most recent wave of asylum seekers may
have been curbed, but Germany will be forced to face the issues
of migration and naturalization. Whether the Germans like it or
not, they have become a multicultural society. Temporarily, related problems may lose urgency but they will not disappear.

## Mass Sentiment

We begin our analysis of mass sentiments by looking at the salience of foreigner-related issues. We use the responses to an
open-ended question routinely included in the monthly
*Politbarometer* surveys conducted by the Forschungsgruppe
Wahlen (Kuechler, 1994). Respondents are asked to name the two
most important problems facing Germany. Unlike importance
ratings in closed question format – where almost everything
turns out to be "important" – the open format truly reflects what

is foremost on the public's mind.[8] Figure 11.1 shows the percentage of issues named that are related to foreigners over time (for more detail on 1994 see Chapter 8). For comparison, the salience of the unemployment issue is displayed.

Obviously, the salience of foreigner-related issues differs considerably between eastern and western Germans. Yet, apart from the marked difference in level, the changes in trend in East and West are strikingly similar. Figure 11.1 also shows that the foreigner issue was certainly not a new phenomenon in the 1990–1994 legislative period. The peak in April 1989 almost matches the high levels in 1991–1992.

As far as the 1994 campaign is concerned, Figure 11.1 shows a very distinct downward trend starting in mid-1993, after the constitutional change affecting the further inflow of asylum seekers (pp. 251). At the same time, we see a dramatic rise in the salience of the unemployment issue for western Germany. Therefore, we cannot safely conclude that the foreigner issue had become moot by early 1994. Given the question format, low or declining levels of one issue may be due to the emergence of another. This question only measures *relative* salience of issues. This same caveat holds for an assessment of the eastern German figures. At any rate, the new spark in spring of 1995 serves as a reminder that the foreigner issue may be dormant at times, but it can gain prominence on the public agenda at any time.[9]

Next we track public attitudes toward foreigners using two questions that have been used repeatedly and thus allows us to track the trend in public opinions. The first indicator of public sentiment towards foreigners is a general question related to the (increasing) numbers of foreigners living in Germany. It concerns the political debate on *Überfremdung*, a German word that has no direct equivalent in English. It encapsulates the view that (too many) foreigners negatively affect the social, political, and cultural fabric of Germany, making Germans feel estranged and alienated in their own native country. Following established rules in survey methodology, the question is worded more simply: "There are many foreigners living in Germany. Do you think that this okay or is it not okay?"[10] Figure 11.2 shows the percentage of respondents that thought that it is "not okay" that many foreigners are living in Germany.

We again find a noticeable difference between Easterners and Westerners. The level of anti-foreigner sentiment, a feeling of

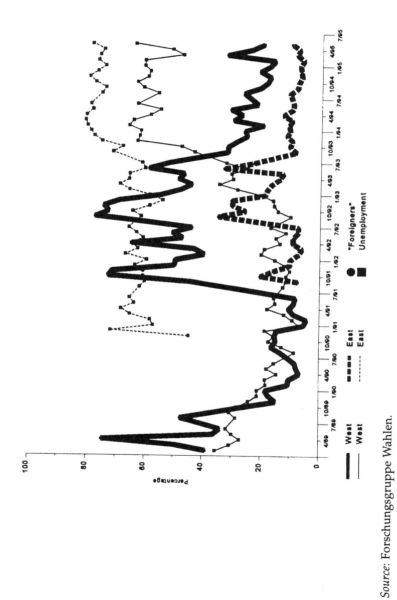

**Figure 11.1** Salience of Selected Issues, 1989–1995

*Source:* Forschungsgruppe Wahlen.

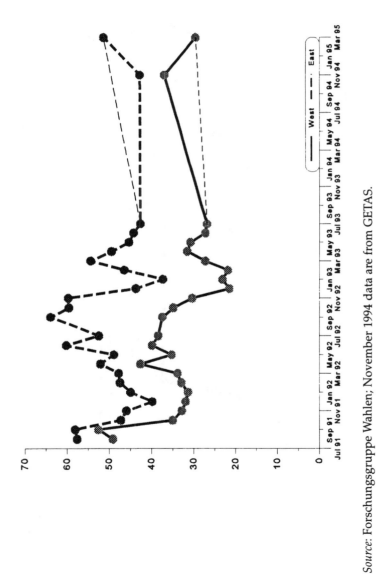

*Source:* Forschungsgruppe Wahlen; November 1994 data are from GETAS.

**Figure 11.2** Negative Feelings toward the Number of Foreigners

"overcrowding" is significantly higher in the East – despite the fact than less than 1 percent of the population in these Länder are foreigners. Obviously, the actual number of foreigners is a very poor indicator of mass sentiment toward *Überfremdung*. Apart from the difference in level, the pattern of the trend curves is rather similar across regions. From mid-1991 to mid-1993, we see roughly parallel movements of the salience and the sentiment curve (see again Figure 11.1). However, the downward trend in the salience curve thereafter is not matched by a similar decline in anti-foreigner sentiment. Unfortunately, we only have two timepoints available for the more recent period. These do suggest, however, a slight increase or at best stagnation, but not a decline of xenophobic sentiment. Currently, between 40 and 50 percent in eastern Germany and at around 30 percent in western Germany express these opinions.

More detailed analysis of the November 1994 GETAS survey finds that the sentiment in western Germany varies considerably between different birth cohorts, while no age effect shows among eastern Germans. In the youngest cohort of Westerners, those born after 1964 or below age 30 at the time of the survey, only 21 percent find fault with the number of foreigners in Germany. In contrast, about half of those born before 1935 or of age 60 and older feel that it is "not okay" to have that many foreigners in Germany (table not shown). As expected, we also find a correlation between party preference and anti-foreigner sentiment with a high of 44 percent (nationwide) among CDU voters and a low of 19 percent among adherents of the Greens. FDP voters, however, come in surprisingly high with 35 percent, a stark discrepancy with the official party position. While the difference between CDU and SPD voters is noticeable, the supporters of the two parties are closer in their sentiments than the official party position would suggest.

The second set of opinion indicators is more specific. It assesses mass sentiment towards *Gastarbeiter*. We draw on data collected by the ALLBUS survey (see Davis et al. (1994) for a general overview). Five surveys conducted between 1980 and 1994 track both contact with *Gastarbeiter* and feelings of Germans towards them over time.[11] A simple dichotomy established whether there was contact with foreigners in four areas: family and close relatives, neighborhood, work, friends and acquaintances. Contact, of course, is a function of both deliberate choice and opportunities. Low levels of contacts, then do not necessarily indicate avoidance (based on negative feelings toward foreigners). Yet contact figures are a valuable indicator of *de facto* integration.

Not surprisingly because of the lower proportions of foreigners in the East, contact between eastern Germans and guest workers is very limited. Over 80 percent of Easterners do not report contact in any of the four areas – compared to under 40 percent among Westerners in 1994. For the latter, the percentages expressing "no contact" have declined slowly but steadily since 1980 when almost 60 percent reported no contact. Yet, in any one of the four areas still more than 60 percent report no contact in 1994. Family and close kinship remains the most segregated area; less than 15 percent of the Westerners and less than 3 percent of the Easterners have a guest worker in their close kin (table not shown).[12]

Attitudes towards guest workers are measured more directly by agree–disagree responses to four normative statements about what guest worker should do: better adjust to the German lifestyle, marry among their own, be barred from political activity, and be sent home when jobs get scarce (see Kuechler (1994) for more details). These four items can be combined into an additive index defined simply as the mean of the four individual responses. To simplify the presentation, the original seven-point scale is dichotomized, contrasting responses on the negative side against the rest. In terms of the additive index, the percentage of negative attitudes has decreased from well over 50 percent in 1980 to under 30 percent in 1994 for West Germans only. The only available 1994 figure for East Germans is slightly higher.

As Figure 11.3 shows, the decrease in negative attitudes is the product of both generational replacement and a learning process for all age cohorts. This is an encouraging sign that the Germans are well on their way to adjusting to the presence of a large contingent of foreign residents. Yet, the current level of xenophobic attitudes is still high. Reconfirming the findings for the general indicator of xenophobia, anti-foreigner sentiment correlates strongly with party preference.

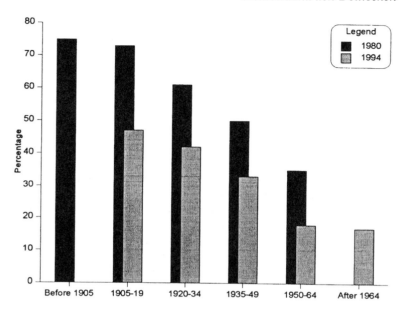

*Source*: 1980 and 1994 ALLBUS surveys; Western Germany only.

**Figure 11.3** Negative Attitudes toward Guest Workers by Birth Cohort (Western Germans)

## Policy Debates and Legal Changes in the 1990–1994 period

As seen previously (Figure 11.1), issues related to foreigners preceded the 1990–1994 legislative period. However, the many problems of German unification all but eclipsed the public debate on foreigners in 1989–1990. During the 1990–1994 period, however, a variety of policy changes altered the nature of the foreigner-related issue.

On 1 January 1991, significant modifications of the laws governing foreigners took effect. Local authorities previously had much discretion (*Ermessensspielraum*) in granting, extending, and upgrading residence and working permits, as well as outright naturalization. The new laws specified concrete criteria for those decisions rather than requiring that naturalization should serve "German interests" or that the applicant must have a good reputation (*unbescholtener Lebenswandel*).[13] In addition, the formerly steep administrative fees were reduced. As shown above, these changes had little if any effect on naturalization statistics. The major impact of these changes lay in the area of extending and upgrading residence permits, giving long-term foreign residents more control over their future. These changes, however, do not show easily in official statistics.

The major debate in the 1990–1994 period did not concern long-term residents or guest workers. Instead, the debate centered on the swelling number of people seeking political asylum in Germany and – to a lesser extent – the resettlers. Figure 11.4 shows the numbers of asylum seekers and resettlers in the broader context of the last fifteen years. The wave of resettlers had reached its crest in 1990 concurrent with the breakdown and/or liberalization of communist regimes across Eastern Europe.

Public support for resettlers had declined in the late 1980s, but none of the major parties openly advocated a change in the constitution granting the right to German citizenship to ethnic Germans. The CDU/CSU was not about to abandon the concept of German citizenship based on blood relations, thus alienating the still influential group of expellees (*Vertriebenenverbände*),

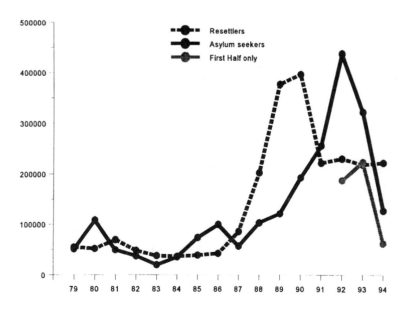

**Figure 11.4** Asylum Seekers and Resettlers, 1979–1994

ethnic Germans driven from territories Germany lost as a consequence of losing the Second World War. However, a basic
reason for the CDU's success – particularly in the era of Chancellor Kohl – is the ability to put pragmatism above ideological
conservatism. Without casting any doubt on maintaining their
rights in principle, the Kohl government created incentives for
ethnic German in foreign countries *not* to return to Germany.
With the Ethnic Settler Reintegration Act (in force since 1 July
1990) and later the War Consequences Consolidation Act (*Kriegs-
folgenbereinigungsgesetz*; effective since 1 January 1993), the re-
migration of ethnic Germans was slowed. Now it is subject to
an annual quota of 220,000. In addition, children born to ethnic
Germans after 1993 do not inherit their parents' rights to German
citizenship – unless the parents also assume German citizenship.
The group of ethnic Germans with a potential claim on German
citizenship, then, is closed. Exact figures are not available, but
most estimates suggest that another 2 million remain eligible to
return to the Federal Republic and automatically claim German
citizenship; most of them now live in the territories of the former
Soviet Union. The resettler issue has been handled by the Kohl
government with great success, alleviating growing public concern without alienating an important constituency (the expellees)
and without compromising an important party position. Kohl's
continued electoral success is in no small part explained by his
ability to plan ahead and defuse problems that otherwise could
become campaign liabilities. The resettler issue is an excellent
example of this.

Unlike the resettler issue, the handling of the asylum problem
caused a major public debate and offered no smooth solution.
Influenced by the experience with the Nazi regime where many
oppositional Germans had to seek asylum abroad, the German
constitution provided very broad and very generous asylum
rights. Article 16 simply stated: "Persons persecuted on political
grounds shall enjoy the right of asylum." As a general principle,
vast majorities of the German public supported this provision
even as the number of asylum seekers rose dramatically. However, the public debate quickly centered on the issue of abuse.
Were these applicants truly seeking *political* asylum or did they
choose to come to Germany for mostly economic reasons? The
answer, of course, depends on how one may define "political."
Official statistics show that in the three-year period from 1990

to 1992 almost half of all applicants came from two countries: (former) Yugoslavia and Romania. Another 10 percent originated from Turkey and Bulgaria (Beauftragte der Bundesregierung für die Belange der Ausländer, 1994). There was a civil war raging in what was Yugoslavia, persecution of Kurds in Turkey, and gypsies in Romania certainly did not benefit from the downfall of the communist regime. There is good reason to believe, then, that the vast majority of the asylum seekers had legitimate reasons to apply for asylum according to the letter of the German constitution. But why Germany, why not Italy, Austria, or Switzerland? Almost 800,000 people applied for asylum in Germany in 1991–1992, but only about 26,000 applied in Italy. It is obvious that apart from the generous provisions in the constitution, the German economy has served as a magnet. It is quite likely that most asylum seekers did not face immediate incarceration, a concentration camp, or even worse, but does this constitute abuse? It would be more honest to say that the Germans' willingness to share their affluence had reached its limits – and who can blame them? After all, the wave of asylum seekers came at a time when western Germans were already concerned about their sacrifices to accommodate their brethren from the East, and Easterners were afraid that they might not get what they duly deserved – at least not as quickly as they had hoped (see e.g., Kuechler, 1993). Abuse or not, the verdict of the masses was clear, the wave of asylum seekers had to be stopped. The parties responded.

To come up with effective measures, the government needed the agreement of at least the major opposition party, the SPD. A two- thirds majority is needed for any change in the constitution, but the consent of the SPD was also needed to implement a series of procedural administrative changes on the Länder level. In contrast to the resettler issue, the CDU/CSU did not face any conflict between its program, the preferences of its clientele, and practical necessities. To avoid a blunt nationalist stance, the CDU developed and cultivated a rhetoric emphasizing political asylum and immigration as problems to be solved within the context of the European Union in the long run while preserving genuine German interests in the short run.

For both the SPD and FDP, the situation was much more difficult. Cutting back asylum rights – if only to a level comparable to its Western European neighbors and in full accord with the Geneva convention – meant seriously comprising previously held programmatic positions and alienating the left wing of their clientele. At the same time, both parties held executive responsibility: the FDP as junior partner in the Federal government, the SPD in several Länder and communities where they routinely had to deal with the stream of asylum seekers. The SPD could not win in this situation. Refusing to participate in a solution would have left SPD-run states and communities in a bind and would have displeased the more centrist wing of their voter base. Participating as the SPD finally did, after long and tedious negotiations, did not promise a gain either. If the compromise was not effective (meaning it did not significantly reduce the number of asylum seekers), the CDU could blame the SPD for having prevented more rigorous measures. If it did work, the CDU would be seen as primarily responsible (by the majority in favor of the change) and the SPD would be blamed for having caved in (by those opposed to a change). To minimize the political damage, the SPD and FDP sought to couple the measures to curb asylum applications with improvements in the residence and naturalization law – pushing the changes that went into effect in 1991 (see pp. 247) a step further. On a limited scale, the SPD and FDP reached some of their goals; enough to quiet intraparty opposition and to prevent more serious damage. However, a major success it was not.

While a basic agreement was reached by the end of 1992, the legal changes did not go into effect before 1 July 1993. The one sentence provision in the old Article 16 was replaced by a lengthy Article 16a. Without going into all details, the new article severely restricts the right to apply for political asylum. In particular, no person entering from a member country of the EU or any other country deemed to observe the Geneva convention on refugees is permitted to apply.[14] By reaching agreements (which include financial compensation) with its non-EU neighbors, like Poland and the Czech Republic, to take back persons trying to enter Germany without sufficient authorization, Germany effectively shut off entrance of asylum seekers by land. Frankfurt airport became the main entry point. Official statistics (see again Figure 11.4) show a marked decrease in the number of asylum seekers after the new regulations took effect. In 1994, over 100,000 persons were registered as seeking political asylum and only a slight decline can be expected for 1995.[15] In addition, the new category of *Kriegs- und Bürgerkriegsflüchtlinge* (refugees due to war and civil war) was created at the same time. To a considerable extent, people seeking refuge have just been moved from one statistical category to another. The steep decline apparent in Figure 11.4, then, is partially due to a change in definition. In addition, it will not continue at the same rate. The public is rarely aware of such subtleties, however, and the dropping statistics shown did quiet mass concern in time for the 1994 campaign.

As part of the interparty compromise, the residence and naturalization laws that had been changed in 1990 were liberalized further. In particular, young adults between the ages of 16 and 23 now have a legal title to naturalization, if they have lived in Germany for eight years and if they have attended a German school for six years. Similarly, all foreigners with at least fifteen years of residence are entitled to naturalization if they are able to support themselves and any dependents. Spouses and children of eligible applicants may be naturalized even if they do not meet the length of residence requirement themselves. The entitlement is void if the applicant did not lawfully reside in Germany, if he or she was convicted of any significant offense,[16] or if he or she has engaged in behavior that constitutes legal grounds for deportation (most notably, violent political behavior). These clauses may appear as fairly common and not subject to any major disagreement. However, they explicitly rule out amnesty for illegal immigrants. Furthermore, "public advocacy of violence to resolve political conflicts" is open to varying interpretation. Critics may see this provision as the continuing attempt to restrict political activism among foreigners. The most important contingency clause, however, is the requirement that applicants for naturalization must give up their current citizenship – some very narrowly defined exceptions notwithstanding. Due to this requirement, the liberalizations in the naturalization law have had little effect on the actual number of naturalizations. The overwhelming majority of eligible foreigners, Turks specifically, are not willing to give up their current citizenship. Apart from emotional and symbolic reasons, manifest economic interests are involved. For example, Turkish laws on property ownership, inheritance, and similar topics put Turks renouncing their Turkish citizenship at a serious disadvantage. Dual citizenship, then, has become the pivotal issue in the debate on the integration of the long-term resident foreign population. Party positions differ sharply on this issue.


## Party Positions in the 1994 Campaign

Having discussed the policy actions of the 1990–1994 period, we now turn our attention to the positions actually taken by the parties during the 1994 campaign.

The CDU position is clearly laid out in the *Grundsatzprogramm* adopted at their party convention in February 1994. Two of the 162 articles in this program deal specifically with foreigners, immigration, and naturalization. To a large extent, these articles reflect the policy the Christian Democrats have pursued earlier. They accept the long-term residence of foreigners as irreversible, and they anticipate a further increase in the number of foreigners, but strictly as a consequence of continuing European integration. All immigration should be based on a general agreement within the EU. Unrestricted geographical mobility within the European Union as well as the constitutional rights of ethnic Germans are given higher priority than accepting (a limited number of) migrants from outside the EU. In essence, then, the CDU still maintains that Germany is not a country of immigration. With respect to long-term residents, the CDU supports their right to naturalization but reaffirms its position that dual citizenship must be restricted to a few exceptions. On a more fundamental level, the CDU views complete assimilation as a prerequisite for naturalization.

Overall, the programmatic statement of the CDU presents a careful balance between: 1) endorsing the rights of foreigners, 2) acknowledging their contribution, 3) stressing the need for peaceful cohabitation between Germans and foreigners, 4) condemning discrimination and violence against foreigners, and 5) emphasizing the priority of native German interests and the limits to which Germany and the EU can respond to the needs of people seeking a better place to live. It caters to the right-wing of their clientele without assuming openly xenophobic positions. Most importantly, while not overly liberal, the position does not create a problem for the CDU's more progressive wing. Put to a (hypothetical) referendum, I suppose a solid majority of German voters would support it. It conforms with prevailing mass sentiment and it is consistent with actions taken in the legislative period.

The position of the FDP is quite different. In its election manifesto (*Program zur Bundestagswahl 1994*), the FDP accepted that Germany is a country of immigration and called for a law addressing this reality (monitoring and limiting immigration). No details were given, but if the positions on foreigners with long-term residence are any indication, substantive differences with the CDU would emerge if such a law was drafted. The FDP has routinely held the office of the Federal Commissioner on Foreigner Affairs – an ombudsman of sorts, a public advocate with little real power or influence. In the 1990–1994 period, Cornelia Schmalz-Jacobsen served in this capacity and she has clashed with the government on several occasions. The most prominent point of contention is dual citizenship, which the FDP supports unequivocally.

The FDP has embraced the foreigner issue as a liberal principle. However, with the re-emergence of a more conservative wing in the party – sometimes referred to as the *Nationalliberalen* – these positions are not unilaterally supported within its own membership and clientele. Also, given the overrepresentation of people from the upper middle class in their clientele ("Partei der Besserverdienenden"), the foreigner issue can hardly serve as a rallying point for the party and a policy challenge to its coalition partner. In fact, the FDP's impact on the agreement to alter asylum rights was quite modest and hardly a major accomplishment for the 1990–1994 legislative period.

In contrast to the CDU, the *Grundsatzprogramm* of the SPD dates back to December 1989. It calls for rather vague improvements in the rights of foreigners residing in Germany, and more specifically for granting foreigners voting rights in municipal elections. Finally, it reaffirms political asylum rights as defined in Article 16 (SPD, 1993: 21). The decisions by the German Constitutional Court in 1990 rendered the first point obsolete. As discussed above, a change of the constitution to provide local voting rights for foreigners was done to accommodate the provisions of the Maastricht Treaty. However, given the CDU's firm stand, there is no chance for further change. As to asylum rights, the SPD effectively reversed its position by participating in the agreement to change Article 16. Not surprisingly, then, the SPD's "1994 Government Programme" adopted in June 1994 is silent on the asylum issue other than simply stating that the SPD wants "to draw up an immigration law" (SPD 1994a: 29). With respect to foreign residents, however, the SPD takes a very clear position: automatic citizenship for all children born in Germany to foreigners legally residing in Germany and acceptance of dual citizenship. However, these programmatic items are not on the list of high priorities. In its German version of a "Contract with America" – the *100-Tage-Program* – the SPD defines the sixteen items that would be addressed first and foremost. These do not include a measure related to foreigners, immigration, or naturalization. Instead, the list includes rather peripheral items like bad-weather compensation for construction workers or a bonus for wrecking old cars and buying a new one (SPD, 1994b).

Quite like the FDP, the SPD advocates a much faster pace and more radical steps toward the integration of foreigners. Like the FDP, it faces the problem that this agenda is somewhat controversial among its own clientele. In contrast to the FDP, however, the SPD's consent to the change in Article 16 is much more embarrassing. Within a coalition, there is an objective need for compromise. If an opposition party agrees, it represents at least a partial recognition that its own position is untenable. Consequently, the SPD did not push for a debate on these issues during the campaign.

In contrast to the SPD and CDU, the Greens do not have a detailed party program. In lieu, there is a *Grundkonsens*, a fairly short and rather general statement of basic political belief. This programmatic statement was drafted in the process of merging the western Greens party with the eastern Alliance 90 (see Chapter 5). In the general context of the full realization of human rights, the Greens call for complete political participation of foreign residents (Bündnis 90, 1993: 22). A campaign document, however, provides specific details (Bündnis 90, 1994: 17–18). They call for a repeal of Article 16a (revised asylum rights) and, short of its realization, a repeal of the accompanying measures. The Greens also advocate an immigration law based on humanitarian and social principles without rigid quotas. Finally, they want a comprehensive reform of the naturalization law granting citizenship to everyone born on German soil and allowing dual citizenship. Foreigners with over five years of (legal) residency should be entitled to full citizen rights (*Bürger-Innenrechte*; note the spelling). This last suggestion would achieve something similar to the legal status of resident aliens ("green–card holders") in the United States.

The position of the Greens is clearly the most extreme position. Unlike the cases of the FDP and SPD, however, the Greens' positions are compatible with the views of the vast majority of their core clientele. Still, from a strategic point of view, the Greens could hardly expect gains from pushing the foreigner issues in the campaign. The Greens were in the process of assuming the role of the FDP with respect to representing the highly educated, urban, liberal segment of the population. A major deterrent for mainstream voters to switch to the Greens, however, is doubt about the economic feasibility of the Green agenda. This is the area where the Greens have to prove themselves, where they have to alleviate fears that their view of the future may be utterly naive and unrealistic, even if it is appealing in principle (see also Chapter 5).

Given the process of disintegration the Republikaner experienced in 1994 (see Chapter 7), I will exclude them as well as other parties with very limited public appeal. However, the PDS warrants attention because of its strong regional base in eastern Germany (see Chapter 6). In its party program – adopted in January 1993 – the PDS called for an elimination of the "völkisch" Article 116 of the German constitution (this article defines the rights of ethnic Germans living outside Germany to citizenship), naturalization rights for foreigners in residence, dual citizenship, expanded asylum rights, and comprehensive rights for minorities including public funding of activities aimed at preserving their cultural identity (PDS, 1994: 10). In theory at least, the PDS position is extremely radical, matching the views of the Greens. Its practical relevance, however, is doubtful given the support base of the party. If the PDS is going to survive, it will survive as a party representing eastern interests. The prevailing mood in the East certainly does not favor foreigners. Consequently, there was no incentive for the PDS to seek an extensive debate of these issues during the campaign.

In comparative terms, only the CDU and Greens entered the 1994 campaign with a consistent record on immigration and naturalization, that is, their programmatic positions were not compromised by actions taken during the legislative period. In addition, their positions enjoyed solid support by their own clientele as demonstrated by public opinion on the singular but pivotal issue of dual citizenship. In November 1994, the *Polit-barometer* data showed that 54 percent of all Westerners favored keeping the single citizenship requirement while 41 percent supported dual citizenship. Broken down by vote intention, 65 percent of CDU voters and 69 percent of Green voters supported the party position whereas only 50 percent of SPD voters and 49 percent of FDP voters were with their party on this issue. Among Easterners, opposition to dual citizenship was markedly stronger. Overall, only 32 percent were in favor of dual citizenship and less than 30 percent among both SPD and FDP voters. Support of dual citizenship was far from unanimous among Green voters in the East as well (53 percent), but the Greens' base is predominantly in the West anyway. There is also dissent on the Left on the issues of dual citizenship and voting rights, as evidenced by a lively debate in the *tageszeitung*. Opponents maintain that a significant portion of the Turks lack sufficient identification with German society, and that they are unduly influenced by the conservative Turkish media, which condones human rights violations and espouses anti-feminist views (e.g., Wiessner, 1994).

Both the SPD and FDP had compromised their programmatic positions in the process of changing political asylum rights, and their positions were not widely supported within their own voter base. Both SPD and FDP had given in to a swelling mass sentiment that called for halting the rising numbers of asylum seekers and stopping the presumed abuse of asylum provisions. In a way, these two parties had no choice, but the compromise left them vulnerable and their credibility in doubt. For different reasons, then, no party was inclined to push issues of immigration and naturalization during the campaign. Consequently, the campaign was silent on these issues despite stark differences in party positions.

The SPD's programmatic push may be driven by an anticipated widening of its voter base – if foreigners are allowed to vote. Conventional wisdom suggests that foreigners will be more likely vote for parties on the Left given their lower average class status.[17] However, there is a little in terms of reliable hard data. Public opinion polls in Germany are often restricted to German citizens; if not excluded by design, lenient sampling procedures fail adequately to represent the foreigners in opinion surveys. Data supposedly showing the party preferences of foreigners may have limited validity. Still, Wiessner (1994) reports that of all foreigners, 42 percent would vote for the SPD, 11 percent for the Greens, and just 7 percent for the CDU, with 35 percent undecided. Her figures for just the Turks are very similar. Unfortunately, no information on the source of these data is given.

More reliable data on the party preferences of foreigners can be found in the 1994 ALLBUS. On an eleven-point party sympathy scale ranging from -5 to +5, the mean rating for the CDU among foreigners is -.4 in contrast to -.1 for FDP, .6 for the Greens, and 1.4 for the SPD. These data point in the same direction, but caution is still advised.[18] Overall, basic principles are much more responsible for determining the different party positions than highly speculative voter arithmetic.

## Outlook: The New Legislative Period

Strictly based on party positions, there should be a solid majority in the Bundestag for a reform of the naturalization law and more specifically for dual citizenship. All parties except the CDU/CSU strongly favor dual citizenship. All parties except the CDU/CSU favor an immigration law for people seeking entry to Germany. Here, of course, the programmatic positions are fairly general and much disagreement could emerge once details are discussed. Assessing majorities, then, is highly speculative. Dual citizenship, however, is a very concrete and clearly defined issue. As discussed above, dual citizenship is the litmus test of true intent to change the status of long-term foreign residents. Important as some of the recent changes are in legal terms, their factual impact will remain rather limited.

What are the chances of significant change, then? Given the German system of formal coalitions and voting strictly along party lines in Bundestag roll calls, they are minimal. The CDU/CSU and FDP form the governing coalition. The new coalition agreement of 11 November 1994 – a lengthy document detailing legislative projects for the next four years – calls for a comprehensive reform of the naturalization law. In particular, it details a plan for a new form of "child citizenship" for third-generation foreign residents. Children born in Germany will receive this "child citizenship" if one parent is born in Germany, and both parents have legally resided in Germany for the last ten years before the birth of the child and have a permanent residence permit. A child can keep the citizenship of his or her parents as well. At age 18, the child citizenship will convert to regular German citizenship if the individual supplies proof that he or she has given up the second citizenship. In addition, gradual improvements in residency laws would establish concrete rights and further reduce the discretion of local authorities. Finally, the office of the Commissioner of Foreigners Affairs would be defined more clearly and written into law.

All in all, the coalition agreement reaffirms the essential policy positions of the CDU with marginal rhetoric concessions to the FDP. If the FDP honors the agreement and the coalition holds, chances are slim that major changes in immigration and naturalization legislation will occur in the current legislative period. However, given the precarious state of the FDP with its devastating losses in state elections in North Rhine-Westphalia and in Bremen in May 1995 (after a successful result in the Hesse elections of February 1995), a change of government mid-stream cannot be ruled out. In June 1995 the FDP elected a new party leadership and quieted intraparty struggles. At the same time, the new leader, Wolfgang Gerhardt, has pledged to push for the realization of liberal positions and to emphasize the unique contribution of the FDP to the coalition government. Similarly, Cornelia Schmalz-Jacobsen who reluctantly agreed to continue as the Commissioner of Foreigner Affairs (based on rather vague promises in the coalition agreement to move ahead with significant reforms), was elected as one of the deputy party leaders and has demanded that her party takes a stronger, more independent stand in the coalition. Yet, with the slim majority left after the 1994 elections, this may be impossible to do without blowing the coalition apart.

If the current coalition fails, the prospects of naturalization and immigration reform may not be much better. The most likely outcome would be a grand coalition between CDU and SPD bridging the time before new elections are due. It is hard to conceive that the CDU would buckle under. After all, while certainly not a model of multiculturalism, the CDU's policy positions are in line with the majority of the German electorate. They are a delicate mix of affirming Germany's commitment to international cooperation and integration (closely tied to the European Union)

– in contrast to national chauvinism – and maintaining native German interests as well as conserving the traditional social and cultural fabric. Chancellor Kohl's careful maneuvering is a significant factor in the failure of right-extremist parties to capitalize on the latent xenophobia in the German public, as Le Pen and his National Front have done with great success in France. In the long run, bolder steps towards the integration of foreigners and towards accommodating migration will be necessary, but they may take more time. The German public is getting ready – but very slowly.

## Notes

As in the past, I am deeply indebted to a number of colleagues in Germany who have supplied me with data. These include the Forschungsgruppe Wahlen (Manfred Berger, Matthias Jung, and Dieter Roth) for the Politbarometer data, Michael Braun (ZUMA) and Michael Terwey (ZA) for ALLBUS data, and Barbara von Harder (GETAS) for a much-needed replication of a trend question. Most importantly, I would like to thank Wolfgang Gibowski (BPA) for making it possible for a group of scholars from the United States to visit Germany around election day in October 1994. The talks with high-ranking party representatives provided invaluable insights into party strategies and the 1994 campaign. I feel most privileged to have been included in this group.

1. Resettlers are ethnic Germans from Eastern Europe (by now mostly from the territory of the former Soviet Union) who are entitled to German citizenship according to Article 116 of the German Basic Law. Legally, resettlers are not foreigners; in sociological terms, however, they are "foreign" and need to be considered as such in an analysis of civility and civic culture.
2. All figures in this section are taken from a report on the situation of foreigners compiled by the Federal Commissioner of Foreigner Affairs (Beauftragte der Bundesregierung, 1994) which in turn draws on official statistics generated by the German Census Bureau and other government agencies. Fig-

ures since 1991 refer to the united Germany, earlier figures refer to West Germany only. For reasons explained above, resettlers are not included in these figures.

3. Of course, these figures are based strictly on legal status and many of the differences are accounted for by the restrictive nature of the German immigration and naturalization laws. In contrast to the United States, France, or Great Britain, German citizenship is based on the principle of *jus sanguinis* (blood relationship) rather than *jus solis* (where all persons born within the territory of a state receive automatic citizenship). See e.g. Brubaker (1992) for a detailed comparison of citizenship laws in France and Germany.

4. Since 1975, German citizenship is awarded if at least one parent is a German citizen. Since 1993, this applies to children born out of wedlock as well.

5. These figures do not include members of foreign armed forces stationed in Germany.

6. These figures do not include *Anspruchseinbürgerungen*, basically naturalizations of ethnic Germans from Eastern Europe who decide to resettle in Germany.

7. In 1990, the German Constitutional Court had voided electoral laws passed in the states of Schleswig-Holstein and Hamburg that granted voting rights to foreigners in municipal elections. The court's decision largely muted a growing debate about granting (limited) voting rights independent of naturalization.

8. Whether this is an effect of more extensive media coverage or whether increasing public concern is the cause for expanded media coverage, is an interesting side issue that I will not pursue. From the point of view of devising party campaign strategies, it is of limited interest.

9. Its reemergence in early 1995 is most likely due to a series of attacks on Turkish institutions. Most of these, however, were not attributed to German right-wing extremists, but to members of the PKK, the Kurdish Worker's Party, spreading the civil war in Turkey to German soil.

10. This is a fairly literal translation of the German question wording: "In Deutschland leben viele Ausländer. Finden Sie das in Ordnung oder finden Sie das nicht in Ordnung?" It may sound somewhat awkward in English, but the German wording is fine.

This question was included in the monthly *Politbarometer* surveys from July 1991 to July 1993, and again in March 1995. In addition, the same question was included in a survey conducted by GETAS in November 1994 shortly after the elections.

11. Recognizing the problematic nature of the very term "Gastarbeiter," the 1994 ALLBUS included a methodological split-half experiment. For one half of the survey, the term "Gastarbeiter" was used to replicate previously used questions without any change. For the other half, the term was replaced by "in Deutschland lebende Ausländer" (foreigners living in Germany). The change in question wording produced significant differences for questions dealing with frequency of contact. For the attitude items, however, the differences are only partly significant when the full seven-point response scale is considered. For the dichotomization used here, the effect of question wording is insignificant.

12. The figures are slightly higher when the alternative wording (n.11) is used.

13. In German legal terms, the revised laws granted a *Regelanspruch* but still not a *Rechtsanspruch*, meaning (on the positive side) that a negative decision by the local authorities could be easily challenged in court and therefore would be less likely, but that meeting the specified criteria did not constitute a legal right to permanent residence or to naturalization.

14. More precisely, the new Article 16a explicitly refers to two conventions: the "Convention Relating to the Status of Refugees" and the "Convention for the Protection of Human Rights and Fundamental Freedoms."

15. Up to May 1995, 49,460 people applied for political asylum; a decline of 7.9 percent compared to the same period in the previous year.

16. The law provides a detailed list of offenses considered as non-minor (*nicht unerheblich*).

17. Conventional wisdom also suggested that the SPD would profit for unification and that voters in the East would strongly support the Social Democrats, which, of course, turned out not to be the case.

18. Despite the small size of N=150, these differences are statistically significant except for the CDU–FDP difference. These figures are for Westerners only; there were only three

foreigners in the eastern subsample. For western Germany, the percentage of foreigners over 18 years of age in the sample was 6.5 compared to an expected 7.5 percent according to official statistics (Koch et al., 1994: 77). However, the foreigner sample may differ from the underlying population in important traits like language abilities, familiarity with German norms and customs, etc. Even the ALLBUS data, then, cannot necessarily be taken at face value.

## References

Beauftragte der Bundesregierung für die Belange der Ausländer, ed. 1994. *Daten und Fakten zur Ausländersituation.* Bonn: Mitteilungen der Beauftragten der Bundesregierung.

Betz, Hans-Georg. 1994. *Radical Right-Wing Populism in Western Europe.* New York: St Martin's Press.

Brubaker, Rogers. 1992. *Citizenship and Nationhood in France and Germany.* Cambridge, MA: Harvard University Press.

Bündnis 90/Die Grünen. 1993. *Politische Grundsätze.* Bornheim: Bündnis 90/Die Grünen – Referat Öffentlichkeitsarbeit.

———. 1994. *Ein Land reformieren – 10 Reformprojekte und ein Finanzierungsvorschlag.* Bornheim: Bundesgeschäftsstelle von Bündnis 90/Die Grünen.

CDU. 1994. *Freiheit in Verantwortung – Grundsatzprogramm der Christlich Demokratischen Union Deutschlands.* Bonn: CDU-Bundesgeschäftsstelle.

Davis, James, Peter Mohler, and Tom Smith. 1994. "Nationwide General Social Surveys," in Ingwer Borg and Peter Mohler, eds. *Trends and Perspectives in Empirical Social Research.* Berlin: de Gruyter.

Edye, Dave. 1987. *Immigrant Labor and Government Policy: The Case of the Federal Republic of Germany and France.* Brookfield, VT: Gower.

Hoskin, Marilyn. 1991. *New Immigrants and Democratic Society.* New York: Praeger.

Inter Nationes. 1994. *Special Election Report – Procedures, Programmes, Profiles.* Bonn: Inter Nationes.

Koch, Achim, Siegfried Gabler, and Michael Braun. 1994. *Konzeption und Durchführung der "Allgemeinen Bevölkerungsumfrage der Sozialwissenschaften" (ALLBUS) 1994*. Mannheim: ZUMA.

Kuechler, Manfred. 1993. "Framing Unification: Issue Salience and Mass Sentiment 1989–1991," in Russell Dalton, ed. *The New Germany Votes*. Oxford/Providence: Berg.

———. 1994. "The Germans and the 'Others': Racism, Xenophobia, or Legitimate Conservatism?" *German Politics* 3: 47–74.

Otto, Hans-Uwe and Roland Merten, eds. 1993. *Rechtsradikale Gewalt im vereinigten Deutschland*. Opladen, Germany: Leske & Budrich.

PDS. 1994. *Programm der Partei des Demokratischen Sozialismus*. Berlin: Wahlbüro der PDS.

SPD. 1993. *Grundsatzprogramm der Sozialdemokratischen Partei Deutschlands*. Bonn: Vorstand der SPD.

———. 1994a. *1994 Government Programme*. Bonn (mimeographed).

———. 1994b. "Für ein gerechtes und friedliches Deutschland – '100-Tage-Programm' der SPD," *Intern – Informationsdienst der SPD* 17.

Wiessner, Irina. 1994. "Konservativ und manipuliert," *Die tageszeitung* 15 October: 18–19.

Wrench, John and John Solomos, eds. 1993. *Racism and Migration in Western Europe*. Oxford/Providence: Berg.

# 12
# Women and the 1994 Federal Election

## *Eva Kolinsky*

When the new Germany voted for the second time in October 1994, unification was in its fifth year. The hopes which had inspired the citizens' movements in the GDR, the exodus of East Germans from their state and the mass demonstration of 1989–1990 had given way to altered sentiments. Women on either side of the former German–German border have been wrong-footed by the social realities since 1990.

Seen from the West, the GDR had seemingly offered a model that combined employment and motherhood by offering child-care facilities for all who wanted to use them. Although few intended to emulate the East German system of moulding children into "socialist personalities," western women with children saw improved access to full-time child-care facilities as a social policy they would welcome. West German women also looked with a certain degree of envy to the apparently equal integration of women into the East German labor market while they continued to encounter unequal employment opportunities in addition to the unresolved conflict between employment and homemaking (Helwig and Nickels, 1993).

In East Germany, this conflict about the role of women was seemingly relegated to history. Employers were obligated to provide child-care for very little cost, and to provide care for children during holiday periods. The state devised an increasingly comprehensive net of support measures for working mothers, a *Muttipolitik* to encourage female employment and childbirth. From the outside, and for women in East Germany before the collapse of state socialism, equality in employment and in society seemed to have been achieved. While women in West Germany had become increasingly sensitive to overt and hidden forms of discrimination and gender stereotyping, most East German women believed themselves equal in all respects: access to employment, pay, qualifications, social prospects, mobility (Kolinsky, 1993a: ch. 7). Of course, women took part in the Monday demonstrations, were prominent in the citizens' movement and challenged (in smaller numbers than men) the GDR by leaving it. Their discontent, however, was not directed at the overall conditions of their lives, their working and family roles, and their way of combining the two. The discontent of women who called for unification ("We are One People") was directed at the shortages dominating their everyday lives, the meager living conditions compared with the West, and the lack of freedom to travel.

The critical agenda of West Germany's women's movement and party activists meant nothing in the East. A critical agenda emerged in the East only after the 1990 elections as the social and economic impact of unification became apparent. Once market principles took effect, the hidden disadvantages of women in eastern Germany turned into open disadvantages: women were concentrated in narrow occupational bands with lower qualifications, lower pay, and less seniority than men; women were hit harder by unemployment and early retirement, and were less likely to be retained in short-term employment or to find new employment. In GDR times, motherhood had been supported by elaborate state policies and social institutions; now it turned into an obstacle to employment as the conflict between family roles and employment roles reopened. In the GDR, women's lower pay had hardly mattered since everyone was earning relatively little and the state supplemented mothers with generous family and child bonuses. In post-unification eastern Germany, four out of five women earn less than average incomes and one in five have fallen into poverty (Kolinsky, 1995a).

Eastern women continue to look to employment as a key dimension of their lives, not only to make ends meet but in a deliberate bid for continuity with the established pattern of the GDR years. In order to diffuse the conflict between family roles and employment opportunities, young eastern women have begun to postpone childbirth and marriage until they are established in their careers. Women with family responsibilities before 1990 could not turn the clock back, and found themselves at the vulnerable end of the newly competitive social climate.

Given women's unexpected social dislocation in eastern Germany, politics has taken a back seat. In the first hour, some women were active in political parties and movements; since unification party membership in the new Länder dropped by at least two-thirds among men and women (Ammer, 1992: 447f.). Post-SED political participation has yet to become an accepted dimension of the eastern political culture. Caught in the new uncertainties about employment and their socioeconomic future, the majority of eastern women are not interested in politics. In 1990, most supported the party which promised unification; in 1994, CDU support in the East still remained higher than in the West, although the other parties – notably the PDS – made some gains among women voters.

The 1994 election was shaped by the priorities and the electoral trends which had emerged in the West, not in the East. In the electorate the major development can be summed up as the erosion of a CDU/CSU women's bonus and a diversification of women's electoral preferences. In the party organizations these developments and the entry of the postwar generations into politics have resulted in a debate and in some parties a formal pledge to insure improved or even equal representation of women in political life. Specific "women's issues" were less relevant in the 1994 campaign than a focus on women's representation in parties and parliaments as a measure of each party's competence to turn pledges of equal opportunities into political reality. This chapter explores the role of women in the 1994 elections under four broad headings: 1) the electoral preferences of women; 2) determinants of women's political participation; 3) women's access to Bundestag representation; and 4) responses by the two *Volksparteien* to women's voting in 1994.

## Women's Party Preferences in the 1994 Election

In 1994 neither of the two *Volksparteien* attracted unusually high support from men or women; the gender balance of their electorates seemed to match that of the population as a whole (Table 12.1). Women were significantly overrepresented among Greens voters and outnumbered in the electorates of the FDP.

*Social and Political Developments*

**Table 12.1** Party Support by Gender and Age, 1994

| Age | Electorate | CDU/CSU | SPD | FDP | A 90/G | PDS |
|---|---|---|---|---|---|---|
| **Total** | | | | | | |
| *men* | 48.0 | 47.1 | 48.2 | 51.3 | 44.2 | 49.9 |
| women | 52.0 | 52.9 | 51.8 | 48.7 | 55.8 | 50.1 |
| **18–24** | | | | | | |
| *men* | 5.2 | 4.4 | 4.6 | 5.0 | 9.0 | 5.6 |
| women | 4.7 | 3.5 | 4.7 | 4.2 | 10.1 | 5.9 |
| **25–34** | | | | | | |
| *men* | 9.1 | 7.7 | 9.1 | 7.5 | 14.2 | 10.6 |
| women | 8.6 | 6.0 | 10.0 | 6.1 | 16.5 | 10.9 |
| **35–44** | | | | | | |
| *men* | 8.1 | 7.0 | 8.7 | 8.3 | 10.4 | 9.2 |
| women | 8.0 | 7.3 | 7.9 | 7.5 | 13.0 | 9.4 |
| **45–59** | | | | | | |
| *men* | 12.4 | 13.3 | 12.4 | 15.6 | 6.6 | 11.0 |
| women | 12.4 | 13.6 | 12.2 | 13.0 | 8.3 | 11.9 |
| **60 and over** | | | | | | |
| *men* | 10.0 | 11.6 | 9.5 | 12.2 | 2.5 | 9.6 |
| women | 15.1 | 19.3 | 13.4 | 15.8 | 6.6 | 8.9 |

*Source*: Forschungsgruppe Wahlen (1994: 20). Contrary to the 1990 elections when men and women used different ballot papers to cast their vote, the 1994 elections were conducted with uniform ballot papers to conform with the Data Protection Act. The analysis of gender specific voting is based on the exit poll conducted by the Forschungsgruppe Wahlen.

The apparent irrelevance of gender for electoral preferences in 1994 hides a more uneven electoral reality. In the first two decades of postwar German democracy, the majority of women had opted for the CDU/CSU. This conservative women's bonus no longer applies (Kolinsky, 1994: 63–75). In society generally, the link has loosened between social position and party orientation leaving more scope for individual and issue-based electoral choices. For women's preferences for the CDU/CSU, a decline in religious observance and the waning of the religious cleavage have been particularly relevant.[1] In 1994, female active churchgoers still supported the CDU/CSU as they had in the past, but their number was not large enough to recapture the women's bonus of yesteryear.

Changes in the social situation of women also modified electoral preferences. Women today are better educated than women in the first twenty years of FRG electoral history. Education broadened occupational and employment opportunities and offered women a more varied spectrum of career choices and lifestyles. In education, women had nearly achieved equality and even overtaken men in a silent revolution at all but the most advanced levels, although equal treatment and equal opportunities in employment proved more elusive. In the West, women experienced a clash between career expectations and employment opportunities. When the first cohort of well-educated women entered the labor market in the early 1970s, unemployment made the successful transformation of educational qualifications into employment more difficult than at any time in the postwar period. In addition, women in West Germany were confronted with an unresolved conflict between motherhood and employment.

That state socialism in East Germany did not offer equal pay or equal employment status and career opportunities to women was little known because of the belief that family and employment roles could be so readily combined (Kolinsky, 1995b: 95–8). Since unification, however, women in the new Länder bore the brunt of unemployment, found themselves under threat of being excluded from the labor market, and feared that they may be forced into a homemaker and family role they did not want and could not accept.

These developments affected younger women more than older women; better-educated women who encountered conflicts between their career and their role as homemaker more than the less well educated who were more inclined towards traditional lifestyles and modes of thinking (Hofmann-Göttig, 1987).

The command of an electoral majority of the two *Volksparteien* depends increasingly on the party preferences of younger women. Until the late 1960s, the CDU/CSU could expect a majority of women's votes in all age groups. The Christian Democratic women's bonus gradually shifted towards the older cohorts, while the SPD made gains among voters under age 35. This turned the SPD's women's deficit into a bonus (Kolinsky, 1994: 118). In the 1980s, the Greens competed with the SPD for the vote of young women and increasingly for the vote of women generally. Since unification, the PDS emerged as a further

269

electoral player on the Left, at least in the new Länder.

The 1994 election revealed this transformed electoral land-scape (see Table 12.1). Young women abandoned the CSU/CSU in increasing numbers, while CDU voters are over-represented among older female voters. For instance, women between the ages of 18 and 24 accounted for 4.7 percent of the 1994 electorate, but just 3.5 percent of the CDU/CSU electorate. The Christian Democrats had a women's bonus among women aged 45–59 years (a 1.2 percent bonus) and among those over 60 (a 4.2 percent bonus).

CDU/CSU losses did not translate directly into SPD gains. The SPD accrued a bonus among 25–34-year-old women but even here it lay only 1.4 percent above average. As mentioned earlier, among the youngest, the party's vote corresponded to the share of 18–24-year-old women in the electorate as a whole. Among women above 35 years of age, however, the SPD continued to incur a small gender deficit between 0.1 percent to 1.7 percent. At first glance, the traditional Social Democratic women's deficit and Christian Democratic women's bonus appear to have survived into the mid-1990s. Yet, the degree of SPD under-representation among older women voters has steadily decreased as the gap narrowed over time.

Competition for women's electoral support is not confined to the two *Volksparteien*. In 1994, the Greens consolidated their position as the only political party with an electorate in which women are significantly overrepresented. The Alliance 90/Greens are the only party in which women outnumber men in all age cohorts and the only political party with women's bonuses in all age cohorts between 18 and 44 (Table 12.2). In the 1980s, the Green electorate had been predominantly male despite the party's commitment to anti-discrimination policies. In 1990, women began to outnumber men in the Green electorate. In 1994, the profile of the Greens as an electoral party for women was consolidated across all age groups.[2]

In 1994 the PDS emerged as an eastern political voice in which women were more strongly represented than men in nearly all age groups.

For the CDU, the new volatility of women's party preferences has all the makings of a crisis. Since 1983, losses among women voters added up to 7 percent overall, and more than 13 percent among women between the ages of 25 and 44 (Table 12.3). In the

**Table 12.2** Green Party Preferences of Women by Age Cohorts, 1990 and 1994

| Age | 1990 | 1994 | Difference |
|---|---|---|---|
| 18–14 years | 11.4 | 15.8 | +4.4 |
| 25–34 years | 10.4 | 14.2 | +3.8 |
| 35–44 years | 6.3 | 12.0 | +5.7 |
| 45–49 years | 2.7 | 5.0 | +2.3 |
| 60 and over | 0.9 | 3.2 | +2.3 |

*Source*: "Frauenbericht." Bericht des Generalsekretärs zur Umsetzung der Essener Leitsätze (1994: 8).

past, the party had taken solace from the expectation that electoral preferences were governed by life-cycles and that women would turn to conservatism as they grew older. Increasingly the CDU realized that electoral preferences within a given generation are unlikely to change substantially as this generation ages (Rhardt-Vahldieck and Möller-Fiedler, 1994). The losses sustained among younger women may not be easily reserved in later years and could eventually erode the CDU's dominant position, even among older voters. Unless the party can improve its standing among young female voters, its *Mehrheitsfähigkeit* looks doubtful.

**Table 12.3** CDU Support among Women by Age, 1983–1994

| Age Group | 1983 | 1987 | 1990 | 1994 | Difference 1983–1994 |
|---|---|---|---|---|---|
| 18–24 | 40.3 | 34.8 | 34.6 | 30.8 | − 9.5 |
| 25–34 | 42.8 | 34.4 | 34.2 | 29.1 | −13.7 |
| 35–44 | 50.9 | 42.5 | 40.2 | 37.6 | −13.3 |
| 45–59 | 50.9 | 47.4 | 47.7 | 45.3 | − 5.6 |
| 60 and over | 53.5 | 53.5 | 53.9 | 52.6 | − 0.9 |
| Overall | 49.2 | 45.1 | 44.9 | 42.2 | − 7.0 |

*Source*: "Frauenbericht." Bericht des Generalsekretärs zur Umsetzung der Essener Leitsätze (1994: 11).

From the SPD perspective, gender had faded as an issue of concern. In its post-election analysis, the SPD head office noted with distinct satisfaction that the "party's election result was nearly identical among men and women" (SPD, 1994: 19). *Hoffnungsträger*, a particularly promising group for the SPD, were

Social and Political Developments

women in the age group 24–34. Here the SPD led the CDU by 12.5 percent. Among the youngest and the oldest female voters, however, the party stagnated or suffered losses since the 1990 Bundestagswahl.

## Taking Part in Politics

Of the 1.4 million women entitled to vote for the first time in 1994, more than half did not exercise their right to vote (Veen, 1994). Although electoral participation among the youngest voters (especially young women) has always been lower than among older voters, the 1990s saw a sharp decline in turnout among women under the age of 25. Interest in politics had generally increased, but the inclination to translate this into electoral participation fell (Feist, 1994: 43). A low turnout, therefore, does not necessarily point to lack of interest in politics but points more often to a sense of detachment from the party system in Germany and from the modes of participation it offers to citizens. Of young female non-voters, 51 percent thought that it would make no difference whether they cast their vote or not. Among young female voters, just 8 percent held that their vote might not have any impact (CDU Generalsekretärs, 1993: 13).

## Interests and Issues

Differences in political interest and socio-demographic indicators such as education, occupational status, locality contribute to the gender gap of electoral participation but they do not reveal the full picture. In key policy areas, women appear to have less confidence than men in government policies. In 1993, for instance, 57 percent of women and 43 percent of men thought that peace in Europe was under threat, more women than men opposed the participation of the *Bundeswehr* in UN military missions, more women than men expressed doubts about the stability of the economy (66 percent and 54 percent respectively) and more women (24 percent) than men (17 percent) favored an immediate halt to all use and production of nuclear energy (CDU Generalsekretärs, 1993; Rhardt-Vahldieck and Möller-Fiedler, 1994).

Two issues in particular may have influenced women's electoral stance in 1994: women felt more strongly threatened by violence and criminality than men (53 percent and 38 percent respectively) and women rated the reform of the abortion legislation in the wake of German unification as a more salient issue than men (Rattinger, 1993). In western Germany, this gender difference did not appear to be wide enough to influence electoral preferences. In eastern Germany, however, abortion had acquired more salience and may have determined electoral choices, although early protests had subsided by the time the legislation was passed. In addition, there is some evidence that eastern women prefer the new advisory centers to the impersonal and uncaring abortion clinics they replaced (Rattinger, 1993: 261–3).

In their public profiles, the contestants in the 1994 elections tended to emphasize more all-embracing and abstract women's issues and evaded direct messages. The CDU slogan "Ohne Frauen ist kein Staat zu machen" was burdened with multiple meanings: women are needed, the CDU is the natural party of government (*Staat*), looking impressive in public (*Staat machen*) is important. The SPD opted for a similar double-speak: "Frauen verdienen mehr," which means women deserve more than they have. However, the SPD slogan could also mean that women earn more than men already. None of these slogans bore any relationship to the issues that might decide the election for women. Female potential SPD voters in particular lost confidence in their party's issue competence. In the course of 1994, the SPD lost credibility in key areas where women would have perceived that party as their voice (Table 12.4). The perceived competency of the SPD to secure the welfare state and assist women in combining family and employment eroded during 1994. Losses were more pronounced in the East than in the West.

The SPD deficit on key women's issues contributed to the party's losses to the PDS in East Germany and to the Greens in the West. While the CDU/CSU also lost heavily among (younger) women in western Germany it was able to capitalize on its better performance in the East.

## The Representation of Women

In their organization and policy agendas, political parties are increasingly perceived as removed from or even hostile to women's

**Table 12.4** Issues and Party Preferences in East and West, 1994

| Issue | Western Germany | | | | Eastern Germany | | | |
|---|---|---|---|---|---|---|---|---|
| | SPD 2/94 | SPD 6/94 | CDU/ CSU 2/94 | CDU/ CSU 6/94 | SPD 2/94 | SPD 6/94 | CDU/ CSU 2/94 | CDU/ CSU 6/94 |
| Economic stability | 30 | 30 | 36 | 43 | 32 | 23 | 31 | 46 |
| Securing welfare state | 48 | 44 | 21 | 27 | 47 | 39 | 11 | 21 |
| Combining family and employment | 38 | 34 | 22 | 25 | 38 | 29 | 12 | 20 |

*Source*: SPD, 1994: 2.

involvement in politics (Kolinsky, 1993b: 126–34). Women, it has been argued, favor team work and cooperation, not hierarchies and competition. Personal relevance and the social context of policies matter more than abstract principles and narrow specialisms (Meyer, 1992). With their established structures, their *Ochsentour* of office holding, their power networks, and not least their traditions of meeting in smoke-filled back rooms of pubs, political parties have placed a myriad of formal and informal obstacles in the paths of those women who want to turn their interest in politics into active political participation through party membership.

In the 1970s, the SPD was the first party to debate the place of women in politics and the discrepancy between women's expectations and their political opportunities. Getting women elected in accordance with their contribution to the party and their acumen and motivation as politicians has been the most urgent demand of the Association of Social Democratic Women (ASF). The ASF became active after the electoral disaster of 1972 when the number of female SPD deputies reached an all-time low of 5 percent, even below the CDU. This was also a time when a new generation of women began to enter the SPD in ever-increasing numbers and brought with them new expectations about their voice in the party and their equal treatment in society and politics.

A decade later, a similar debate began in the CDU, fuelled by discontent about the prospects for politically active female party members to hold a political office, gain a parliamentary seat, and make politics their career alongside and equal to men. By the mid-1980s, the Greens had intensified the debate about the parties' treatment of women by imposing a minimum quota of 50 percent women for all party and parliamentary positions. The 1985 CDU congress in Essen passed a recommendation that women should be represented at all levels of the party organization and in parliaments in accordance with their share of the membership. Three years later, the SPD amended its party statutes and prescribed that by 1994, 40 percent of party posts and no less than 30 percent of parliamentary seats should be held by women. The FDP contented itself with recommending that more women should be active in the party and hold an office. The CSU refused to embark on a formal discussion, but brought more women forward (Naßmacher, 1994: 62–4).

In the 1987 election, the nomination of candidates and their chances to gain seats was turned into an election issue, although there is no evidence that women were more inclined to support female candidates over males. Instead, party preferences followed established electoral patterns. Women candidates did not mobilize votes from women against the grain of party orientations. In the 1990 election, the issue of women's equality in politics continued to occupy the political parties and their female members and office holders. However, for much of the electorate these matters were eclipsed by the turmoil of unification. The 1994 election took place at a time when the emphasis on equal opportunities had already transformed the party organizations of the Greens and the SPD and given women a more prominent place among their front-bench leadership. By contrast, the CDU, CSU and FDP had rejected quota regulations and little had occurred to extend women's roles in their organizations, parliament or the government.

The intraparty debate on the representation of women and the uses of women's quotas hardly spread from the parties to the public domain. The nomination of parliamentary candidates put the spotlight on women's place in German party- and parliamentary politics, although this spotlight did not focus on issues that may have determined women's electoral choices. For the political parties seeking re-election in 1994, the success or failure of women in winning Bundestag seats, gaining leadership positions in their parliamentary parties, or obtaining government posts constituted a hidden agenda of the campaign. The women's issue was hotly contested within the parties, and each party tried to project itself as the party with women's interests at heart.

In the 1994 federal election, a record number of 3,923 individuals contested parliamentary seats, one in three of them women (Der Bundeswahlleiter, 1994; *Das Parlament*, 23 September 1994: 1). At no time in German political history had so many women entered the hustings. The outcome of the elections also secured a place in the history books: with 176 female members, the new Bundestag includes more women than any of its predecessors. With 26 percent of the seats, women achieved a breakthrough at national level, although several regional parliaments already include a higher proportion of women members (Figure 12.1).[3] Looking back at the changes in women's representation in the Bundestag since the quota debate placed a new emphasis on equal access, the 1994 increase is not so much a peak as the most recent point in a continuing trend. Since 1983, the representation of women in the Bundestag has increased gradually (by approximately 5 percent at a time) from election to election.

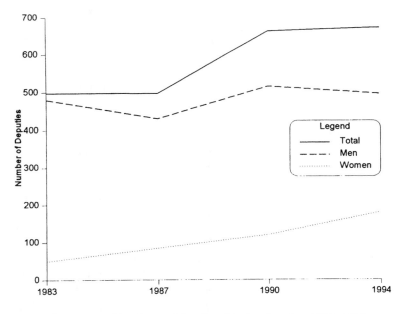

**Figure 12.1** Bundestag Membership by Gender, 1983–1994

The German electoral system is based on proportional representation linked to plurality voting by district. The citizen thus casts two votes, one for a constituency candidate who is elected to parliament by a plurality, the other for a political party. This electoral system results in two candidacy tracks for would-be parliamentarians: a *Wahlkreiskandidat* competes for the votes in a given constituency, and candidates nominated on regional party lists may enter the Bundestag if their party gains a sufficient number of votes. For women candidates, party lists have always been the more important route. Since the early 1980s up to four times as many women were elected to the Bundestag via party lists than as direct candidates in their constituencies.

There are several reasons for this. The first concerns the limited access to constituency seats. They have been the preserve of bigger parties since smaller parties stand little chance of gaining the majority of the votes in a given locality. Between 1961 and 1990, only the *Volksparteien* held constituency seats and the CDU/CSU did considerably better than the SPD in securing them. In 1990, the FDP won a surprise constituency victory in Halle, Hans-Dietrich Genscher's hometown; this was a flurry of Genscherism that could not be sustained in 1994. In 1994, the PDS won four East Berlin constituencies; among the *Direktkandidaten* was Christa Luft, the first woman in German political history to be directly elected to the Bundestag from a small party. The Greens, by contrast, have never harnessed a majority at the constituency level. They have based their parliamentary representation exclusively on *Zweitstimmen* and the distribution of party list seats among the political parties.

Efforts to improve women's access to parliamentary seats concentrated on influencing the composition of party lists and ensuring the nomination of women to positions that might result in parliamentary seats. In the past, women tended to be bunched at the lower end of the list where they made up the numbers but where electoral chances were poor. This began to change in the mid-1980s in the wake of the quota debate. Party lists for the 1994 federal elections reflect these developments. Taking the first thirty names on a regional party list as the group from which the parliamentary representatives will be recruited, the lists included women in accordance with the party's self-proclaimed or prescribed quota: 25 percent in the CDU/CSU, just over 30 percent in the SPD, between zero and 50 percent in the FDP, at least 50 percent in the Greens, and up to 60 percent in the PDS.

Women headed four of the CDU regional lists and nine for the SPD. In the SPD, a woman tended to hold one of the first three places, in the CDU placements on the lists were more uneven and generally less favorable. Three of the CDU women heading a Land list were public figures: Rita Süßmuth, President of the Bundestag, Angela Merkel, the (outgoing) Minister for Women, Youth, and Claudia Nolte, the young eastern Catholic who had achieved rapid political stardom since first entering politics through her success in the 1990 Volkskammer and 1990 Bundestag elections. In Bavaria, Ursula Männle stood as number two on the CSU list but was elected for her constituency. In Berlin, Hesse, North Rhine-Westphalia and Schleswig-Holstein, the highest female place on the CDU list was number three; in Brandenburg and Bremen, CDU women failed to gain a nomination among the first three and none were elected for these regions. Overall, nineteen women entered the Bundestag as list candidates for the CDU/CSU, two for the CSU in Bavaria and seventeen for the CDU from the other fifteen Länder. In clear contrast to the other political parties, the number of female constituency deputies for the CDU/CSU is higher than the number elected via party lists and also higher than the number of women directly elected for any of the other parties (Figure 12.2). Since the CDU and CSU have won most constituency seats in Bundestag elections and won 12 additional mandates in 1994 (to the SPD's four), CDU/CSU women appear to enjoy better chances than women in the other parties to obtain a constituency nomination that may result in a parliamentary seat. However, their poor positioning on CDU and CSU party lists is reflected in the low number who can turn their nomination into a Bundestag seat.

For the small parties, party lists have been lifelines to the parliamentary participation of women and an effective device to demonstrate their commitment to women's equal access. Between them, the PDS and Alliance 90/Greens elected forty-two women to the Bundestag via their Land lists. As mentioned earlier, the FDP refused to adopt a quota system. The twin effect of poor positioning of FDP women on party lists and the loss of thirty-two seats compared with the 1990 elections reduced the number of FDP women from sixteen to eight.

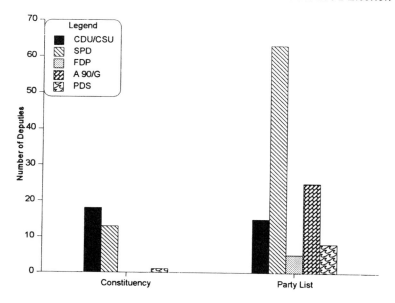

**Figure 12.2** Women Members of the Bundestag (District and List Candidates), 1994

## Equal Opportunities in the SPD and CDU During the 1994 Campaign and After

On paper, the SPD met its women's quota of 33 percent of Bundestag deputies although the party failed to increase its share of women when compared to 1990. The 1994 result highlights the extent to which women's access to the Bundestag has improved within the SPD, but the uneven distribution of successful constituency and list candidacies also shows that inequalities persist. Women would have fared less well without the feminist muscle shown by the ASF and the obligation placed on the party organization to ensure that women get elected.

In 1990, SPD gains were also based on a special effort to nominate women for safe constituency seats which had fallen vacant. In the round of nominations for the 1994 elections, the SPD increased its number of female constituency candidates from 76 to 101, but few of these nominations resulted in seats (ASF, 1994: 10–11). In order to honor its pledge about women's representation in the Bundestag, the SPD had to utilize its party list and secure one in three of the top places for women.

Of the 176 women elected to the thirteenth Bundestag, nearly half (48.3 percent) belong to the SPD (Figure 12.3). Between them, the opposition parties make up over 70 percent of the Bundestag's female membership. A comparison with the composition of the Bundestag after the elections in 1990 may serve to put the gains and losses of women's representation into perspective. Then, 44 percent of the female members of the Bundestag belonged to a party of the government coalition, and the CDU/CSU alone included one-third of the women in the Bundestag. The SPD increased the number of women delegates by twenty-one, that is, 48.3 percent of women members of the Bundestag. The Greens, who were down to three women members (2 percent) when the West German Greens failed at the 5 percent hurdle in 1990, entered the Bundestag with twenty-nine women in 1994, 16.5 percent of the total female membership. The number of women in the PDS faction rose from eight to thirteen, that is, 7.3 percent of women delegates. With 3.7 percent and 4.9 percent respectively, the CSU and FDP bring up the rear (Figure 12.3).

In the 1994 election women clearly enjoyed better access to parliamentary seats in the political parties of the opposition than in those of the governing coalition. The parliamentary parties of the Greens and the PDS include more women members than men. Although a women's majority in a parliamentary party is not altogether new in German electoral politics, a women's majority never had occurred above the regional level. Compared with the representation of women in the Alliance 90/Greens and the PDS, the 33 percent mark reached by the SPD appears as a shortfall and the party barely managed to meet the 30 percent target prescribed in the statute.

From the vantage point of women in the SPD, the 1994 campaign did not go fully to plan and its outcome was no better than it should have been. One of the high-points of the campaign was the nomination of seven women in Scharping's prospective government team of fifteen. In the past, the SPD had been under pressure to honor the expectations of office holding voiced by long-established party members. The majority of female Bundestag deputies and office holders in the parliamentary party had been party members since the 1970s and worked their way up through the organization. In 1994, a backlog of long-standing

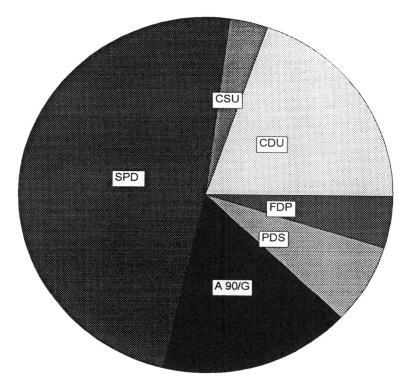

**Figure 12.3** Women in the Thirteenth Bundestag by Political Party

female members without a senior political office no longer
existed to the same degree since the SPD's regional electoral successes increased representation in Land parliaments and yielded
a record number of government posts for women, including the
office of minister-president for Heide Simonis in Schleswig-
Holstein (ASF, 1993b: 9–21; Hürdenlauf an die Macht, 1993). It
therefore became easier for new female members in the SPD to
gain access to a political office without having to subject themselves to an *Ochsentour* of party service. Unification also changed
the significance of organizational involvement since almost all
eastern SPD members are novices in the political and parliamentary arena.

Yet, the SPD "government" team was little more than a publicity device to project a progressive image and persuade female
voters that women had a place and a voice in the SPD. Beyond

the glossy front, the campaign hardly included women. In her post-election reckoning, Karin Junker from the ASF complained:

> The men in the SPD do not consider that women's policy has anything to do with them, they know very little about the contents of this policy and they frequently regard "woman" as the equivalent of "family." This means that female voters feel that the SPD has nothing on offer for them. When female and male members of the SPD talk about the same topic it often sounds as if they are speaking for two totally different political parties. (Junker, 1994: 6)

The majority of media events, discussion groups, and advertising spots only included men. If women were present, they addressed women's issues while the men dealt with "real" policies. When the SPD decided to boost the faltering candidacy of Scharping, it was a troika leading the SPD, not an integrated team of men and women. When the original SPD chancellor candidate, Björn Engholm, resigned in 1993, three women contested the position of party leader, although none got past a vice-chairman's position (Leinemann, 1993: 24). Women in the SPD perceive themselves as capable and ready to take on the leadership, a claim first voiced in 1976 when the ASF fielded an alternative all-female cabinet with a woman as would-be chancellor. However, the party is not ready to go beyond administering a quota within its party organization. Women continue to be treated as the second gender with improved chances but ultimately in a supporting role. In this respect, the SPD remains sharply different from the Greens where gender has ceased to matter and where women have taken as prominent a role as men at the parliamentary and party levels. If allocating women frontbench roles is seen as a device to placate female party activists, the SPD is making headway. If dismembering the gender barrier extends to the party culture itself in order to regain the confidence of Germany's youngest female voters, the SPD has yet to find a formula that will convince an electorate sensitized by feminism that the party will advance equality and not just (additional) "jobs for girls" in an essentially male party organization.

The Christian Democratic Union has had a much different experience. For the first time since 1983, the number of Christian Democratic women elected to the Bundestag in 1994 went down rather than up. The 1990 elections in particular had brought a leap from 18 female CDU/CSU members of the Bundestag to 44. In 1994, 41 women gained seats, 35 for the CDU and 6 for the CSU. Although women's share of the parliamentary *Fraktion* remained virtually unchanged at 13 percent and 14 percent respectively, this stagnation combined with the reduction in numbers was perceived by women within the party (and particularly by the *Frauenunion*) as a defeat, and a direct outcome of the CDU hesitancy to underwrite a women's quota.

On the regional party lists, some 25 percent of CDU/CSU parliamentary candidates were women, but most were positioned too low to stand a chance of getting elected, especially in an election where their party suffered overall losses. The disappointment of *Frauenunion* activists at their failure to have more women elected to parliament surfaced during a *Frauendebatte*, a formal debate on the situation of women in the CDU during the party's first post-election congress on 28 November 1994 in Bonn. Had the problem been confined to its female members and their unmet expectations, little might have changed (*Frau und Politik*, 1994: 19–23). The party had bypassed women members in the past, be it in selecting female ministers from outside the party organization, or by refusing to promote women and close the gender gap in office holding. This time, however, the electoral debacle of CDU losses among women of all ages persuaded the leadership that a forceful gesture was required to regain the initiative through *Umbau* – internal reorganization – or a *neuer Ruck*, a new drive for innovation (*Frau und Politik*, 1994: 19-23). In his congress address, Helmut Kohl admitted that he had been wrong to oppose a women's quota: "I failed in my view that we do not need a stipulated procedure" (*Frankfurter Rundschau*, 29 November 1994: 3)

Using a new term, *Quorum*, to describe a system of positive discrimination, Kohl attempted to set the CDU apart linguistically and politically from parties with established anti-discrimination practices where the term *Quote* had been used. In the CDU, the *Quote* had been opposed on the grounds that it was allegedly detrimental to women who were included to make up the numbers rather than as equals and in recognition of their political calibre (Rössler, 1994: 10). The CDU post-election congress floated the idea of introducing what it called a *Quorum* but refrained from doing so. Actual steps toward improving women's representation in the party will not be put into place before the 1996 congress.

To re-establish its credibility among German women, the CDU appointed Claudia Nolte as Minister for Women and Youth. She combines two electoral strengths: she is a member of the younger generation of women that the CDU is appealing to, and she is an Easterner and thus presumably qualified to address the most disaffected members of Germany's female population. After unification, Kohl had chosen another Easterner, Angela Merkel, as the minister addressing the pressing consequences of social transformation facing women in the new Länder. In the test case during her period of office – the abortion debate – she towed the government line and failed to meet the expectations of younger women in the West and women in the East to decriminalize abortion and make it available in the early stages of pregnancy. Claudia Nolte, her successor, has gone on record as opposing abortion altogether and demanding that women who had had an abortion should work in a hospital for a year as a punishment (Prützel-Thomas, 1993; Kolinsky, 1995b: 281–97). Such views, however, differ sharply from those of most women of her own generation and the generations the CDU hopes to win back (*Frankfurter Rundschau*, 18 November 1994: 4). Moreover, Claudia Nolte is an outspoken opponent of either a quota or a quorum. She will not become a torchbearer for CDU women who have pressed for an organizational and parliamentary voice, or for German women who consider women's equal participation in politics as a yardstick of party competence in matters of equal opportunities.

## Conclusion

In the first two decades of postwar (West) German history, women were kingmakers of conservative-led governments. When women of the postwar generations began to perceive the SPD as guardian of equal opportunities, the Social Democrats also built their government role on women's support. In the 1980s and 1990s, both *Volksparteien* have been less able to meet the expectations of female voters. In 1994, the CDU lost voting support in all age groups, and the SPD all but stagnated. The two parties with oppositional agendas, the Alliance 90/Greens and the PDS, found an electoral stronghold among women under the age of 35.

In the old Länder, the New Politics agenda of the Alliance 90/Greens includes a commitment to anti-discrimination policies and women's quotas. The Greens have long been perceived as the party most competent to address women's issues. Many female voters who rank these issue high on their personal list of priorities tend to prefer Alliance 90/Greens to the established parties.

In the new Länder, the PDS built its electoral fortunes on its perception as an eastern interest party. For women with previous SED/PDS loyalties and in particular for women who feel short-changed by the economic transformations and social un-certainties in their lives, the PDS is a means to express their discontent with unification and, to some extent, with the established process of (West) German policy making.

The 1994 election results indicate that women of the younger generations – in the old Länder for slightly different reasons than in the new – lack confidence in mainstream politics and are turning to the smaller parties that appear to address their con-cerns. Or, women abstain from political participation altogether. Given the narrow margins that make or break the government role of either of the two big *Volksparteien*, the weakening of their support among younger women has as much a kingmaker-function as the solid CDU/CSU bonus had in the founding years of the Federal Republic.

"Women's issues" in the 1994 election cannot be narrowed down to specific policy themes such as child-care or similar measures to reduce women's conflict between family and employment roles. Nor did the abortion issue retain the political salience it seemed to have in 1993, since most eastern women accepted the format of obligatory counselling as a positive innovation. Abortion itself had lost its former GDR-function as a realm for women's self-determination. In the East, the "women's issue" in 1994 consisted of disaffection which turned into support for the PDS. In the West, it consisted of the expectation that policies and party organizations should no longer define separate areas for women or exclude them from political office, but grant equality. In this perspective, women's issues are them-selves discriminatory while a party's competence to represent the interests of women depends on the place for women in the party organization, in parliament, and in leadership and government positions.

The 1994 election revealed an uneven track record: the CDU, CSU, and FDP failed to improve women's representation despite promises to do so, while the SPD met its quota commitments but tended to relegate women to special women's realms in policy debates during the campaign. In their reluctance to support the *Volksparteien* or the FDP, women under the age of 35 signaled that declaration that intent alone no longer suffices. Moreover, women in the younger age groups regard party organizations and their policy aims as ill-suited to their own preferences about policy styles and themes. In 1994, the Alliance 90/Greens, whose earlier women's policy has been displaced by a broad front against discrimination, emerged as the party receiving the strongest electoral gains among the cohort of women who have been increasingly skeptical of the benefits of women-specific policies.

In present-day Germany, all political parties are challenged to recast their organizations and party cultures and include women as equals in parliaments and politics. Without such changes, women will withdraw their confidence from established political parties and turn to alternatives which may serve them better, or they may turn away from political participation altogether. In the 1994 election, Germany's young women voiced their demands for a better democracy, a democracy which removes role-stereotypes, involves them as equals in the political process, and allows them to lead the lives they choose. In West and East, the actual choices differ, but have the same aim of recasting policy agendas in order to meet women's expectations: a life of social and political equality and self-realization in the West, a life of employment, material security, and social opportunity in the East. On both sides of the former German–German border, the established parties have yet to respond to these expectations while the relevance of the Alliance 90/Greens and PDS for women voters shows them to be beacons of hope that women's place in society and in politics can be changed for the better.

**Notes**

1. Religious observance never carried the same weight in the new Länder, since only a minority of the Easterners identify with a religious denomination (see Chapter 9).
2. The following figures describe the growth in the percentage of women favoring the Greens between 1990 and 1994, by age cohort (CDU Generalsekretärs, 1993: 8):

|  | 18–24 | 25–34 | 35–44 | 45–59 | 60+ |
|---|---|---|---|---|---|
| 1990 | 11.4 | 10.4 | 6.3 | 2.7 | 0.9 |
| 1994 | 15.6 | 14.2 | 12.0 | 5.0 | 3.2 |
| Difference | +4.4 | +3.8 | +5.7 | +2.3 | +2.3 |

3. Among the women elected to the thirteenth Bundestag, 85 are from the SPD, 35 are from the CDU, 29 are from the Alliance 90/Greens, 13 are from the PDS, 8 are from the FDP, and 6 are from the CSU.

**References**

Ammer, Thomas. 1992. "Die Parteien in der DDR und in den neuen Bundesländer," in Alf Mintzel und Heinrich Oberreuter, eds. *Parteien in der Bundesrepublik Deutschland*. Bonn: Bundeszentrale für politische Bildung.

ASF. 1993a. "Hürdenlauf an die Macht. Die SPD Frauen fünf Jahre nach der Quote," in Arbeitsgemeinschaft Sozialdemokratischer Frauen (ASF), ed. *Frauenthemen* 9 (September).

———. 1993b. "Bericht zur Lage der Frauen in der SPD." Gleichstellungsbericht vorgelegt auf dem Wiesbadener Parteitag am 17. 11. 1993," in Arbeitsgemeinschaft Sozialdemokratischer Frauen (ASF), ed. *Frauenthemen* 10 (December).

———. 1994. "Frauen haben die Wahl. Politik für Frauen – mit Frauen," in Arbeitsgemeinschaft Sozialdemokratischer Frauen (ASF), ed. *Frauenthemen* 13 (September).

CDU Generalsekretärs. 1993. "CDU Frauenbericht," Bericht des Generalsekretärs zur Umsetzung des Essener Leitsätze, vorgelegt auf dem 6. Parteitag der CDU Deutschlands 1994 in Bonn (28 November), unpublished manuscript).

Der Bundeswahlleiter, ed. 1994. *Die Kandidaten der Bundestagswahl 1994.* Wiesbaden.

Feist, Ursula. 1994. "Nichtwähler 1994. Eine Analyse der Bundestagswahl 1994," *Aus Politik und Zeitgeschichte* B 51–2.

Helwig, Gisela, and Hildegard Nickels, eds. 1993. *Frauen in Deutschland 1945–1992.* Berlin: Aufbau Verlag.

Hofmann-Göttig, Joachim. 1987. *Emanzipation mit dem Stimmzettel. 70 Jahre Frauenstimmrecht.* Bonn: Neue Gesellschaft.

Junker, Karin. 1994. "Jetzt ist eine frauenpolitische Offensive angesagt," in Arbeitsgemeinschaft Sozialdemokratischer Frauen (ASF), ed. *Frauenthemen. Special Issue Superwahljahr* 14 (December).

Kolinsky, Eva. 1993a. *Women in Contemporary Germany – Life, Work and Politics.* Oxford: Berg.

——. 1993b. "Party Change and Women's Representation in Unified Germany," in Joni Lovenduski and Pippa Norris, eds. *Gender and Party Politics.* London: Sage.

——. 1994. "Women and Politics in Western Germany," in Marilyn Rueschemeyer, ed. *Women in the Politics of Postcommunist Eastern Europe.* New York: Sharpe.

——, ed. 1995a. *Between Hope and Fear. Everyday Life in Post-Unification East Germany.* Keele: Keele University Press.

——. 1995b. *Women in 20th Century Germany. A Reader.* Manchester: Manchester University Press.

Leinemann, Jürgen. 1993. "Mächtig am Kommen," *Der Spiegel* (Title: "Wer rettet die SPD? Die Frauen ran") 19 (10 May): 24–9.

Meyer, Birgit. 1992. "Die 'unpolitische' Frau. Politische Partizipation von Frauen oder: Haben Frauen ein anderes Verständnis von Politik?" *Aus Politik und Zeitgeschichte* B 25–6.

Naßmacher, Hiltrud. 1994. "Frauen in die Politik?!" in Elke Biester et al., eds. *Demokratie oder Androkratie? Theorie und Praxis demokratischer Herrschaft in der feministischen Diskussion.* Frankfurt/Main: Campus.

Prützel-Thomas, Monika. 1993. "The Abortion Issue and the Federal Constitutional Court" *German Politics* 2: 467–84.

Rattinger, Hans. 1993. "Attitudes Towards the Abortion Law in Germany," *German Politics* 2: 261–3.

Rhardt-Vahldieck, Susanne, and Sybille Möller-Fiedler. 1994. "Die Abkehr jüngerer Frauen von der CDU. Ausmaß, Gründe und Konsequenzen." Unpublished manuscript, Hamburg.

Rössler, Beate. 1994. "Ohne Quotendebatte keine Demokratie. Hier mit der Debatte," *taz* 4258 (8 March): 10.

SPD. 1994. "SPD Analyse der Bundestagswahl 1994." Parteivorstand der SPD, Stand 24. November 1994, Bonn (unpublished manuscript).

Veen, Hans-Joachim. 1994. *Die Bundestagswahl vom 16. Oktober 1994. Eine erste Analyse.* Bonn/Sankt Augustin: Konrad Adenauer Foundation.

# V Conclusion

# 13

# Looking Ahead: Politics in Germany After the 1994 Bundestag Election

## *Max Kaase*

On election night and the days thereafter, the electoral losses of the CDU/CSU and FDP triggered a heated public debate on the future of the conservative–liberal coalition. The SPD and Greens questioned the formal legitimacy of the government's parliamentary majority of 10 seats based on the 12 "surplus mandates" (*Überhangmandate*) for the CDU (the SPD had 4 such mandates), and promised a permanent challenge to the government. The opposition predicted that the coalition would not make it intact to the end of the legislative period in 1998.

Contrary to such claims and expectations, at least until the end of summer 1995 the coalition was in firm control. This situation was not the least due to the SPD's internal conflicts and particularly the publicly "celebrated" conflict between Rudolf Scharping, the SPD opposition leader in the Bundestag, and Gerhardt Schröder, his rival and minister president of the state of Lower Saxony. As a result of these internal struggles and the continuously strong showing of Chancellor Helmut Kohl, the CDU/CSU by September 1995 had found public support to an extent that would have rendered an absolute CDU/CSU majority (in seats) possible if a Bundestag election had been called then.

Of course, there is little point in pursuing further speculations based on electoral moods and not on real votes. I only addressed this situation because the German climate of opinion in the summer of 1995 displayed little, if anything, of the strains and problems the outcome of the election seemed to forecast. Political tides come and go, however, and it therefore seems appropriate to place the 1994 Bundestag election in the context of more general sociopolitical developments on both a national and a transnational scale.

Conclusion

## Becoming and Staying Democratic

The breakdown of the Weimar Republic, Hitler's rise to power and Germany's role in provoking the Second World War cast long shadows on the early years of the Federal Republic. Doubts regarding the democratic habits of the Germans prevailed for a long time. Only with the first peaceful government turnover from the CDU/CSU to the Social Democrats after the general election of 1969 did Germany pass an essential democratic test (Huntington, 1991: 266–7). A thorough analysis of the political orientations of the West German citizenry in the late 1970s and the resulting conclusion that West Germany had finally entered the ranks of other established democracies (Conradt, 1980) went unchallenged in the literature and seemed to square well with the concrete operation of German democracy. David Conradt notes, however, "it is ironic that West Germany has become a 'model stable democracy' almost exactly at the time when this model both in Germany and elsewhere in the West has come under increasing challenge from both scholars and political activists" (Conradt, 1980: 265).

The "quiet" years of postwar reconstruction in the OECD countries, based on the foreign policy impasse of the Cold War between the democratic and the socialist bloc as well as on the enormous growth in economic well-being, was coming to an end in the 1960s. In West Germany, even the sudden political outbursts of the student movement, the temporary economic downswing after 1965, the short-lived rise of the right-wing National Democrats (NPD), and the Grand Coalition of CDU/CSU and SPD (1966–1969) had only faintly – and more outside than inside the country – evoked fears of the Weimar syndrome. Rather, Willy Brandt's famous dictum to "risk more democracy" (*mehr Demokratie wagen*) in his first speech in the Bundestag after his election as chancellor pointed to new frontiers in democratic government. Such thoughts, however, were in no way unique to Germany.

The late 1960s and the 1970s were also the years when leftist critics proclaimed the imminent breakdown of late capitalism and its twin, the political system of liberal democracy. The protagonists of those legitimacy crisis speculations were not quite clear what political order would emerge after the predicted breakdown, although they expressed little doubt that some sort of socialist state would ensue (Offe, 1972: 169). These views never became politically consequential, but they had a substantial impact on the intellectual climate in the Federal Republic, an impact that even in the mid-1990s is still felt particularly in cultural discourse.[1]

The legitimacy crisis debate and its conservative equivalent, the ungovernability theme (for details see Kaase and Newton, 1995: 17–39), had so little political effect not least because of the economic advantage Western capitalist states so obviously possessed over their communist adversaries. Still, the communist political option of the (benevolent) totalitarian state remained a very vivid and attractive one to many people. This belief was reinforced by the left ideological underpinnings of images of an egalitarian society.

The support for the *idea* of socialism in the West was one factor which prevented a more realistic assessment of the nature and status of the political system that had emerged under the label of socialism. Even more important, however, was the tight control the totalitarian states of the East exercised over access to those polities, as well as to the free flow of information. The latter point is particularly relevant for the empirical social sciences, which were prevented from establishing an apparatus of systematic observation of social and political phenomena.[2]

Both aspects may help to understand why the successful self-transformation of authoritarian regimes in South America and Southern Europe in the 1970s into pluralist democracies and the mutation of orthodox communists into euro-communist parties in Italy and France were not interpreted in the West, at that time, as signs of a waning in strength of communist ideology and power. It should be noted that for the West German electorate at large, other than for some members of the cultural intelligentsia, communism at no point was a viable option. Real socialism, in the form of the German Democratic Republic as a "negative reference society" (Lepsius, 1981: 436), was simply too present and too observable to muster any public support for a communist alternative in the West (Kudera et al., 1979: 362–8).

In general, the breakdown of totalitarian communism caught the world by surprise. For Germany, these developments suddenly opened an avenue to unification of the two German states that almost everybody had believed closed for many years to come. The story how, under Kohl's guidance and with President

295

*Conclusion*

Bush's support, this road was successfully travelled to 3 October 1990, the day of unification, has been told many times and need not be repeated here. However, for the united Germany two problems arose from the truly epochal processes of political transition in Central and Eastern Europe: a general and a specific one, and both are pertinent for the future of the German polity.

*The General Dimension*

Francis Fukuyama's (1992) book on the end of history reflects the breakdown of communism in a very basic fashion, namely as the exhaustion of available counter-models to the liberal democratic state. One need not dwell on the problem that predicting the future (which was not intended by Fukuyama, but was held against him by some of his critics anyway) is a close to impossible enterprise. Obviously, alternative modes of political organization can emerge in the future because of social, political, cultural, and technological changes which are beyond contemporary imagination. What is important today, however, is that the eclipse of communism has bereaved liberal democracy of its "easy" ideological and institutional antipode.

It was mentioned before that an important ideological element in the communist belief system was the emphasis on equality. This ideology, when put into effect, suppressed all economic and social dynamics in the communist countries. In addition, the sheer existence of the claim for equality, supported by the USSR as the hegemonic state incorporating that belief, also was an important precondition for the consensual acceptance of equality as one societal goal in the West. The Scandinavian welfare state, dismantled as it may have been lately, always embodied this idea under democratic rule. Democracy and welfare statism, at least in Europe, became almost synonymous. This observation leads to the general argument that for democracies to obtain peaceful change in the distribution of wealth and/or power, a believable threat (ideological or otherwise) to those advantaged under the status quo is necessary (even if not sufficient). Communism was the epitome of such a threat. Without this threat, it is questionable whether capitalism would have survived and transformed itself economically, socially (e.g., into the *soziale Marktwirtschaft*), and politically.

There is more to the loss of the ideological antipode, however.

The visible physical, economic, and political conditions of life under communism were so abhorrent for the vast majority of citizens in the West that their governments could easily point to those conditions in order to distract attention from the many problems within pluralist democracies. With the negative referent of communism missing, the questions will now be how democracies fare without it, whether they need a replacement for this void, and what such a replacement might look like.

The impact of the waning of communism as an alternative institutional political order to democracy may be further aggravated by two processes going on within liberal democracies. For one, Joachim Fest (1993; 1994) has pointed out that as democracies age and cohort replacement takes place, liberalism and human rights have become so universal and taken for granted that pluralist democracy with its constituent value relativism and without noteworthy external threats is increasingly becoming a "cold project." This raises the question of where citizens will find their emotional attachment to democracy and to their state in the future. Even more basically, is such an attachment, be it Easton's (1965; 1975) diffuse support for the political community, Bellah's (1967) civil religion, Sternberger's (1990) *Verfassungspatriotismus* (constitutional patriotism), or the communitarians' emphasis on citizens who accept responsibility for their political community (a revival of republican thought), necessary and possible in modern, differentiated societies (a question Dubiel [1992; 1994], with support from Hirschman [1994] answers negatively)? Such controversies are typical for the situation of normative ambiguity about their self-ideology into which Western democracies seem to be moving. The extent to which Germany has already been touched by this debate is clearly signaled by the enormous public success of a book (1994) by TV journalist Ulrich Wickert on the loss of values.

The second factor pertains to the encompassing sociopolitical changes Western democracies have experienced over a period of almost three decades.[3] Individually and in interaction, structural factors like economic growth, the expansion of higher education, the growth of the service/communication and the decline of the agricultural and industrial sectors, have reshaped the contours of the OECD countries in many ways. For the domain of political beliefs, probably the most consequential developments were secularization, that is, the loss of religious ties by citizens in

Europe – both as declining religious values and formal attachment to a church, and the Inglehart-type value change which
emphasizes a generational shift from material to nonmaterial
concerns (van Deth and Scarbrough, 1995).

In sum, the OECD democracies in general have been
undergoing some very basic changes in their environment and
their internal characteristics. Given their similarity in economic,
social and political structure, these processes took place more or
less at about the same time in the various countries. In addition,
in a world which is rapidly becoming the once proclaimed global
village, individual countries no longer have the leverage to
determine their fate mostly by themselves. Both aspects, of
course, also hold for the German case. However, the unification
of the two formerly independent German states poses a series of
additional questions. This topic will be taken up in the next
section.

### The Specific Dimension

As more and more societies are linked through trade, business,
transnational unions and parties, international political organizations and – foremost – communication, issue agendas also
become more and more transnational (like environmental
concerns). Thus, the synchronic decline in the European Union
(EU) countries in satisfaction with democracy in 1992 and 1993
may reflect the extent to which all EU countries are bothered by
structural unemployment, the overarching problem in Europe.
However, German unification produced two additional issues
which will most likely continue to bother the country: the
economic problems accompanying unification, and the merging
of two populations that had lived for more than forty years under
vastly different political and social systems.

Of course, a thorough treatment of the economic problems
resulting from the fusion of a planned economy and a market
economy under truly breathtaking time constraints is impossible
in the context of this chapter. The scale of the annual transfers
from the old to the new Länder since 1991 (about $100 billion per
year on a continuing basis) provides a sense of the magnitude of
the problem. The completely rundown infrastructure of the GDR,
the disappearance of one-third of the GDR's jobs, the resulting
(real) unemployment of 30 to 35 percent of the workforce, and

high levels of forced job mobility all quickly added up to a picture of gloom and strain that eastern Germans already antici- pated in 1990 before unification (Kaase, 1993: 52) and which gained full force only after 1990. After a while, the repercussions of the eastern situation also were felt by Westerners. This is a major factor in the steep decline in government popularity in both the East and the West that began shortly after the December 1990 Bundestag election (the data are displayed by Jung and Roth, 1994: 4). It is important to note here – this point will be taken up again later in the chapter – that the decline in govern- ment popularity was not made up for – as democratic theory would suggest – by a corresponding increase in opposition support. Rather, both curves developed more or less in unison, an indication of a deep-seated dissatisfaction with all political actors, although for different reasons in the West (fear of loosing previous privileges) and in the East (economic turmoil and deprivation). The strengthening relationship between economic and political dissatisfaction sometimes made one wonder whether Germany had returned to the early phases of establishing democracy in the "old" Federal Republic. Renate Köcher (1994: 18) rightly points to the fact that the 1992/93 data on political attitudes did indeed imply what quickly became a catchword for the way citizens felt politically: *Politikver- drossenheit*.

Next to economics, the second major concern was how the eastern and western Germans would manage the problem of be- coming one people again. Among political scientists, the most interesting question appeared to be how politically different both populations really felt and what would follow from the diagnosis to be given. A first wave of findings emphasized, against the plausible expectation of substantial differences in basic political orientations, a surprising amount of convergence (Bauer, 1991; Weil, 1993; Bauer-Kaase, 1994; Dalton, 1994). Later research, however, has qualified this picture considerably. As Easterners became more and more frustrated with the (economic) con- sequences of unification, dissatisfaction grew with the incumbent parties and with German democracy in general; and reident- ification with the former GDR followed suit (Westle, 1992a; 1992b; 1994). Noelle-Neumann (1995) observes that despite a distinct sense of optimism in the new Länder, a broadly based attachment to the political system of democracy cannot be found.

Also, western and eastern Germans differ in the extent to which they blamed their own or the other side for problems arising in the unification process. These perceptions were quite different in 1992, became even more different in 1993, receded somewhat in 1994, but are still substantial (Kaase, 1995a).

Interpretations of the evidence that the two German populations are getting more distant or closer together are not without elements of wishful thinking on the side of the protagonists of either position (Veen and Zelle, 1995; Noelle-Neumann, 1994a; 1994b). However, the eager search for differences or commonalities is increasingly replaced by a more patient acceptance of the fact that both the different life histories and the different problem agendas of the two populations will, for some time to come, necessarily result in differences in outlook and behavior in many life domains that have to be accepted in their own right. Another question is for how long public concerns about the *Befindlichkeiten* of eastern and western Germans will prevail. Much can be said in favor of the hypothesis that the existence of substantial difficulties arising from unification is now so generally accepted that its news value, as the economic situation in eastern Germany improves and time passes, is substantially deflated. This routinization probably owes a lot also to the fact that both populations are getting tired of that topic and finally want to return to their own lives – different as they may look like in the East and in the West.

It may or may not happen that this divide becomes politically relevant again, for example, if the economic situation in the new Länder drastically worsens. However, in the political realm the simple datum must not be overlooked that both Germanies have been operating for some time now under the same constitutional and institutional framework. At the December 1990 Bundestagswahl this situation had just started to shape the voters' orientations (not to speak of the fact that the two Germanies were treated by the electoral law as two separate electoral areas). The 1994 election came at the end of a unified campaign (with, of course, different regional emphases) and was channelled into a unified party system. It sometimes appears as if the strength of the postcommunist PDS in the East and the (not very surprising) fact that the vote in the old and in the new Länder is still determined by different factors (Dalton and Bürklin in Chapter 9 speak of the "two electorates") make observers underestimate the constraints originating from the common institutional foundations which govern not only elections, but also the political process at large in a unified Germany.

## Political Structure and Political Culture

The functionalist approach to the analysis of political processes (Almond and Powell, 1978) has provided a useful heuristic device for the study of system perseverance and change (Fuchs, 1989; Westle, 1989). Quite simplistically, and with little sound empirical testing, one could venture the argument that as structure and culture get out of synchronization, a threat to the perseverance (stability) of a political system would follow. Of course, one can avoid the potential that this becomes a circular argument only when "culture" and "structure" are measured independently and when "stability" can be validly conceptualized as an ordinal variable with system change (that is, change in the basic political order) as one end point and ultra-stability as the other.

Political science has yet to come up with a set of theory-guided indicators that gives a reasonably precise and encompassing account of what the basic structure of a given political system is and how it can be empirically assessed. This is particularly true with respect to comparisons between democracies (a noteworthy exception is the work by Lijphart; see 1984; 1991; 1994). This deficiency makes it difficult to tell to what extent a given democratic system has changed its institutions and procedures over time, perhaps as a reaction from culturally derived pressures and strains in the system.

A look at the culture dimension provides a completely different picture. When political culture is conceptualized in the tradition of the Almond and Verba *Civic Culture* Study (1963; 1980) as "a particular pattern of orientations to political action" (Almond, 1956: 396), then the confinement to individual properties, that is, the micro level, brings the whole breadth of survey research into play.

Max Kaase (1979) and David Conradt (1980) were among the first to point out, on empirical grounds, that German democracy in the 1970s was not suffering from the proclaimed legitimacy crisis. Dieter Fuchs (1989) and Bettina Westle (1989), working within the Eastonian theoretical framework, conducted sophisticated analyses that demonstrated that a reservoir of diffuse support for the system of democracy (the regime level in Easton's words) had accumulated over the years. This shielded the German political system from the ups and downs of partisan moods built into the democratic political process through the government–opposition antinomy (Luhmann, 1986; Weil, 1989). This antinomy, again in Easton's words, pertains to the political authorities and in particular to specific political parties.

In democratic theory the structure–culture relationship becomes relevant. The legitimacy of the overall political system is not endangered as long as the ever-present dissatisfaction in parts of the citizenry is not becoming so universal *across party lines* that the built-up reservoir of diffuse support for democracy as a political system is effected.

Given the empirical evidence already discussed, this topic did not return to the research agenda until German unification was taking place. One question asked how the new Germany would integrate the East Germans, who had been socialized for forty-five years into a totalitarian doctrine, into an internationally praised democratic West German culture. Findings referred to before, speaking to a surprising amount of democratic creed also in the East Germans, took much of the heat away from this problem. In addition, a factor not always made explicit, certainly also played an important role here. Unification according to Article 21 of the German Basic Law was *de facto* a complete surrender of the GDR to the FRG; little wonder that the term *Kolonialisierung* gained so much currency particularly among critics of unification (in the West parts of the left cultural intelligentsia and the Greens; in the East the devoted communists, and that to a large extent meant the PDS). The West Germans certainly could not have demanded this mode of unification and the East German government would not have accepted it, except for the population ratios between the two Germanies: 20 percent Easterners and 80 percent Westerners. Given these numbers and the stable institutional and constitutional framework of West Germany, it was not very likely that a major impact on overall German political culture would ensue.

This optimistic scenario, however, quickly took a negative turn after the 1990 election. Quite unexpectedly, the eastern economy broke down almost completely because of the instant change from a planned to a market system. This breakdown resulted in strong demands on the western economy that were aggravated by an international recession; this caught Germans unaware because they had been mislead by the burst of economic activity induced by the initial consumer demand from the new Länder. Helmut Kohl's false promise of blossoming landscapes in the East, the realization that the costs of unification would not be paid out of western pockets, and a series of political scandals, combined to create a climate of political anger. It did not take long before this mood found expression. As both Hans Rattinger (1993: 24) and Hildegard Hamm-Brücher (1993: 3) report, *Politikverdrossenheit* (frustration with politics) became the 1992 "word of the year."

It is worth recalling that the catchword "frustration with parties" (*Parteienverdrossenheit*) has been used since the 1980s (Rattinger, 1993: 24–5 gives some examples), although the empirical evidence had been sketchy. Westle (1990: 282) emphasizes that the critique against specific parties at that time was *not* generalized to the party system at large. The topic, though, was "in the air" (Wildenmann, 1989). Not only had the 1987 Bundestag election for the first time resulted in a substantial decline in turnout (minus 4.8 percent compared to 1983), but this drop continued in 1990 (minus 5.7 percent) despite the enormous politicization in the unification year. The 1990 turnout almost equaled the turnout level at the first Bundestag election in 1949. In the end, however, it was only in the aftermath of unification that feelings of political dissatisfaction crystallized in the debate on "*Politikverdrossenheit*."

As is quite usual in these matters, journalists and social scientists alike quickly jumped on to the bandwagon, thereby creating a self-reinforcing image that people were deeply dissatisfied with not only parties, but also democratic politics at large. Especially among those who were addressing this topic in a speculative manner, visions of an imminent political breakdown surfaced again, as in the old "crisis of legitimacy" days.[4] Even empirically minded social scientists, who usually are more cautious in jumping to far-reaching conclusions, noted that citizen dissatisfaction with politics had dramatically risen since 1991 (Rattinger, 1993; for summaries of the available literature see Ehrhardt and Sandschneider, 1994; Rieger, 1994).

More recent reflections on this topic have introduced a note of reservation about the indiscriminate use of *Parteien-*, *Politik-* and *Demokratieverdrossenheit* (Lösche, 1995), and one should be careful not to misread temporary results as structural phenomena (Welzel, 1995: 143). Indeed, Renate Köcher's (1994: 18) analysis points to the fact that the dissatisfaction with the *whole set of parties* had fallen in mid-1994 to levels prevalent in the early 1980s as quickly as it had risen in 1992 and 1993.

There is overwhelming empirical evidence that this change is directly related to the perceived (and real) improvement in the economic situation which was reported by all of the German economic research institutes in the spring of 1994 (Jung and Roth, 1994; Rohrschneider and Fuchs, 1995; Schultze, 1995; Norpoth and Roth, Chapter 10). However, although *Politikverdrossenheit* no longer seems to be *en vogue*, the question remains whether the well-founded belief that democracy in the Federal Republic is insulated from economic ups and downs is still valid. Here, the answer seems to be ambivalent at best. Preliminary analyses (Kaase, 1995a) indicate that satisfaction with the democratic system of government has again become dependent on economic satisfaction, as in the pre-1969 days. The dramatic post-1990 decline in satisfaction with the way democracy works in one's country in practically all European Union countries is an important phenomenon (Fuchs and Klingemann, 1995). The indicator used in the Eurobarometer studies is not quite measuring what it should – attachment to democracy as a system of political order – and caution is always advised in making quick *ad hoc* interpretations of fresh survey data. Nevertheless, it may be that the pervasiveness of economic strains in Europe (being, of course, aggravated in Germany by the cost of unification) is indeed gnawing at the reservoir of diffuse support for democracy. Here, then, the evaporation of the communist antipode may help to reinforce that process. While an alternative option to democracy is obviously not in sight, support of democracy may still be suffering and might eventually lead either to outbursts of apathy or rebellion.

The debate about the declining turnout in Germany, however, is a good example with which to show that only systematic longitudinal studies can properly unfold the determinants of such a decline and its eventual longevity. Thomas Kleinhenz (1994) analyzed public opinion surveys over the past decade; he concludes that non-voting is a multi-faceted phenomenon. His main finding is that both dealignment and normalization (in the sense of a reduction in the number of those who believe that voting is a citizen duty) are important factors in the decline in West German turnout (the new Länder are a different and difficult extra case) (Kleinhenz, 1994: 224). Party frustration is less important as an explanatory factor. Thus, a return to levels of turnout in national elections typical for the 1960s and 1970s is quite unlikely (see also Rattinger and Krämer, 1995: 284).

In sum, then, democratic governance is facing interesting future challenges, which, in one form or another, have accompanied the rise of the democratic political order to prominence and have strengthened its past development. Yet, five years after 1990 the conclusion seems justified that both the economic strains and the problem of two still quite distant German peoples will preoccupy the political process in the unified Federal Republic for some time to come. However, the available evidence certainly does not reveal a particular threat to German democracy in the aftermath of unification.

## The German Party System in Context – Present and Future

Structural stability of the political system in no way precludes changes in important elements of that system. Since postwar Germany was constructed very much as a party democracy, a look at the present state of the party system is mandatory.

Parties are living, active organisms which are not helplessly subjected to changes in their environment. And yet such changes may, despite a party's efforts, deeply influence a party's fortune in the middle to long run. There is no question that social change has affected the ease and the probability with which parties can obtain electoral support. Even if Carsten Zelle (1995) finds little empirical support for the claim that the German electorate has become increasingly volatile – measured as the share of the floating vote among those who voted at two consecutive elections – at least the secular decline in turnout already points to the impact of social change. Dealignment, according to Kleinhenz (1995), is a major factor. This process has helped to erode the levels and intensity of identification with the parties (see Chapter 10), not least because the number of citizens belonging to the social milieus supporting specific parties has shrunk dramatically (one need only think of the number of Catholics regularly attending church services, the classic CDU/ CSU clientele). Also, as turnout drops, the switch between party voting and non-voting becomes ever more important in the analysis of electoral behavior.

Bearing all this in mind, one cannot help but be amazed at the consistently high level of electoral success the CDU and CSU secured over four decades. The return of the economy, Chancellor Kohl's standing, and the singular event of unification all have contributed to this success. In addition, the CDU's support for social programs in the conservative–liberal coalition was a major factor in its retaining a fair share of the working-class vote. Furthermore, both Christian parties, especially the CSU, worked hard to strengthen their organizational infra-structure.

The almost complete lack of such an infrastructure for the FDP is one of the reasons why the FDP now seems doomed for oblivion. The Free Democrats have hardly any parliamentary representation in the Länder and in many communes. The party's survival in the 1994 Bundestag election depended almost exclusively on votes obtained by CDU/CSU (see Chapter 10), an obviously untenable situation in the long run.

Counter to many predictions (which seemed to be supported by its 1990 exit from the Bundestag), the Greens have become an established party. The Greens might now even enter a phase where a durable voter alignment based on a value cleavage (epitomized by its emphasis on environmental concern) seems possible. The environment has long been a valence issue that is represented in the manifesto of every party. However, the Greens' exclusive concern with that domain and their generally acknowledged role as a pioneer for that issue give them a lead over all other parties among a distinct voter bloc: the state-paid public service, teachers, social workers, and students. It remains to be seen, though, how they would fare without their present leader, Joschka Fischer, and what effect the need to develop policy stances on other issues than the environment will have on the party (e.g., the debate on the use of force to end the conflict in former Yugoslavia). This broader agenda follows from their participation in an increasing number of Länder governments and their quest for governmental representation in Bonn.

Undoubtedly, the party that has suffered most from social change is the SPD. Almost fifteen years ago, Max Kaase and Hans-Dieter Klingemann (1982) empirically demonstrated that the SPD is, for all practical purposes, two parties in one: the Old Left (trade union organized workers), and the New Left (service class). Being thrown out of the Bonn government in 1982 has enabled the SPD verbally to bridge that gap, although at the price of waning electoral support from both camps and the strengthening of the Greens. The return of the economic dimension as a priority issue is now forcing the SPD to develop a new position on economic policy. In 1995, it is difficult to see how the party will be able to reconcile the demands from its structurally differing clienteles.

Given the Holocaust, it cannot come as a surprise that right-wing extremism is an extremely sensitive topic in German politics (viewed both from the inside and from the outside). From the beginnings of the Federal Republic, right-wing support has always come and gone in waves. Much, therefore, can be said in favor of an interpretation that looks at right-wing voting more as a safety valve than a stable identification with right-wing ideologies. Voting for a right-wing party effectively channels political protest, given the immediate attention that accompanies any real or constructed resort to the German Nazi past. The asylum problem and its solution, as Jürgen Falter (1994: 160–3) points out, probably was the *one* most important factor in producing the rise and the fall of the Republikaner since 1989 (see also Kuechler, 1994 and Chapter 11). Obviously, the problem with right-wing voting in Germany is that even though only a small share of the population hold deep-seated right-wing authoritarian attitudes (this is not different from other countries; see Falter, 1994: 163; Kuechler, 1994), their ranks can, almost at will, be augmented by a floating protest vote.

Undoubtedly, the most interesting "innovation" in the German party system has been the rise of the postcommunist PDS. Jürgen Falter and Markus Klein (1994: 34) have concluded that subjective factors more than objective (structural) factors determined the PDS vote in 1994. PDS voters could be characterized by a "mixture of ideology, nostalgia and protest." Under these circumstances, it would appear only logical to predict, as normalization in the new Länder continues, that the PDS will increasingly lose electoral support.

However, there is one structural factor that is missing in this equation and has already been very consequential for the revitalized electoral fortunes of postcommunist parties in the new democracies in Central and Eastern Europe: the existence of a strong and effective party organization infrastructure. Jürgen Lang and Patrick Moreau (1994: 10) point out that the PDS membership in the new Länder almost equals that of all other parties together. During the 1994 Superwahljahr, reports abounded that PDS party members were instrumental in many eastern communities in helping citizens to find their way through the complex new regulations resulting from the administrative reform after unification. This engagement is even the more understandable, given the fact that almost half of the PDS members are pensioners (Lang and Moreau, 1994: 11).

In the past, predictions that the PDS would quickly disappear from the German party system turned out to be premature. Nevertheless, the ongoing political normalization in the new Länder, the inability of the PDS to establish itself in the old Länder, and the age composition of its membership all point in the direction that the PDS will find it difficult to retain its electoral strength in the long run.

One factor which limits this speculation, but also pertains to the FDP and any right-wing party, is the German electoral law with its 5 percent clause and the option to split one's vote between the first ballot (for a constituency candidate) and the second ballot (for the party list). The PDS, with 4.4 percent of the second ballot vote, would not have regained parliamentary representation, had it not been for the provision that a party winning three constituency seats could share in the proportional representation of seats. This gave the PDS thirty seats in the Bundestag. The FDP got just 3.3 percent on the first ballot; with 6.9 percent of the second ballot the party jumped over the 5 percent hurdle only with strong support form CDU/CSU adherents. How would these people have voted had it been uncertain that the FDP would obtain at least 5 percent of the second ballot? Considerations for these two parties point to general instability in the German party system which, under the specific circumstances of the next election, can end up with between three (CDU/CSU; SPD; Greens) and six (FDP; PDS; Republikaner) parties represented in the next Bundestag.

The more parties that gain parliamentary representation despite the 5 percent clause, the less likely it is that governments will be constructed as minimal winning coalitions. In addition, the more parties that participate in a government, the more likely it is that non-decisions or policy compromises will result and that parties will attribute this to the other coalition partners. One particularly problematic example of oversized coalitions is the "große Koalition" of CDU/CSU and SPD, which almost had to be formed in Bonn in 1994 because of the PDS parliamentary presence and is presently (autumn of 1995) in effect in four of the sixteen Länder (Baden-Württemberg, Berlin, Mecklenburg-Western Pomerania, and Thuringia).

Little wonder, then, that analysts are cautiously suggesting a reform of the German electoral law in the direction of some variant of majority rule (e.g. absolute majority vote with two ballots). This would install single-party governments and thereby institutionalize a higher degree of government accountability to the citizenry (Kaase, 1995b; see also Powell, 1989). This structural element of democratic politics is not the least important because, as Frederick Weil (1989: 688–9) has shown, a clear government–opposition structure (single-party government, minimal winning coalition) is conducive to system legitimacy.

Such thoughts also may gain in currency because other developments limit the chances for political accountability: the decline of parliamentary politics through the rise of direct political participation, the growing internationalization of governance (in Europe most notably through the European Union), the fusion between political parties and new social movements (Kriesi, 1993), and the creation of party-based power cartels at the local level (Scheuch and Scheuch, 1992). All this contributes to the neutralization of the central factor conducive to political innovation and control in democracies: a working government–opposition mechanism in the sense of 'throwing the rascals out' (Kaase, 1995b: 18–19).

While these are general developments, one additional, specifically German element has to be explicitly addressed: cooperative federalism and the relationship between the Bundestag and the Bundesrat in legislative matters. Given the divergent party coloring of the majorities in the Bundestag and the Bundesrat, the *Vermittlungsausschuß* (Mediation Committee) gains an ever-increasing weight. This results in a situation where policy positions are so watered down as to destroy even the few remaining traces of government accountability (the growing administrative nexus between Bonn and the Länder – *Politikverflechtung* – is another aspect of the phenomenon in question). Grimm (1994: 354) summarizes the problem very aptly:

> Without the public display of competing concepts the formation of public opinion and interest articulation are lacking. The policy outcomes of these fused politics can no longer be attributed to any one specific political competitor. The difference between majority and minority constantly shrinks. Critical assessments of government policies can be neutralized by pointing to shared responsibilities. The opposition can claim that they rendered planned government initiatives ineffective, the majority can claim that it was prevented from pursuing its policies. Under these circumstances it becomes increasingly difficult to use the vote to evaluate past government performance or to give an advanced trust check for declared government programs. (Author's translation)

## The 1994 Bundestag Election and Beyond

Germany more than any other Western democracy was directly affected by the demise of communism. The Bundestag election on 2 December 1990 was the first general election in unified Germany. In the foreword to the edited volume looking at the 1987 general election and written in the spring of 1990, Max Kaase and Hans-Dieter Klingemann (1990: 11) raised the question "to what extent are the available theories and concepts in electoral research capable also of analyzing and understanding such deep-seated and fast changes in the political landscape of Germany" (author's translation) as were induced by the union of the two Germanies.

By now, this question can receive a tentative affirmative answer, with some important qualifications. In general, the extension of the constitutional and institutional structures of the old Federal Republic to the new Länder and the almost complete – with the exception of the PDS – transfer of the West German party system into the East have created a stable electoral environment for balloting in the new Länder. Below this macro stability, however, momentous changes have taken place particularly in the intermediary infrastructure of the former GDR.

The GDR mass organizations (e.g. Free German Youth, Free Trade Union Association) were dissolved, the mass media system was restructured, party organizations either disappeared or were transformed (SED to PDS, the former block parties of CDU and LDP merged with their sister parties in the West). The rebuilding of that intermediary structure is still going on, but under these circumstances it is little wonder that the traditional West German linkages between organizations and voters which are epitomized in the social cleavage model are almost non-existent in the East, thereby producing counterintuitive findings (like the CDU working-class vote). While the concept of the two electorates is justified on empirical grounds as indicating that voting in the old and new Länder does not follow an identical logic, this does *not* imply that electoral research has to break completely new theoretical ground to understand the eastern vote. Rather, a general explanatory model needs to consider the same variables. These variables just behave differently and carry different weight in explaining party choice in the East and in the West. As a consequence, for some time to come the vote will have to be analyzed separately in order to avoid artificial findings that disguise the different political behavior in the two Germanies.

This situation, however, opens up fascinating opportunities for analyses of how changes on the macro and meso level influence individual behavior, as well as the impact of long-term socialization on behavior, almost as with a time machine (*Zeitraffer*).

Politically speaking, the 1994 election results signaled stability for Germany, but the outcome was narrow and fragile. The present CDU/CSU–FDP government undoubtedly was reinstalled because the economic outlook substantially improved during the spring of 1994. This gave some delayed credence to the government's claim in 1990 that it would manage the economic problems of unification.

Unification is not the only reason why economics will determine the political agenda in Germany for years to come. The globalization of production and thereby the economic competition between countries with enormous differences in their standard of living (and labor costs) are creating new debates about the future of the welfare state in Germany and beyond. It is telling that the 1995 conflict within the SPD is essentially on that topic, or as Gerhard Schröder phrased it, on modern versus old-fashioned economic policy. For the SPD this conflict touches on the historical and ideological roots of that party. Joschka Fischer even forced the Greens to discuss this problem on ideological as well as practical grounds. The SPD, trade unions, social welfare organizations, and governments at all levels and of all colors are accepting the principle of cost reduction, a situation inconceivable in the 1980s. No wonder that the decrease in public spending on social policies and the ensuing threat of a new poverty rate high among citizen concerns.

These German developments take place in a context which is becoming more and more transnational. Since most of world trade is still between OECD countries – and that means democracies – future international competition may increasingly involve competition between institutional variants of democracy (Moe and Caldwell, 1994). It is ironic, given the ideological battles on legitimacy of the 1970s and 1980s within democracies, that this will revive the concept of political effectiveness which Lipset (1960) had formulated as a twin to legitimacy – a concept that had lost almost all currency in the last three decades.

**Notes**

1. A good example is the controversy over Günter Grass' new book, *Ein weites Feld*.
2. This is why von Beyme's (1994) criticism of the lack of predictive qualities of the social sciences with respect to the political transition in Central and Eastern Europe is ill-taken.
3. For a detailed account see the five volumes in the Beliefs in Government series published in 1995 by Oxford University Press; see also Kaase and Kohut (1996).
4. *Aus Politik und Zeitgeschichte* (Issue B 31, 3 July 1993), issued by the Bonn Bundeszentrale für Politische Bildung, is full of examples of these doomsday associations).

# References

Almond, Gabriel. 1956. "Comparative Political Systems," *Journal of Politics* 18: 391–409.

—— and G. Bingham Powell Jr. 1978. *Comparative Politics. System, Process, and Policy*. 2nd ed. Boston-Toronto: Little, Brown and Company.

—— and Sidney Verba. 1963. *The Civic Culture*. Princeton: Princeton University Press.

—— and Sidney Verba, eds. 1980. *The Civic Culture Revisited*. Boston and Toronto: Little, Brown and Company.

Bauer, Petra. 1991. "Freiheit und Demokratie in der Wahrnehmung der Bürger in der Bundesrepublik und der ehemaligen DDR." In Rudolf Wildenmann, ed. *Nation und Demokratie*. Baden-Baden: Nomos Verlagsgesellschaft.

Bauer-Kaase, Petra. 1994. "Germany in Transition: The Challenge of Coping With Unification." In M. Donald Hancock and Helga Welsh, eds. *German Unification*. Boulder, CO: Westview Press.

Bellah, Robert N. 1967. "Civil Religion in America," *Daedalus* 96: 1–21.

Beyme, Klaus von. 1994. "Der Zusammenbruch des Sozialismus und die Folgen für die sozialwissenschaftliche Theoriebildung," *WZB-Mitteilungen* 63, Berlin: Wissenschaftszentrum Berlin für Sozialforschung.

Conradt, David P. 1980. "The Changing German Political Culture." In Gabriel Almond and Sidney Verba, eds. *The Civic Culture Revisited*. Boston: Little Brown.

Dalton, Russell J. 1994. "Communists and Democrats: Democratic Attitudes in the Two Germanies," *British Journal of Political Science* 24: 469–93.

Deth, Jan W. van, and Elinor Scarbrough, eds. 1995. *The Impact of Values*. Beliefs in Government, vol. 4. Oxford: Oxford University Press.

Dubiel, Helmut. 1992. "Konsens oder Konflikt? Die normative Integration des demokratischen Staats." In Beate Kohler-Koch, ed. *Staat und Demokratie in Europa*. Opladen: Leske & Budrich.

——. 1994. *Ungewißheit und Politik*. Frankfurt am Main: Suhrkamp.

Easton, David. 1965. *A Systems Analysis of Political Life*. New York: John Wiley.

——. 1975. "A Re-Assessment of the Concept of Political Sup-

Conclusion

port." *British Journal of Political Science* 5: 435–57.

Ehrhardt, Christoph, and Eberhard Sandschneider. 1994. "Politikverdrossenheit: Kritische Anmerkungen zur Empirie, Wahrnehmung und Interpretation abnehmender politischer Partizipation," *Zeitschrift für Parlamentsfragen* 25: 441–58.

Falter, Jürgen W. 1994. *Wer wählt rechts? Die Wähler und Anhänger rechtsextremistischer Parteien im vereinigten Deutschland.* München: C. H. Beck.

—— and Markus Klein. 1994. "Die Wähler der PDS bei der Bundestagswahl 1994," *Aus Politik und Zeitgeschichte.* Beilage zur Wochenzeitung *Das Parlament,* B 51/52–94, 22–34.

Fest, Joachim. 1993. *Die schwierige Freiheit. Über die offene Flanke der offenen Gesellschaft.* Berlin: Siedler Verlag.

——. 1994. "Nach dem Scheitern der großen Entwürfe." In Werner Weidenfeld, Dirk Rumberg, eds. *Orientierungsverlust – Zur Bindungskrise der modernen Gesellschaft.* Gütersloh: Verlag Bertelsmann Stiftung.

Fuchs, Dieter. 1989. *Die Unterstützung des politischen Systems der Bundesrepublik Deutschland.* Opladen: Westdeutscher Verlag.

—— and Hans-Dieter Klingemann. 1995. "Citizens and the State: A Relationship Transformed." In Hans-Dieter Klingemann, Dieter Fuchs, eds. *Citizens and the State.* Beliefs in Governments, vol. 1. Oxford: Oxford University Press.

Fukuyama, Francis. 1992. *The End of History and the Last Man.* New York: The Free Press.

Grimm, Dieter. 1994. *Die Zukunft der Verfassung,* 2nd ed., Frankfurt am Main: Suhrkamp.

Hamm-Brücher, Hildegard. 1993. "Wege in die und Wege aus der Politik(er)verdrossenheit." *Aus Politik und Zeitgeschichte.* Beilage zur Wochenzeitung *Das Parlament,* B 31/93. Bonn: Bundeszentrale für Politische Bildung, 3–6.

Hirschman, Albert O. 1994. "Wieviel Gemeinsinn braucht die liberale Gesellschaft?" *Leviathan* 22: 293–304.

Huntington, Samuel. 1991. *The Third Wave: Democratization in the Late Twentieth Century.* Norman and London: University of Oklahoma Press.

Jung, Mathias, and Dieter Roth. 1994. "Kohls knappster Sieg. Eine Analyse der Bundestagswahl 1994." *Aus Politik und Zeitgeschichte.* Beilage zur Wochenzeitung *Das Parlament,* B 51–52/94. Bonn: Bundeszentrale für Politische Bildung, 3–15.

Kaase, Max. 1979. "Legitimitätskrise in westlichen demokratischen Industriegesellschaften: Mythos oder Realität." In Helmut Klages and Peter Kmieciak, eds. *Wertewandel und gesellschaftlicher Wandel*. Frankfurt and New York: Campus.

——. 1993. "Electoral Politics in the New Germany: Public Opinion and the Bundestag Election of December 2, 1990." In Christopher Anderson, Karl Kaltenthaler, Wolfgang Luthardt (eds.), *The Domestic Politics of German Unification*. Boulder, CO and London: Lynn Rienner Publishers.

——. 1995a. "Die Deutschen auf dem Weg zur inneren Einheit? Eine Längsschnittanalyse von Selbst- und Fremdwahrnehmungen bei Ost- und Westdeutschen." In Hedwig Rudolph, ed. *Geplanter Wandel, ungeplante Wirkungen. Handlungslogiken und -ressourcen im Prozess der Transformation*. Berlin: Sigma Verlag.

——. 1995b. "Demokratie im Spannungsfeld von politischer Kultur und politischer Struktur." In Werner Link, Eberhard Schütt-Wetschky, Gesine Schwan, eds. *Jahrbuch für Politik*, 5, Halbband 2, Baden-Baden: Nomos.

—— and Hans-Dieter Klingemann. 1982. "Social Structure, Value Orientations, and the Party System," *European Journal of Political Research* 10: 367–86.

—— and Hans-Dieter Klingemann. 1990. "Einführung." In Max Kaase, Hans-Dieter Klingemann, eds. *Wahlen und Wähler. Analysen aus Anlaß der Bundestagswahl 1987*. Opladen: Westdeutscher Verlag.

—— and Andrew Kohut. 1996. *Estranged Friends? Societal Change and Transatlantic Consequences*. New York: Council on Foreign Relations.

—— and Kenneth Newton. 1995. *Beliefs in Government*. Beliefs in Government, vol. 5. Oxford: Oxford University Press.

Kleinhenz, Thomas. 1994. *Die Nichtwähler. Ursachen der sinkenden Wahlbeteiligung in Deutschland*. Opladen: Westdeutscher Verlag.

Köcher, Renate. 1994. "Auf einer Woge der Euphorie. Veränderungen der Stimmungslage und des Meinungsklimas im Wahljahr 1994." *Aus Politik und Zeitgeschichte*. Beilage zur Wochenzeitung *Das Parlament*, B 51–52/94. Bonn: Bundeszentrale für Politische Bildung, 16–21.

Kriesi, Hanspeter. 1993. *Political Mobilization and Social Change. The Dutch Case in Comparative Perspective*. Aldershot: Avebury.

Kudera, Werner, et al. 1979. *Gesellschaftliches und politisches Bewußtsein von Arbeitern. Eine empirische Untersuchung*. Frankfurt am Main: Europäische Verlagsanstalt.

Kuechler, Manfred. 1994. "Germans and 'Others': Racism, Xenophobia, or 'Legitimate Conservativism?" *German Studies* 3: 47–74.

Lang, Jürgen P., and Patrick Moreau. 1994. "PDS. Das Erbe der Diktatur." *Politische Studien*. Special Issue No. 1, 45, Munich: Hanns Seidel Stiftung.

Lepsius, M. Rainer. 1981. "Die Teilung Deutschlands und die deutsche Nation." In Lothar Albertin and Werner Link, eds. *Politische Parteien auf dem Wege zur parlamentarischen Demokratie in Deutschland*. Düsseldorf: Droste-Verlag.

Lijphart, Arend. 1984. *Democracies*. New Haven and London: Yale University Press.

———. 1991. "Constitutional Choices for New Democracies," *Journal of Democracy* 2: 72–84.

———. 1994. "Democracies: Forms, Performance and Constitutional Engineering," *European Journal of Political Research* 25: 1–17.

Lipset, Seymour Martin. 1960. *Political Man*. New York: Doubleday.

Lösche, Peter. 1995. "Parteienverdrossenheit ohne Ende? Polemik gegen das Lamentieren deutscher Politiker, Journalisten, Politikwissenschaftler und Staatsrechtler." *Zeitschrift für Parlamentsfragen* 26: 149–59.

Luhmann, Niklas. 1986. *Ökologische Kommunikation. Kann die moderne Gesellschaft sich auf ökologische Gefährdungen einstellen?* Opladen: Westdeutscher Verlag.

Moe, Terry M., and Michael Caldwell. 1994. "The Institutional Foundations of Democratic Government," *Journal of Institutional and Theoretical Economics/Zeitschrift für die gesamte Staatswissenschaft* 150: 171–95.

Noelle-Neumann, Elisabeth. 1994a. "Problems with Democracy in Eastern Germany after the Downfall of the GDR." In Frederick D. Weil and Mary Gautier, eds. *Political Culture and Political Structure: Theoretical and Empirical Studies*. Research on Democracy and Society, vol. 2. Greenwich: JAI Press.

———. 1994b. "Eine Nation zu werden ist schwer," *Frankfurter Allgemeine Zeitung*, 10 August 1994: 5.

———. 1995. "Das demokratische Defizit. Zum fünften Jahrestag der deutschen Einheit," *Frankfurter Allgemeine Zeitung*, 20 September 1995: 5.

Offe, Claus. 1972. *Strukturprobleme des kapitalistischen Staates.* Frankfurt am Main: Suhrkamp.

Powell, G. Bingham Jr. 1989. "Constitutional Design and Citizen Electoral Control," *Journal of Theoretical Politics* 1: 107–30.

Rattinger, Hans. 1993. "Abkehr von den Parteien. Dimensionen der Parteiverdrossenheit." *Aus Politik und Zeitgeschichte.* Beilage zur Wochenzeitung *Das Parlament*, B 11/93. Bonn: Bundeszentrale für Politische Bildung, 24–35.

—— and Jürgen Krämer. 1995. "Wahlnorm und Wahlbeteiligung in der Bundesrepublik Deutschland: Eine Kausalanalyse," *Politische Vierteljahreszeitschrift* 36: 267–85.

Rieger, Günter. 1994. "'Parteienverdrossenheit' und 'Parteienkritik' in der Bundesrepublik Deutschland," *Zeitschrift für Parlamentsfragen* 25: 459–71.

Rohrschneider, Robert, and Dieter Fuchs. 1995. "A New Electorate? The Economic Trends and Electoral Choice in the 1994 Federal Election," *German Politics and Society* 34: 100–22.

Scheuch, Erwin K., und Ute Scheuch. 1992. *Cliquen, Klüngel und Karrieren. Über den Verfall der politischen Parteien – eine Studie.* Reinbek bei Hamburg: Rowohlt Taschenbuch Verlag.

Schultze, Rainer-Olaf. 1995. "Widersprüchliches, Ungleichzeitiges und kein Ende in Sicht: Die Bundestagswahl vom 16. Oktober 1994," *Zeitschrift für Parlamentsfragen* 26: 325–52.

Sternberger, Dolf. 1990. *Verfassungspatriotismus.* Frankfurt am Main: Insel Verlag.

Veen, Hans-Joachim, and Carsten Zelle. 1995. "National Identity and Political Priorities in Eastern and Western Germany." *German Politics* 4: 1–26.

Weil, Frederick D. 1989. "The Sources and Structure of Legitimation in Western Democracies," *American Sociological Review* 54: 682–706.

——. 1993. "The Development of Democratic Attitudes in Eastern and Western Germany in a Comparative Perspective." In Frederick Weil, Jeffrey Huffman, Mary Gautier, eds. *Democratization in Eastern and Western Europe.* Research on Democracy and Society, vol. 1, Greenwich, CT: JAI Press.

Welzel, Christian. 1995. "Politikverdrossenheit und der Wandel des Partizipationsverhaltens. Zum Nutzen direkt-demokratischer Beteiligungsformen," *Zeitschrift für Parlamentsfragen* 26: 141–9.

Westle, Bettina. 1989. *Politische Legitimität – Theorien, Konzepte, empirische Befunde*. Baden-Baden: Nomos.

——. 1990. "Zur Akzeptanz der politischen Parteien und der Demokratie in der Bundesrepublik Deutschland." In Max Kaase and Hans-Dieter Klingemann, eds. *Wahlen und Wähler. Analysen aus Anlaß der Bundestagswahl 1987*. Opladen: West- deutscher Verlag.

——. 1992a. "Strukturen nationaler Identität in Ost- und West- deutschland," *Kölner Zeitschrift für Soziologie und Sozial- psychologie* 44: 461–88.

——. 1992b. "Unterstützung des politischen Systems des vere- inten Deutschland." In P. Mohler and W. Bandilla, eds. *Blick- punkt Gesellschaft 2. Einstellungen und Verhalten der Bundesbürger in Ost und West*. Opladen: Westdeutscher Verlag.

——. 1994. "Demokratie und Sozialismus. Politische Ordnungs- vorstellungen im vereinigten Deutschland zwischen Ideologie, Protest und Nostalgie," *Kölner Zeitschrift für Soziologie und Soz- ialpsychologie* 46: 571–96.

Wickert, Ulrich. 1994. *Der Ehrliche ist der Dumme. Über den Verlust der Werte*. Hamburg: Hoffmann & Campe.

Wildenmann, Rudolf. 1989. *Volksparteien. Ratlose Riesen?* Baden- Baden: Nomos.

Zelle, Carsten. 1995. "Social Dealignment versus Political Frus- tration: Contrasting Explanations of the Floating Vote in Germany," *European Journal of Political Research* 27: 319–345.

# Appendix: Voting Statistics

**Table A.1** 1994 European Parliament Election Results by State

| Parties | Baden-Württemberg | Bavaria | Berlin | Brandenburg | Bremen | Hamburg | Hesse | Lower Saxony |
|---|---|---|---|---|---|---|---|---|
| CDU/CSU | 42.0% | 48.9% | 28.4% | 23.4% | 28.0% | 32.1% | 37.0% | 39.7% |
| SPD | 26.6 | 23.7 | 28.1 | 36.9 | 40.7 | 34.6 | 34.9 | 39.6 |
| FDP | 5.2 | 3.3 | 3.2 | 2.7 | 4.6 | 3.7 | 4.7 | 3.9 |
| Alliance 90/G | 13.2 | 8.7 | 14.3 | 4.6 | 16.0 | 18.4 | 12.2 | 9.8 |
| PDS | 0.5 | 0.4 | 15.9 | 22.6 | 2.1 | 1.4 | 0.8 | 0.7 |
| REP | 5.9 | 6.6 | 3.3 | 2.3 | 3.0 | 3.1 | 4.6 | 2.4 |
| Other parties | 6.6 | 8.4 | 6.8 | 7.5 | 5.6 | 6.7 | 5.8 | 3.9 |
| Turnout | 66.4% | 56.4% | 53.5% | 41.5% | 52.7% | 51.7% | 56.4% | 52.7% |

| Parties | Mecklenberg-West. Pomerania | North Rhine-Westphalia | Rhineland-Palatinate | Saar | Saxony | Saxony-Anhalt | Schleswig-Holstein | Thuringia |
|---|---|---|---|---|---|---|---|---|
| CDU/CSU | 33.6% | 37.0% | 40.7% | 35.6% | 39.2% | 30.1% | 40.6% | 35.8% |
| SPD | 22.5 | 40.1 | 38.2 | 43.4 | 21.0 | 27.9 | 35.5 | 26.0 |
| FDP | 2.3 | 4.3 | 4.0 | 3.7 | 3.8 | 4.7 | 3.8 | 4.3 |
| Alliance 90/G | 4.8 | 11.2 | 8.7 | 8.2 | 5.6 | 5.7 | 11.9 | 6.0 |
| PDS | 27.3 | 0.6 | 0.4 | 0.4 | 16.6 | 18.9 | 0.7 | 16.9 |
| REP | 2.6 | 2.7 | 3.7 | 4.3 | 3.5 | 2.8 | 2.1 | 2.9 |
| Other parties | 6.9 | 4.1 | 4.3 | 4.4 | 10.3 | 9.9 | 5.4 | 8.1 |
| Turnout | 65.8% | 59.5% | 74.3% | 74.1% | 70.2% | 66.1% | 51.3% | 71.9% |

*Source: Statistisches Jahrbuch der Bundesrepublik, 1994* (Stuttgart: Metzler-Poeschel): 96.

**Table A.2** 1994 Bundestag Election Results by State

| Parties | Baden-Württemberg | Bavaria | Berlin | Brandenburg | Bremen | Hamburg | Hesse | Lower Saxony |
|---|---|---|---|---|---|---|---|---|
| CDU/CSU | 43.3% | 51.2% | 31.4% | 28.1% | 30.2% | 34.9% | 40.7% | 41.3% |
| SPD | 30.7 | 29.6 | 34.0 | 45.0 | 45.5 | 39.7 | 37.2 | 40.6 |
| FDP | 9.9 | 6.4 | 5.2 | 2.6 | 7.2 | 7.2 | 8.1 | 7.6 |
| Alliance 90/G | 9.6 | 6.3 | 10.2 | 2.9 | 11.1 | 12.6 | 9.3 | 7.1 |
| PDS | 0.8 | 0.6 | 14.8 | 19.3 | 2.7 | 2.2 | 1.1 | 1.0 |
| REP | 3.3 | 2.8 | 1.9 | 1.1 | 1.7 | 1.7 | 2.4 | 1.2 |
| Other parties | 2.4 | 3.1 | 2.5 | 1.6 | 1.6 | 1.7 | 1.2 | 1.1 |
| Turnout | 79.7% | 77.0% | 78.7% | 71.9% | 78.6% | 79.8% | 82.4% | 81.9% |

| Parties | Mecklenburg-West. Pomerania | North Rhine-Westphalia | Rhineland-Palatinate | Saar | Saxony | Saxony-Anhalt | Schleswig-Holstein | Thuringia |
|---|---|---|---|---|---|---|---|---|
| CDU/CSU | 38.5% | 38.0% | 43.8% | 37.2% | 48.0 | 38.8% | 41.5% | 48.0% |
| SPD | 28.8 | 43.1 | 39.4 | 48.8 | 24.3 | 33.4 | 39.6 | 24.3 |
| FDP | 3.4 | 7.6 | 6.9 | 4.3 | 3.8 | 4.1 | 7.4 | 3.8 |
| Alliance 90/G | 3.6 | 7.4 | 6.2 | 5.8 | 4.8 | 3.6 | 8.3 | 4.8 |
| PDS | 23.6 | 1.0 | 0.6 | 0.7 | 16.7 | 18.0 | 1.1 | 16.7 |
| REP | 1.2 | 1.3 | 1.9 | 1.6 | 1.4 | 1.0 | 1.0 | 1.4 |
| Other parties | 0.9 | 1.6 | 1.2 | 1.6 | 1.0 | 1.1 | 1.1 | 1.0 |
| Turnout | 73.0% | 81.9% | 82.3% | 83.5% | 72.0% | 70.6% | 81.0% | 75.5% |

*Source: Frankfurter Allgemeine Zeitung,* 18 October 1994: 36–37.

*Appendix*

**Table A.3** State Election Results (West)

**Baden-Württemberg**

| Parties | 1988 Land | 1990 Bundestag | 1992 Land | 1994 Bundestag | 1996 Land |
|---|---|---|---|---|---|
| CDU | 49.0% | 46.5% | 39.6% | 43.3% | 41.3% |
| SPD | 32.0 | 29.1 | 29.4 | 30.7 | 25.1 |
| FDP | 5.9 | 12.3 | 5.9 | 9.9 | 9.6 |
| Alliance 90/G | 7.9 | 5.7 | 9.5 | 9.6 | 12.1 |
| PDS | – | 0.3 | – | 0.8 | – |
| REPS | – | 3.2 | 10.9 | 3.3 | 9.1 |
| Other parties | 5.2 | 3.0 | 4.8 | 2.4 | 2.8 |
| Turnout | 90.0% | 77.4% | 70.1% | 79.7% | 67.5% |

**Bavaria**

| Parties | 1990 Land | 1990 Bundestag | 1994 Land | 1994 Bundestag |
|---|---|---|---|---|
| CDU | 54.9% | 51.9% | 52.8% | 51.2% |
| SPD | 26.0 | 26.7 | 30.1 | 29.6 |
| FDP | 5.2 | 8.7 | 2.8 | 6.4 |
| Alliance 90/G | 6.4 | 4.6 | 6.1 | 6.3 |
| PDS | – | 0.2 | – | 0.6 |
| REPS | 4.9 | 5.0 | 3.9 | 2.8 |
| Other parties | 2.6 | 3.0 | 4.3 | 3.1 |
| Turnout | 65.9% | 74.4% | 67.9% | 77.0% |

**Bremen**

| Parties | 1987 Land | 1990 Bundestag | 1991 Land | 1994 Bundestag | 1995 Land |
|---|---|---|---|---|---|
| CDU | 23.4% | 30.9% | 30.7% | 30.2% | 32.6 |
| SPD | 50.5 | 42.5 | 38.8 | 45.5 | 33.4 |
| FDP | 10.0 | 12.8 | 9.5 | 7.2 | 3.4 |
| Alliance 90/G | 10.2 | 8.3 | 11.4 | 11.1 | 13.1 |
| PDS | – | 1.1 | – | 2.7 | 2.4 |
| REPS | – | 2.1 | 1.5 | 1.7 | – |
| Other parties | 5.8 | 2.3 | 8.2 | 1.6 | 15.1 |
| Turnout | 75.6% | 76.5% | 72.2% | 78.6% | 68.6 |

**Table A.3** Continued

**Hamburg**

| Parties | 1987 Land | 1990 Bundestag | 1991 Land | 1993 Land | 1994 Bundestag |
|---|---|---|---|---|---|
| CDU | 40.5% | 36.6% | 35.1% | 25.1% | 34.9% |
| SPD | 45.0 | 41.0 | 48.0 | 40.4 | 39.7 |
| FDP | 6.5 | 12.0 | 5.4 | 4.2 | 7.2 |
| Alliance 90/G | 7.0 | 5.0 | 7.2 | 13.5 | 12.6 |
| PDS | – | 1.1 | 0.5 | – | 2.2 |
| REPS | – | 1.7 | 1.2 | 4.8 | 1.7 |
| Other parties | 1.0 | 1.8 | 2.6 | 11.9 | 1.7 |
| Turnout | 79.5% | 78.2% | 66.1 | 69.6% | 79.8% |

**Hesse**

| Parties | 1987 Land | 1990 Bundestag | 1991 Land | 1994 Bundestag | 1995 Land |
|---|---|---|---|---|---|
| CDU | 42.1% | 41.3% | 40.2% | 40.7% | 39.2% |
| SPD | 40.2 | 38.0 | 40.8 | 37.2 | 38.0 |
| FDP | 7.8 | 10.9 | 7.4 | 8.1 | 7.4 |
| Alliance 90/G | 9.4 | 5.6 | 8.8 | 9.3 | 11.2 |
| PDS | – | 0.4 | – | 1.1 | – |
| REPS | – | 2.1 | 1.7 | 2.4 | 2.0 |
| Other parties | 0.5 | 1.8 | 1.1 | 1.2 | 2.2 |
| Turnout | 80.3% | 81.1% | 70.8% | 82.4% | 66.6% |

**Lower Saxony**

| Parties | 1990 Land | 1990 Bundestag | 1994 Land | 1994 Bundestag |
|---|---|---|---|---|
| CDU | 42.0% | 44.3% | 36.4% | 41.3% |
| SPD | 44.2 | 38.4 | 44.3 | 40.6 |
| FDP | 6.0 | 10.3 | 4.4 | 7.7 |
| Alliance 90/G | 5.5 | 4.5 | 7.4 | 7.1 |
| PDS | – | 0.3 | – | 1.0 |
| REPS | 1.5 | 1.0 | – | 1.2 |
| Other parties | 0.8 | 1.2 | 7.5 | 1.1 |
| Turnout | 74.6% | 80.6% | 73.8% | 81.9% |

**Table A.3** Continued

### North Rhine-Westphalia

| Parties | 1990 Land | 1990 Bundestag | 1994 Bundestag | 1995 Land |
|---|---|---|---|---|
| CDU | 36.7% | 40.5% | 38.0% | 37.7% |
| SPD | 50.0 | 41.1 | 43.1 | 46.0 |
| FDP | 5.8 | 11.0 | 7.6 | 4.0 |
| Alliance 90/G | 5.0 | 4.3 | 7.4 | 10.0 |
| PDS | – | 0.3 | 1.0 | – |
| REPS | 1.8 | 1.3 | 1.3 | 0.8 |
| Other parties | 0.7 | 1.6 | 1.6 | 1.5 |
| Turnout | 71.8% | 78.7% | 81.9% | 64.1% |

### Rhineland-Palatinate

| Parties | 1987 Land | 1990 Bundestag | 1991 Land | 1994 Bundestag | 1996 Land |
|---|---|---|---|---|---|
| CDU | 45.1% | 45.6% | 38.7% | 43.8% | 38.7% |
| SPD | 38.8 | 36.1 | 44.8 | 39.4 | 39.8 |
| FDP | 7.3 | 10.4 | 6.9 | 6.9 | 8.9 |
| Alliance 90/G | 5.9 | 4.0 | 6.5 | 6.2 | 6.9 |
| PDS | – | 0.2 | – | 0.6 | – |
| REPS | – | 1.7 | 2.0 | 1.9 | – |
| Other parties | 2.9 | 1.9 | 1.1 | 1.2 | 5.7 |
| Turnout | 77.0% | 81.7% | 73.9% | 82.3% | 71.0% |

### Saar

| Parties | 1990 Land | 1990 Bundestag | 1994 Land | 1994 Bundestag |
|---|---|---|---|---|
| CDU | 33.4% | 38.1% | 38.6% | 37.2% |
| SPD | 54.4 | 51.2 | 49.4 | 48.8 |
| FDP | 5.6 | 6.0 | 2.1 | 4.3 |
| Alliance 90/G | 2.6 | 2.3 | 5.5 | 5.8 |
| PDS | – | 0.2 | – | 0.7 |
| REPS | 3.4 | 0.9 | – | 1.6 |
| Other parties | 0.6 | 1.4 | 4.4 | 1.6 |
| Turnout | 83.2% | 85.1% | 83.5% | 83.5% |

**Table A.3** Continued

**Schleswig-Holstein**

| Parties | 1988 Land | 1990 Bundestag | 1992 Land | 1994 Bundestag | 1996 Land |
|---|---|---|---|---|---|
| CDU | 33.3% | 43.5% | 33.8% | 41.5% | 37.2% |
| SPD | 54.8 | 38.5 | 46.2 | 39.6 | 39.8 |
| FDP | 4.4 | 11.4 | 5.6 | 7.4 | 5.7 |
| Alliance 90/G | 2.9 | 4.0 | 4.9 | 8.3 | 8.1 |
| PDS | – | 0.3 | – | 1.1 | – |
| REPS | – | 1.2 | 1.2 | 1.0 | – |
| Other parties | 4.7 | 1.1 | 8.2 | 1.1 | 9.1 |
| Turnout | 77.4% | 78.6% | 71.7% | 81.0% | 67.5% |

*Sources*: Wilhelm Bürklin and Dieter Roth, eds. *Das Superwahljahr* (Cologne: Bund Verlag, 1994): 324–9; *Statistisches Jahrbuch der Bundesrepublik, 1989* (Stuttgart: Metzler-Poeschel): 80; *Statistisches Jahrbuch der Bundesrepublik, 1994* (Stuttgart: Metzler-Poeschel): 96–100.

**Table A.4** State Election Results (East)

**Brandenburg**

| Parties | Volks-kammer | 1990 Land | 1990 Bundestag | 1994 Land | 1994 Bundestag |
|---|---|---|---|---|---|
| CDU | 34.3% | 29.4% | 36.3% | 18.7% | 28.1% |
| SPD | 29.9 | 38.2 | 32.9 | 54.1 | 45.0 |
| FDP/BFD | 5.2 | 6.6 | 9.7 | 2.2 | 2.6 |
| Alliance 90/G | 5.4 | 9.3 | 6.6 | 2.9 | 2.9 |
| PDS | 18.3 | 13.4 | 11.0 | 18.7 | 19.3 |
| REP | – | 1.2 | 1.7 | 1.1 | 1.1 |
| DSU | 3.3 | 1.0 | – | 0.2 | – |
| Other parties | 3.6 | 0.9 | 1.8 | 2.1 | 1.0 |
| Turnout | 93.5% | 67.1% | 73.8% | 56.2% | 71.9% |

**Mecklenburg-Western Pomerania**

| Parties | Volks-kammer | 1990 Land | 1990 Bundestag | 1994 Land | 1994 Bundestag |
|---|---|---|---|---|---|
| CDU | 36.9% | 38.3% | 41.2% | 37.7% | 38.5% |
| SPD | 23.4 | 27.0 | 26.5 | 29.5 | 28.8 |
| FDP/BFD | 4.1 | 5.5 | 9.1 | 3.8 | 3.4 |
| Alliance 90/G | 4.4 | 9.3 | 5.9 | 3.7 | 3.6 |
| PDS | 22.8 | 15.7 | 14.2 | 22.7 | 23.6 |
| REP | – | 0.9 | 1.4 | 1.0 | 1.2 |
| DSU | 2.4 | 0.8 | – | – | – |
| Other parties | 6.0 | 2.5 | 1.5 | 1.6 | 0.9 |
| Turnout | 92.3% | 64.7% | 70.9% | 73.1% | 73.0% |

**Saxony**

| Parties | Volks-kammer | 1990 Land | 1990 Bundestag | 1994 Land | 1994 Bundestag |
|---|---|---|---|---|---|
| CDU | 44.3% | 54.4% | 49.5% | 58.1% | 48.0% |
| SPD | 15.1 | 19.1 | 18.2 | 16.6 | 24.3 |
| FDP/BFD | 6.1 | 5.3 | 12.4 | 1.7 | 3.8 |
| Alliance 90/G | 4.7 | 5.6 | 5.9 | 4.1 | 4.8 |
| PDS | 13.6 | 10.2 | 9.0 | 16.5 | 16.7 |
| REP | – | – | 1.2 | 1.3 | 1.4 |
| DSU | 13.1 | 3.6 | – | 0.6 | – |
| Other parties | 3.1 | 1.8 | 3.8 | 1.1 | – |
| Turnout | 93.6% | 72.8% | 76.2% | 58.4% | 72.0% |

**Table A.4** Continued

**Saxony-Anhalt**

| Parties | Volks-kammer | 1990 Land | 1990 Bundestag | 1994 Land | 1994 Bundestag |
|---|---|---|---|---|---|
| CDU | 45.1% | 39.0% | 38.6% | 34.4% | 38.8% |
| SPD | 23.7 | 26.0 | 24.7 | 34.0 | 33.4 |
| FDP/BFD | 8.1 | 13.5 | 19.7 | 3.6 | 4.1 |
| Alliance 90/G | 4.0 | 5.3 | 5.3 | 5.1 | 3.6 |
| PDS | 14.0 | 12.0 | 9.4 | 19.9 | 18.0 |
| REP | – | 0.6 | 1.0 | 1.4 | 1.0 |
| DSU | 2.4 | 1.7 | – | 0.2 | – |
| Other parties | 2.7 | 1.9 | 1.4 | 1.4 | 1.1 |
| Turnout | 93.4% | 65.1% | 72.2% | 54.9% | 70.6% |

**Thuringia**

| Parties | Volks-kammer | 1990 Land | 1990 Bundestag | 1994 Land | 1994 Bundestag |
|---|---|---|---|---|---|
| CDU | 54.1% | 45.4% | 45.2% | 42.6% | 41.0% |
| SPD | 17.5 | 22.8 | 21.9 | 29.6 | 30.2 |
| FDP/BFD | 5.0 | 9.3 | 14.6 | 3.2 | 4.2 |
| Alliance 90/G | 4.1 | 7.2 | 6.1 | 4.5 | 4.9 |
| PDS | 11.4 | 9.7 | 8.3 | 16.6 | 17.1 |
| REP | – | 0.8 | 1.2 | 1.3 | 1.4 |
| DSU | 5.8 | 3.3 | – | 0.2 | – |
| Other parties | 2.1 | 1.6 | 2.6 | 2.0 | 1.2 |
| Turnout | 94.5% | 71.7% | 76.4% | 75.3% | 75.5% |

*Sources*: Wilhelm Bürklin and Dieter Roth, eds. *Das Superwahljahr* (Cologne: Bund Verlag, 1994): 324–329; *Frankfurter Allgemeine Zeitung*, 18 October, 1994: 36–7; *Berichte der Forschungsgruppe Wahlen* (Mannheim: Forschungsgruppe Wahlen): #72 (30 June, 1994), #73 (14 August, 1994), #74 (16 August, 1994), #78 (8 October, 1994), #79 (October 11, 1994).

**Table A.5** Berlin Election Results

| Parties | 1990 Volkskammer | East Berlin | | | | West Berlin | | | | Total Berlin | | | |
|---|---|---|---|---|---|---|---|---|---|---|---|---|---|
| | | 1990 Ab-haus | 1990 Bund-estag | 1994 Bund-estag | 1995 Ab-haus | 1990 Ab-haus | 1990 Bund-estag | 1994 Bund-estag | 1995 Ab-haus | 1990 Ab-haus | 1990 Bund-estag | 1994 Bund-estag | 1995 Ab-haus |
| CDU | 19.4% | 25.0% | 24.3% | 19.5% | 23.6% | 49.0% | 47.7% | 38.7% | 45.4% | 40.4% | 39.4% | 31.4% | 37.4% |
| SPD | 34.9 | 32.1 | 31.3 | 33.1 | 20.2 | 29.5 | 30.0 | 34.6 | 25.5 | 30.4 | 30.6 | 34.0 | 23.6 |
| FDP | 3.2* | 5.6 | 7.8 | 1.9 | 1.1 | 7.9 | 10.1 | 7.2 | 3.4 | 7.1 | 9.1 | 5.2 | 2.5 |
| Greens/ Alliance 90 | 9.0 | 11.4 | 8.8 | 6.9 | 10.0 | 6.9 | 6.4 | 12.3 | 15.0 | 9.4 | 7.2 | 10.2 | 13.2 |
| PDS | 30.0 | 23.6 | 24.8 | 34.7 | 36.3 | 1.1 | 1.3 | 2.6 | 2.1 | 9.2 | 9.7 | 14.8 | 14.6 |
| Republikaner | – | 1.9 | 1.5 | 1.9 | 2.9 | 3.7 | 3.0 | 2.8 | 2.6 | 3.1 | 2.5 | 1.9 | 2.7 |
| Other parties | 3.5 | 0.4 | 1.5 | 2.0 | 5.9 | 2.0 | 1.5 | 1.8 | 0.6 | 0.5 | 1.5 | 2.5 | 6.0 |
| Turnout | 90.7% | 76.2% | 76.6% | 77.2% | 63.9% | 83.4% | 83.9% | 79.5% | 71.1% | 80.8% | 80.6% | 78.7% | 68.4% |

*Sources*: Forschungsgruppe Wahlen (1990); Bürklin and Roth (1994: 324–329) *Frankfurter Allgemeine Zeitung* (18 October, 1994): 36–37; Jesse (1991: 397).

# Notes on Contributors

**Gerard Braunthal** is Professor Emeritus of Political Science at the University of Massachusetts, Amherst. He has written extensively on German political parties, interest groups, and civil liberties. His latest books include: *Political Loyalty and Public Service in West Germany* (1990), *The German Social Democrats Since 1969* (1994), and *Parties and Politics in Modern Germany* (1996).

**Wilhelm Bürklin** holds the Chair in the Political System of Germany/Domestic Politics at the University of Potsdam. His major research interests are political elites, party systems, voting behavior, and democratic theory. He is the author of *Grüne Politik* (1984), *Wählerverhalten und Wertwandel* (1988), and *Die vier kleinen Tiger* (1993); he is the co-editor of *Superwahljahr* (1994), and has published widely in German and international political science journals.

**Alexandra Cole** is a student in the political science doctoral program at the University of California, Irvine. Her research interests include political parties and social movements in advanced industrial democracies, as well as theories of media effects on political behavior. She is currently working on a comparative study of New Right parties in Europe, focusing on explanations of their emergence and popularity.

**David P. Conradt** is Professor and Chair of Political Science at East Carolina University. He has written widely on German political culture, parties, and elections. His most recent books are *Germany's New Politics* (1995) and *The German Polity*, 3rd ed. (1993).

**Russell J. Dalton** is Professor of Political Science at the University of California, Irvine and Chair of the Department of Politics and Society. His scholarly interests include comparative political behavior, political parties, social movements, and political change in democratic societies. He is author of *The Green Rainbow: Environmental Groups in Western Europe* (1994), *Citizen Politics in Western Democracies*, 2nd ed. (1996), and *Politics in*

*Germany*, 2nd ed. (1992); co-author of *Germany Transformed* (1981); editor of *The New Germany Votes* (1993), *Challenging the Political Order* (1990), and *Electoral Change in Advanced Industrial Democracies* (1984).

**E. Gene Frankland** is Professor of Political Science at Ball State University. His primary teaching and research interests are comparative politics and environmental law and policy. He has written scholarly articles on parliamentary recruitment, political socialization, and Green parties. He co-authored with Donald Schoonmaker *Between Protest and Power: The Green Party in Germany* (1992). Most recently, he has contributed chapters to *The Green Challenge* (1995) and *Green Politics Three* (1995).

**Max Kaase** is on leave from the University of Mannheim; he is presently a research professor at the Berlin Wissenschafts-zentrum für Sozialforschung. He has published widely in comparative politics, electoral sociology, and mass communication. Among his books are *Political Action* (1979) and *Beliefs in Government* (1995). With Hans-Dieter Klingemann he has edited analyses of all German national elections since 1980. He is currently working on the problems of social and political transformation in the context of German unification.

**Hans-Dieter Klingemann** is Professor of Political Science, Freie Universität Berlin, and Director of the Research Unit on Institutions and Social Change at the Berlin Wissenschaftszentrum für Sozialforschung, and Research Fellow, Department of Political and Society, University of California at Irvine. He has served as president of the International Society of Political Psychology, president of the German Paul Lazarsfeld Society, and vice-president of the International Political Science Association. His most recent books include *A New Handbook of Political Science* (with Robert Goodin, 1996), *Citizens and the State* (with Dieter Fuchs, 1995), *Parties, Policies and Democracy* (with Richard Hofferbert and Ian Budge, 1994).

**Eva Kolinsky** is Professor of Modern German Studies and Director of the Centre for the Study of German Culture and Society at Keele University. Recent books include *Women in Contemporary Germany* (1993), *Women in 20th century Germany* (1995), *Between*

*Hope and Fear. Everyday Life in Post-Unification Germany* (1995), *Turkish Culture in German Society* (1996, with D. Horrocks). She is general editor of the *German Studies* series with Berg, co-editor with D. Horrocks of a new book series on *Culture and Society in Germany* with Berghahn Books and co-editor of the journal *German Politics*. Books in progress include *Social Transformation and the Family in Post-Communist Germany* (Gower), *Jewish Culture in German Society* (Berghahn) and a social history of Germany from 1945 to the present (Macmillan).

**Henry Krisch** is Professor of Political Science at the University of Connecticut, Storrs and was President of the Eastern German Study Group (1989–1995). He is the author of *German Politics Under Soviet Occupation* (1974) and *The German Democratic Republic* (1985), as well as articles and chapters on GDR politics. He is currently working on the relationship between political culture and political change, particularly within the SED.

**Manfred Kuechler** is Professor of Sociology at Hunter College and the Graduate Center for the City University of New York (CUNY). Before he took residence in the United States in 1985, he was a professor at the University of Frankfurt, Germany. His numerous articles in scholarly journals and contributions to edited volumes are in the areas of voting behavior, social movements, and research methodology. He is co-editor and contributor to *Challenging the Political Order* (1990).

**Juergen Lass** is a research assistant at the Berlin Wissenschaftszentrum für Sozialforschung. He has written several articles about German political culture and political parties. His most recent publication is *Vorstellungsbilder über Kanzlerkandidaten* (1995). This book discusses images of the chancellor candidates and their impact on voting behavior. He is currently working on the problem of the perception of media coverage and political thinking.

**Helmut Norpoth** is Professor of Political Science at the State University of New York at Stony Brook. His research interests include electoral behavior, public opinion, and political parties in Western democracies. He is co-author of *Politics and Government in Europe Today* (1995), co-editor of *Economics and Politics* (1991), and author of *Confidence Regained* (1992). He served as president of the Conference Group on German Politics from 1988 to 1990, and as vice-president from 1986 to 1988.

**Geoffrey K. Roberts** is Reader in German Politics at the University of Manchester (UK). His research interests are concerned with German parties and elections, with special emphasis on the Free Democratic Party. He has published several articles and book chapters on German parties and elections. He edited and contributed to the special issue of *German Politics* on "Superwahljahr 1994." He is currently completing a book on the German party system in relation to German unification to be published by Pinter Press. He is co-founder and former chairperson of the Association for the Study of German Politics.

**Dieter Roth** is a co-director of the Forschungsgruppe Wahlen and a lecturer at the University of Heidelberg. He is one of the leading analysts of electoral behavior in Germany, and co-host of the monthly Politbarometer program on the Second German Television Network (ZDF). Roth has written widely on the development of the German party system over the past twenty years, based on the extensive opinion surveys of the Forschungsgruppe. He is co-editor (with Wilhelm Bürklin) and contributor to *Das Superwahljahr* (1994).

# Index

# Index